THE POLITICS OF TRADE PRESSURE

To Asifa

The Politics of Trade Pressure

American-Soviet relations 1980-88

MOHAMMED ISHAQ
University of Paisley

Routledge
Taylor & Francis Group
LONDON AND NEW YORK

First published 1999 by Ashgate Publishing

Reissued 2018 by Routledge
2 Park Square, Milton Park, Abingdon, Oxon, OX14 4RN
52 Vanderbilt Avenue, New York, NY 10017

Routledge is an imprint of the Taylor & Francis Group, an informa business

A Library of Congress record exists under LC control number: 99073628

ISBN 13: 978-1-138-33779-4 (hbk)
ISBN 13: 978-0-429-44214-8 (ebk)

Contents

List of Figures

List of Tables

Preface

The United States government, first under the Presidency of Jimmy Carter, and then most notably under a fervent anti - communist Ronald Reagan, adopted a policy of using economic pressure in order to achieve political objectives. These political goals were to reduce or eliminate Soviet involvement in the third world and regional conflicts, and to foster an improvement in Soviet domestic policy on human rights, including dissent and Jewish emigration.

Specific studies of trade pressure in the context of Soviet-American relations have been relatively few. Most (such as those of Philip Hanson and Gordon Smith) have tended to concentrate on trade pressure applied in the framework of East-West relations (i.e. collective Western measures against the Eastern bloc). Since this study offers an analysis of trade pressure on the USSR applied solely by the United States rather than the West as a whole - acknowledging the fact that fundamental differences of opinion and approach existed within the Western alliance, particularly between the United States and its allies, which justify a separate study of trade pressure applied by a single nation like the United States - it has aimed to rectify this shortcoming. This book, while offering an analysis of the economic impact of trade pressure, more importantly offers an in depth analysis of the political success of trade pressure, using evidence from governmental as well as non-governmental sources.

This book was prompted by the acknowledgment that in the modern age the use of trade pressure or as David Baldwin calls it 'economic statecraft' has become an important tool of foreign policy, whether applied by individual countries or by international organisations. One can recollect a number of examples of both unilateral and multilateral trade pressure in the 1990s itself such as UN sanctions against Iraq and Serbia, U.S. sanctions against Haiti, and U.S. sanctions against India and Pakistan. My reason for choosing U.S. trade pressure on the Soviet Union was based on my personal interest in superpower politics, and the Soviet Union in particular, and in the unique intensity of trade pressure applied in the period concerned.

The conventional view that trade pressure very rarely works, if at all, is I believe largely sustained by this book, which notes the limits of applying any sort of pressure on a global power like the former Soviet Union.

The book draws on both Soviet and American sources. A wealth of published Soviet sources were available for consultation in the Soviet Studies section of Glasgow University library, including official documents, statistics and other documentation. These were supplemented by some unpublished archival material acquired from the Centre for Contemporary Documentation in Moscow. Data from the Soviet treaties project recently undertaken at the University of Glasgow was also consulted. American sources were available from a variety of places such as the National Library of Scotland in Edinburgh and the British Library document supply centre, which incidentally coped with my regular demand for sources rather well.

Acknowledgements

I owe a debt of gratitude to a number of individuals. I would firstly like to express my thanks to certain numbers of the academic and research staff at Glasgow University who with great kindness offered me advice and general help on matters or questions which arose from the subject matter of this book. They were Fred Hay and Ljubo Sirc (Department of Political Economy) and Stephen Revell (Department of Politics), and of course Stephen White who provided me with very useful guidance.

Last but not least a word of thanks to my dear parents for their moral support. And of course to my lovely fiancée, Asifa, the most important person in my life, whose inspiration was behind this book and without whose loving support it would have been pointless to have proceeded with it.

1 Soviet-American Relations from Afghanistan to Gorbachev: An Overview

Introduction

The concept of trade pressure involves the manipulation of economic measures, and the utilization of economic instruments to influence the behaviour and actions of another nation with the hope of satisfying designated political goals. In other words it has to be remembered that economics is the means and politics is the intended end.

It should be understood that judging the success of trade pressure is really a two-part task. The first task is to see whether economic pressure had the desired economic impact, since this will go a long way in determining whether trade pressure will be successful from a political standpoint, which is then the second task.

In this respect, as most writers on the issue also appear to recognise, "the political success of sanctions is an independent variable separate from the economic impact of sanctions".[1] The term economic sanctions is used very readily in most discussions of trade pressure. Although it is only one form of trade pressure, it is the form in which trade pressure manifests itself more than any other way.

The true measurement of whether trade pressure is successful from an overall perspective has to be whether the political aims of the practising state are met, and to what extent. This is because the ability of trade pressure to have the intended negative economic impact on the target state will not in itself guarantee that political objectives will be met. Although economic measures such as embargoes and sanctions can be used, and have been used for purely economic reasons, when they are deployed as part of trade pressure then they are being used in a political capacity.

It is fair to say that if trade pressure fails to have the desired negative economic impact on the target nation the chances of it having the desired political impact are virtually zero. Its economic failure will only serve to boost the political will and morale of the target country, which will become less inclined to alter its policies. The only hope then, is that other factors such as leadership changes or changes in government, may force the target to alter its behaviour. The exception to this idea, that if trade pressure fails to have the intended economic effects its chances of achieving the political objectives are low, would be when trade pressure measures such as sanctions are imposed which are of a purely symbolic nature and where no change in political behaviour of the target is expected.

However, although the success of trade pressure from an economic viewpoint boosts the chances of it altering the political behaviour of the target state, this need not be the case since pride, reputation, and sheer stubbornness may make the target state unwilling to budge even in the face of economic adversity brought on by trade pressure measures like sanctions. Also the target may hope to hold out and hope that trade pressure may be relaxed in the near future. Certainly in the case of US trade pressure against the Soviet Union throughout the 1980's its failure to impose significant economic costs on the USSR made the chances of it succeeding in satisfying its political objectives much more difficult.

Although this book looks at the use of trade pressure by the U.S. against the USSR in a specific time period (1980 - 88), it is worth stressing that the use of this policy of trade pressure was not new in US - Soviet relations and had in fact been part of US strategy towards the Soviet Union in the early days of the Cold War, and it is even fair to argue that Ronald Reagan's policy bordering on economic warfare bears striking resemblance to US policy in the early years of the cold war.

As Mastanduno points out, part of US economic containment policy in the years immediately after 1945 involved the "...use of US economic instruments..."[2] to shape Soviet behaviour. The end of the Second World War saw the emergence of the United States as a leading economic as well as military power. The US sought to use its economic power against the Soviet Union as part of its cold war conflict and rivalry with Moscow. As can be witnessed from the U.S. at the time, it became clear that a policy of economic containment would be part of US strategy toward the USSR which was not as powerful economically. Taking into account the fact that trading with an adversary can be detrimental as it can contribute towards its military strength, for these reasons as Mastanduno indicates "....throughout the Cold War US officials treated trade with the Soviet Union and its allies differently from US trade with other destinations ..."[3] The historical debate in the West on trade with the Soviet Union centred largely on the question of the export of goods to the Soviet Union which would contribute to the military potential of Moscow. Western efforts to coordinate allied controls over exports to the Soviet Union and its allies, saw the formation of COCOM in 1949 at a time when the West recognised the strategic risks of trading with the Soviet bloc. In decades to come COCOM came to represent the strategic embargo, the aim of which was to hinder Warsaw Pact access to militarily useful technology in which the West had a lead.

While the allies of America in Western Europe accepted the dangers of trading with the USSR particularly in strategic items and technology and were as a result willing to cooperate with the US in controlling strategic exports they had initially been wary of using economic means as a policy instrument especially to the extreme of economic warfare. From the 1945 period up to the late 1950s the West denied the Soviet Union the benefits of any significant trade with the West. Clearly at this time international or Western Security assumed priority over economic interests. This period from 1945 well into the 1950's was generally depicted as the period of economic containment. The force that initially brought COCOM into being and held it together in the early years was the enormous economic leverage the US could exert on its Western allies in the immediate aftermath of the Cold War.

This was typified by the 1951 US Mutual Defence Assistance Act which was seen as an attempt by the US to use aid to Western Europe as a lever to compel allied compliance on export controls by providing for the discontinuance of US financial assistance to countries that exported restricted commodities to communist countries. As Mastanduno points out[4] Western European nations were not entirely happy with the strategy of economic warfare which was adopted through such means as COCOM but were virtually compelled to participate through US pressure and coercion, even though they acknowledged the principle behind the need to control the export of strategic items. A major concern for Western European nations was that the US was overstating the problem of strategic exports to the Soviet bloc to the extent that items with little or no strategic significance would be restricted, and that this would prove an unnecessary detriment to already minute East - West trade that there was.

Indeed initial COCOM controls saw a compromise between a longer US control list and a shorter list proposed by Britain and France. For Western Europe the desire was "...to limit controls to those of a more narrow strategic embargo". As highlighted by Mastanduno[5] there was somewhat of a retreat from Economic Warfare beginning to take place from 1953. This saw West European nations in particular calling for a liberalisation of COCOM export controls and cuts in the COCOM control list.

This trend or movement towards liberalisation of the western strategic embargo was viewed with alarm by the United States who continued to stress the overwhelming security threat posed by the Soviet Union as well as China.

However, the West Europeans got their way to a great extent and in 1945 during negotiations the COCOM control list was reduced by 50%. Furthermore there was a narrowing of control criteria that would in future cover only those items which made a direct contribution to the Soviet military sector.

In addition to this, in 1958 there was a review of the COCOM list which "...resulted in a significant liberalisation of controls".[6] This was much to the delight of the West European governments who had been unhappy about the inclusion in the control list of many items which were not regarded as strategically important.

The period beginning from the 1960s saw changes in East - West trade. Trade ties began to emerge on a measurable scale by the 1960s and were to benefit greatly from detente during the 1970s. Much of this change was due to Western European governments beginning to reestablish traditional links with markets in Eastern Europe. The United States no longer exercised leadership of Western policies on East - West trade. In view of this the West Europeans moved towards liberalisation of controls within COCOM. This saw the number of items on the COCOM lists decline. The US attempted to stave off this movement towards liberalisation or easing of controls by maintaining its more extensive national controls.

The end of the 1960s to the mid 1970s saw or witnessed what can be called a further liberalisation of East - West trade. It was the period of economic détente (in line with the political detente at the time) with the belief in the West that increased economic ties between East and West may help to foster improved political relations. Even in the United States this view or line was being promoted, and there were calls for a relaxation of controls.

During the 1970s COCOM had almost threatened to become obsolete. Member States had in fact become rather casual in their enforcement of controls. At the same time East - West trade had increased in comparison to previous years. The second half of the 1970s witnessed problems in Western policies towards economic relations with the Soviet bloc. Disagreements once again began emerging within the Western alliance. The U.S. had began to end its liberal approach of the early 1970s to trade with the Soviet Union in response to concerns over Moscow's behaviour. The new more stricter US approach was not to the liking of the West Europeans who by now had considerable economic interests at stake in their trade links with the Soviet bloc. The divisions primarily between the US and its European allies intensified going into the 1980s. On top of this, as we shall see, the renewed period of conflict in East - West relations in the early 1980s proved a disaster for Soviet American economic relations in particular, and saw economic warfare one of the initial features of the cold war dictate Soviet - American issues.

It might be appropriate to briefly look at the reason for the development of Soviet - American relations in the manner in which they did in particular the reasoning behind the Cold War, which actually contributed in attracting the use of U.S. trade pressure in the post - 1945 period.

Since 1945 the Soviet-American relationship has oscillated rather like a business or trade cycle. The period immediately following the Second World War saw the onset of what became known as the 'Cold War'.[7] This term was used to describe the extreme state of tension and hostility that developed between the Western powers led by the United States, and the Communist bloc of Eastern Europe led in turn by the Soviet Union. The 'Cold War' in fact became the norm by which Soviet-American (and East-West relations which were naturally closely interconnected) were governed, and was characterised for much of the post-war period by: political manoeuvring; diplomatic wrangling, psychological warfare; ideological hostility; economic warfare; a major arms race; peripheral wars; and other power contests; falling short of an actual 'hot war'.

It can be said that the Cold War which emerged between the United States and the USSR was waiting to happen long before major developments in Europe after the Second World War made it a reality. The fact is that suspicion and dislike between the two countries could be traced as far back as the Russian Revolution. American troops had took part in the abortive 'White' counter revolution against the Bolsheviks during 1918 - 19. The U.S. as a major capitalist state was in ideological terms in clear conflict with the communist ideology of the Bolsheviks. The Americans continued to oppose diplomatic links with the USSR, and it was only the mutual objective to defeat Hitler's Germany that brought the Soviets and Americans together during the Second World War.

However, once Germany had been defeated the uneasy American - Soviet cooperation soon began to disintegrate and the two faced each other suspicious of each other's motives and intentions. Could the Cold War have been avoided? From the point of view that there existed a dislike between the two well before 1945 maybe not. However, having fought alongside each other could have acted as a catalyst towards a possible reconciliation. This did not materialize because the traditional hatred resurfaced, and hopes of rapprochement were dashed by a series of events and developments which took place in the years immediately after the Second World War.

A significant development was the Soviet 'take – over' of Eastern Europe between 1945 - 47. As the Red Army advanced through Eastern Europe, pro - communist temporary governments were set up. Post - war elections in these countries were held under the watchful eyes of the Red Army which had not yet withdrawn. The West did not regard them as free elections and disliked even more the subsequent communisation of the coalition governments which were elected. They saw Stalin as having broken his promise of free elections he had made at the Yalta Conference. Western leaders had clearly become concerned that Western Europe might suffer the same fate as Eastern Europe.

This concern was highlighted in 1946 by Winston Churchill in his speech in the USA where he warned that an 'Iron Curtain' had descended across Europe and that the USSR wanted indefinite expansion of their power and doctrines. He proposed an Anglo - American military alliance to prevent this.

In 1947 came the Truman Doctrine which said that America would aid 'free peoples' to resist threats by armed minorities or by 'outside pressures'. Truman carefully did not name communism as the enemy but no one had any doubt as to what he meant. The doctrine was applied and American aid sent to any government which could prove itself anti - communist. The Truman doctrine became the cornerstone of America's entire Cold War policy. In June 1947 came the Marshall Plan, a vast programme of American economic aid to Europe. In effect this was the economic arm of the Truman Doctrine in Europe.

The setting up of the North Atlantic Treaty Organisation in 1949 - a military alliance of Western nations - can be seen as providing final proof that the West under principally American leadership, and Eastern Europe under the Soviet Union were now in direct opposition and hostility to each other.

Many rival views had developed as to the origins of the Cold War. The Traditionalist or Orthodox view was that Soviet aggression and expansionism was responsible and further that this aggressive Soviet behaviour came from communist ideology, Russian imperialist traditions and Stalin's personality. The view of the Revisionists was that it was actually Western distrust of the Soviet Union, and attempts by the West to try and establish economic control of Europe that was the cause.

However, the Post - revisionist view adopted a more neutral stance and I believe a more accurate one. It blamed both sides for inaugurating the cold war.

Nevertheless the cold war did not always dictate the thrust of Soviet-American relations, and gave way to detente by about 1969, a concept denoting a relaxation of tensions.[8] This period of detente was at its peak between 1969 and 1976. Detente was based on a recognition that peaceful coexistence was an essential ingredient in American - Soviet relations, and that in its absence the cold war and an expanding arms race could lead to the calamity of a nuclear war.

After two decades of confrontational cold war politics, the two superpowers began to negotiate their differences in the 1960's as a result of the military situational factors.

The period of detente produced a number of arms limitation agreements, increased East - West trade, the Helsinki Accord aimed at obtaining a general agreement to the post - World War II European Status quo, and an increase in cultural exchanges. It began to encounter problems from 1977-79 and eventually collapsed following the Soviet invasion of Afghanistan in December 1979.

Having now outlined the general framework behind this book, we come to the purpose of this chapter, which is to chart the state of Soviet-American relations beginning from the events in Afghanistan in December 1979 through to Mikhail Gorbachev's rise to power in March 1985. With this in mind the chapter is divided for convenience into three sections. Section one has as its starting point the Soviet invasion of Afghanistan, which triggered off a massive deterioration in Soviet-American relations during the course of 1980 in what was to be President Carter's final year in office. Section two analyses the superpower relationship under Reagan's first three years in office, during which time there was a marked intensification in the renewed conflict generated since the end of 1979, and which shattered any hopes of a possible revival of detente, instead inaugurating what commonly became known as the Second cold war. And finally section three looks at the first signs of a possible thaw in the newly invigorated Cold war, which began to emerge or take shape at the outset of 1984 with Reagan's more conciliatory tone towards Moscow and the subsequent ascent to the Soviet leadership of a strong past advocate of detente, Konstantin Chernenko. This slowly developing rapprochement in Soviet-American relations continued through to 1985, and was still very much alive when Chernenko's death brought Gorbachev to power.

1. The Disintegration of Detente

Soviet-American relations during the course of 1980 were shaped by a number of key developments in the last few months of 1979 which were later to culminate in the eventual downfall of an already weakened detente.

Among these developments were U.S. charges in September 1979 concerning a Soviet Combat brigade in Cuba, the North Atlantic Treaty Organisation's unanimous approval of the two track plan for development of American medium range missiles in Europe coupled with simultaneous negotiations on arms control, and perhaps the most significant of all the Soviet invasion of Afghanistan in December 1979.

The Soviet intervention in Afghanistan was to mark the instant death of detente and crumbling of the fragile consensus which had begun to emerge under detente during most of the 1970s. The 'Cold War' appeared to be returning from self-imposed exile.[9] The events in Afghanistan attracted a stiff response from the United States. President Carter called it a "radical and aggressive invasion" which "could pose the most serious threat to the peace since the Second World War".[10] The United states took steps to isolate Moscow including mobilising the international community against the Soviet invasion of Afghanistan and the subsequent American sponsored resolution of censure at the United Nations which was vetoed by the Soviet Union.

President Carter's state of the Union address to a joint session of Congress on January 23, 1980, made it abundantly clear that the American response would not be confined to mere verbal condemnation. Carter emphasised that "the Soviet Union must pay a concrete price for their aggression".[11] The American president announced a package of economic sanctions against the USSR.[12] These included: an embargo on future grain exports leading to a cancellation of an offer of 17 million metric tonnes of wheat and corn; suspension of licensing of all high technology and other products requiring validated export licences pending review; reduction of Soviet fishing privileges in U.S. waters; and limitation of the Aeroflot service to the United States. On top of these Carter threatened to pull the U.S. out of the 1980 Olympic games which were to be held in Moscow. These measures were clearly intended to send a message to the Soviet Union that "....its decision to use military force in Afghanistan will be costly to every political and economic relationship it values."[13] Carter backed up the American economic and political response with a stern warning emphasising that the United States would be willing to use military force if necessary to protect its vital interests such as those in the Persian Gulf region which Washington saw as being threatened by the Soviet presence in Afghanistan. This reaffirmation of the geo-strategic importance of the Persian Gulf and the area immediately surrounding it to American interests became known as the 'Carter Doctrine'.[14]

A major casualty of the renewed confrontation in Soviet-American relations following Afghanistan was the Strategic Arms Limitations Treaty

(SALT 11),[15] signed by Carter and Brezhnev at the Vienna Summit on 18 June 1979 but yet to be ratified by the U.S. Senate. Ratification of the treaty was already in a precarious position even before the events in Afghanistan, the treaty having been 'fatally wounded' during the 1979 hearings held by the Senate Foreign relations and Armed Services Committees. Under much debate and scrutiny regarding the SALT 11 treaty, and despite Carter's support for it,[16] the president stated that "...... because of the Soviet invasion of Afghanistan, I do not believe it is advisable to have the senate consider the treaty now".[17] Despite the fact that Carter had only asked the Senate to temporarily delay consideration of the treaty it never again received formal attention. President Carter's decision was simply a response to the political reality in the U.S., and the prevailing anti-Soviet sentiment which would not only have made ratification of the treaty impossible[18] but would have been construed as sending the wrong signal to Moscow at the wrong time.

The Soviet response to the sharp deterioration in bilateral relations was to place the blame for this solely on the Unites States and exonerate itself. There was total disagreement between both sides as to the version of events in Afghanistan. The Soviets launched their own verbal offensive against Washington, coupled with fervent defiance, accusing the United States of misrepresenting the events in Afghanistan. According to the official Soviet view "..... there has been, and is, no Russian intervention in Afghanistan. The USSR acted on the basis of the Soviet-Afghan treaty of friendship".[19] Moscow's version of events was that it was giving help to the Afghan people to assist them in their struggle to repel ".... outside imperialist interference .....".[20] Indeed at the Central Committee Plenum on 23 June 1980[21], Brezhnev stated the Soviet view of the events in Afghanistan accusing the US of armed aggression against the Afghan people, and all the USSR did was help its neighbour to repel this aggression. He staunchly defended the decision to send in Soviet troops as the correct one. The USSR further assailed the economic sanctions imposed by the United States as a ".... continuation of the old policy of using trade as an instrument of political pressure".[22]

The American decision to postpone ratification of the SALT 11 treaty came under heavy Soviet criticism. Moscow argued that the decision was hard to justify considering that the treaty ".... is in the interests of the US no less than those of the USSR".[23] Indeed Leonid Brezhnev, answering questions from a *Pravda* correspondent, claimed that the American decision to shelve the treaty meant that major progress in the field of disarmament had been lost.[24] The USSR increasingly believed that Soviet-American relations were back on the 'Cold War' track, and that the gains from detente were lost because of a new militaristic course adopted by America. At the heart of Soviet accusations against the United States was the view that Washington was on a irreversible path aimed at attaining military superiority over the Soviet state. Such Soviet charges were not altogether unfounded. The Soviet invasion of Afghanistan had turned Soviet-American relations on their head and confrontation had replaced cooperation. It also encouraged the Carter administration to pursue a more hardline and vigorous defence policy. So it came as no surprise when Congress, without much opposition, approved development of two weapons - the MX missile and new nerve gas weapons labelled binary munitions, a move said to be a serious blow to the future success of arms control efforts. Moreover, Congress increased the level of defence appropriations suggested by the administration for the first time in thirteen years.[25] Commenting on Carter's state of the Union address, a *Pravda* editorial accused the U.S. of seeking outright military superiority and claimed that Washington was pursuing a course aimed at disrupting the present military balance between the U.S. and the USSR.[26] A leading Soviet academician, Georgi Arbatov, dismissed Afghanistan as the issue which was responsible for the downturn in Soviet-American relations and the consequent policy adopted by the United States which was characterised by an accelerated build-up of military power. Instead he argued that the American reversion to this militaristic approach was the root cause of the deteriorating international climate and that this policy was not the result of Soviet action in Afghanistan but in fact was based on a number of decisions taken by the U.S. and its allies prior to the events in Afghanistan. He cited the NATO decision to increase military budgets over a period of fifteen years, and to deploy new American medium range missiles in Europe.[27]

As the year progressed there appeared to be no sign of dissipation of the cold war climate created at the start of the year. In a speech on May 10 to the World Affairs Council in Philadelphia, President Carter pinned any hopes of an improvement in American-Soviet relations on an improvement in Soviet behaviour.[28] In light of the US administration's current policy of enhancing America's military capabilities, this speech was judged as hypocritical as well as hostile to the Soviet Union by the Soviet press. In remarks made at the Central Committee Plenum on 23 June 1980[29] Andrei Gromyko reiterated the Soviet view that the West had been responsible for the rise in tension and hostility, and that this could be seen in the decision of the western countries "to increase their military budgets, stepping up the arms race, and placing new American medium range missiles in Western Europe". He went on to note that the reason why the West had initiated such measures, which had contributed to East-West tension, was because of its quest “to attain a military-strategic predominance over the Soviet Union” and secondly because of its “concern that global developments were not proceeding....” as they would like. He underlined that military supremacy remained the overriding goal of the US government.

Soviet apprehension about what it saw as the dangerous militaristic course embarked upon by the United States was compounded by Presidential Directive No. 59 signed by Carter on July 25, 1980, and later leaked to the press. According to Moscow the directive essentially amounted to a new U.S. nuclear strategy.[30] This so called new nuclear strategy was viewed as particularly provocative since it appeared that the United States had acceded to the concept that waging a ‘limited nuclear war’ was possible. On October 14 Brezhnev received at the Kremlin a prominent U.S. businessman, Dr Armand Hammer, to whom he expressed his deep concern at the poor state of Soviet-American relations.[31] He reiterated comments made earlier in the year “..... that continuation by the United States of a policy of exacerbating international tension and whipping up the arms race will lead to further disorder in international relations and an increase in the threat of war”.[32] He went on to stress that a U.S. policy geared to dialogue with the Soviet Union would be more desirable and would “.... meet with a positive response on the part of the Soviet Union”. This was typical of the echoes from Moscow which tended to combine harsh critique of U.S. policy with support for cooperation and dialogue on an ‘equitable basis’.

The Soviet use of military force in Afghanistan had “..... produced a virtual cut off in substantive contact between the United States and the Soviet Union”.[33] It was not surprising therefore that there was no progress on bilateral issues, illustrated by the fact that no bilateral documents were signed during the whole of 1980.[34] Many Americans felt a sense of betrayal on the part of the USSR for the faith they had invested in detente during the 1970s only to see Moscow (as they believed) exploit the period of relaxed tensions for its own ends. The American nation appeared to have descended into a state or mood of belligerency epitomized on election day when voters opted for “..... politicians whose chief foreign policy prescriptions were more defence spending and a tougher stance against the Soviets”,[35] thus shattering any prospect of a Soviet-American rapprochement for the time being. It appears as though the Soviet leadership did not fully comprehend the scale of anti-Soviet feeling prevailing in the United States or were unwilling to accept it. Indeed the initial Soviet reaction to Reagan’s victory was one of optimism.[36] Moscow presumed that Carter’s defeat was the result of voters rejecting his bellicose foreign policy, while at the same time Moscow detected moderation in Reagan’s rhetoric. It was not until Reagan took office in January 1981 that the USSR fully appreciated his administration's strong anti-Soviet credentials. No doubt Moscow had hoped that by adopting a more moderate tone in response to Reagan's victory it might be able to dissuade the new administration from continuing with its predecessor's confrontational stance.

The chance to salvage something from a disastrous year for Soviet-American relations came with the opening of the second stage of talks on European security and cooperation under the CSCE Helsinki accord in Madrid on 11 November 1980. However no headway was made, and instead the conference provided both sides with a forum from which to launch their own propaganda offensive, thus concluding Carter's final year in office in much the same way as it had began. The Carter administration was to leave behind many pressing points of contention on its Soviet policy. The confidence and trust between the superpowers, one of the hallmarks of detente, had vanished[37] and a steady return to the cold war left the next President Ronald Reagan, with a major foreign policy challenge with which to contend.

2. Confrontation Intensified: The Reagan Presidency - The First Three Years (1981-1983)

Ronald Reagan's early pronouncements regarding the Soviet Union set an ominous precedent for the future conduct of Soviet-American relations. Having ascended to the presidency on a crest of anti-Soviet fervour Reagan proceeded with plans which would put the United States on a new collision course with Moscow. While attempting to woo Reagan at the start the Soviet leadership soon came to realise the futility of such efforts. The Reagan administration arrived in office against a backdrop of failure in American foreign policy (such as the Iran hostage crisis). Therefore at the core of the new administration's foreign policy was the need to reassert America once again including militarily, particularly in response to charges that the United States was lagging behind the Soviet Union in the military arena with the overall balance of forces favouring Moscow. The Reagan administration quickly embraced a policy of containment reminiscent of the immediate post-second world war period. It was becoming clear from the utterances emanating from Washington that Soviet-American global rivalry was back on the agenda with Washington's clear espousal of a policy aimed at rolling back Soviet gains in the third world and with Reagan more willing to intervene in regional conflicts in order to check Soviet expansionism and add credibility to his anti-communist commitments. The provision of economic, humanitarian, and military assistance were the means by which this indirect interventionist policy was to be executed, with the main beneficiaries of this aid being right wing governments and rebel movements in Central America and Africa.[38]

Any hopes of a positive breakthrough in Soviet-American relations and a relaxation of tension had been dashed by the new administration's unequivocal rejection of the concept of detente.[39] During his first press conference Reagan had slammed detente as being a one way street which the Soviet Union had used to foster its own aims, and that it was more advantageous to the USSR than to the United States.[40] The Reagan administration's harsh rhetoric towards the Soviet Union was a common feature early on.

Also in his first press conference on January 31, President Reagan accused the Soviet Union of pursuing world domination. He further added that the Soviets "reserve unto themselves the right to commit any crime, to lie, to cheat, in order to attain that, and that is moral (in their view), not immoral, and we operate on a different set of standards".[41] The Secretary of State, Alexander Haig, continued the bitter attacks on the USSR by claiming that Moscow was "training, funding and equipping international terrorism". The Haig and Reagan remarks drew an angry response from the Soviet Union who accused the administration of deliberately trying "....to discredit the peace-loving policy of the Soviet Union..." and for dragging the world into a cold war situation by hurling unsubstantiated accusations at it.[42]

Soviet-American relations suffered not only as a result of the bitter exchanges at the start of the year but also from what Moscow saw as a concerted policy of the Reagan administration to rebuild America's military capabilities, thus altering what the USSR saw as the existing equilibrium. This view was given further credence when Reagan rejected outright the SALT 11 treaty, calling it 'fatally flawed', and appeared to make no suggestions about modifying or amending the treaty.

In late March 1981 a *Pravda* article accused the United States of plunging into a new arms race with plans to increase defence spending to $178 billion. Commenting on the new U.S. government the newspaper said that the Reagan administration had set itself "..... the goal not of correcting but of multiplying the mistakes made by the preceding administration....".[43]

On the important issue of arms control and disarmament both Reagan and Secretary of State Haig had earlier in the year declared that further negotiations with the Soviets would depend on Soviet behaviour around the world. This policy of linking Soviet behaviour in specific areas with progress on particular Soviet-American issues was rejected outright by the Soviet Union. A leading member of the Politburo, Konstantin Chernenko, poured scorn over this policy of linkage arguing that it was a U.S. ploy to avoid arms talks and to exacerbate existing points of conflict in Soviet-American relations, and that it served no purpose since progress hampered by such a policy would be a mutual loss.[44] Throughout the course of the year the USSR had constantly accused Washington of being uninterested in arms control.

In August 1981 the Soviet Union took the opportunity to attack Reagan for his decision to start production of the neutron bomb, warning of the dangerous consequences of this step.[45] Reagan further left himself open to the charge of insensitivity since the decision to proceed with manufacture of the bomb came on August 6 which was the memorial day for the victims of Hiroshima. More to the point, the U.S. decision to proceed with the neutron bomb played into Soviet hands since it gave some credence to Moscow's earlier pronouncements that the Reagan administration was not committed to arms control.

When taking office President Reagan and Alexander Haig had made it clear that on arms control their emphasis would be on the need to negotiate from a position of strength[46] since only then could they persuade the USSR to take arms control seriously. This approach was highlighted by Reagan on October 2 when he announced his strategic arms policy.[47] During this he "pledged to halt the decline in America's military strength" and presented a comprehensive plan to strengthen and modernize the strategic triad of forces. He went on to clarify that such a programme would provide "the keystone to any genuine arms reduction agreement with the Soviets". This American approach to arms control did nothing to quell tense exchanges with Moscow over this issue, and was probably a major determinant in the growing peace movement in Europe and the United States.

The Soviet Union itself, while in need of a substantial arms accord, was never going to allow itself to be dictated to by the United States and was willing to negotiate only once major obstacles in the arms control field were removed. Moscow continued to campaign to reverse the NATO two track decision for deployment of Pershing and Cruise missiles in Western Europe. This issue, which had been largely overshadowed during Carter's final year by the Soviet invasion of Afghanistan and the adverse repercussions which stemmed from that, always proved to be a major irritant during questions of arms control and disarmament. The USSR welcomed with much satisfaction the upsurge in pacifist sentiment in Western Europe which culminated in demonstrations on a large scale in major cities such as London, Bonn and Rome during October 1981 against the NATO plans to deploy new U.S. missiles in Europe.[48] This increasing wave of protest and the concern portrayed by arms control advocates in the United States were prompted to a large extent by "the strong anti-Soviet line adopted" by the Reagan administration and the extensive programme of rearmament which Reagan had committed himself to undertake which in turn "had raised fears of nuclear war".[49] The USSR attempted to outfox Washington by playing the advent of peace. America thus risked forfeiting the peace card to Moscow if it totally ignored the peace movement, at the same time as the Soviet Union was calling for arms talks and tabling arms proposals.

In view of all this Reagan made an attempt to regain the initiative when he delivered a major foreign policy address before the National Press Club on November 18.[50] During this occasion he announced the so called 'zero option' according to which the United States would forgo entirely deployment of the planned missiles in Europe if the Soviet Union was prepared to dismantle its own similar weapons. Not surprisingly[51] this proposal was rejected outright by the Soviet Union as not serious, and many in the West did not expect Moscow to agree to this latest Reagan initiative.

The unacceptability of Reagan's 'zero option' is not entirely difficult to comprehend, particularly from a Soviet viewpoint. In short, Reagan's proposal for a 'zero option' meant in effect that NATO would not go ahead with the planned deployment of 572 or so U.S. missiles in Europe on condition that the Soviets would be required to eliminate all their deployment of SS-20 missiles including dismantling the 600 or so intermediate range missiles installed since the 1950s. Furthermore the proposal excluded British and French missile systems which the Soviets reminded were also pointed at them. The Soviet newspaper *Izvestia* called the Reagan arms cut proposal a 'propaganda ploy' to show that the American President wanted peace.[52] Furthermore his proposals were viewed by the Soviets as not in good faith and were according to them deliberately framed to be unacceptable. The Soviet press referring to the Reagan proposal once again in 1982 cynically dubbed it as 'zero-option again' in conjunction with new U.S. proposals.[53]

Aside from the zero option offered by Reagan, he used the November 18 address as a platform from which to illustrate his concern at what he described as a steady Soviet military build-up over the past decade which had allowed Moscow to develop an overwhelming advantage. He rejected the Soviet claim that a balance of Intermediate Nuclear forces already existed in Europe, and announced that he had proposed a defence programme "which will remedy the neglect of the past decade ......" All in all this Reagan address combining unacceptable arms proposals with plans for strengthening America's military capabilities, did not go down as well in

Soviet eyes as one would have expected.

Negotiations on Intermediate Nuclear forces officially opened in Geneva on November 30. Arms talks particularly those involving INF in Europe were always a contentious issue in Soviet-American relations. This was because Europe was regarded as the major theatre of operation in the event of any future world war and both sides were therefore anxious to avoid being perceived as having a military-strategic disadvantage in Europe. The importance of Europe was spelled out by Reagan during his afore mentioned November 18 address when he talked about the growing threat to Western Europe posed by Soviet intermediate range missile systems, and explained that this reason was paramount in the NATO two track decision to deploy missiles capable of reaching targets in the Soviet Union. Any hope of serious progress at the Geneva negotiations had been severely dented by Reagan's controversial 'zero option' proposal which was heavily weighted against the Soviet Union, and which the American side restated at the negotiations. The American delegation led by Paul Nitze[54] presented Reagan's proposals in detail. The Soviet team headed by Yuli Kvitsinsky insisted that only weapons deployed in Europe be discussed, a move aimed at deflecting the talks away from the Soviet SS-20s stationed in Siberia (outside European Russia) but still capable of striking targets in Western Europe. Moreover they demanded that British and French nuclear systems be counted in the overall Western tally of forces. As a result the failure of these latest INF negotiations, plagued as they were by major differences, was no surprise.

The downhill course which Soviet-American relations had assumed since December 1979 showed no signs of abating throughout 1981, a year which was rife with charge and countercharge. Towards the end of the year Soviet-American relations plunged to an even deeper level of hostility when on December 13 the authorities in Poland imposed martial law. During the course of the year the United States had warned Moscow not to intervene in the Polish crisis amidst increasing concern that the Soviet Union might send troops to quash the Solidarity movement. Despite the fact that the USSR did not intervene, at least not directly, to determine the events in Poland, the military crack-down was blamed on Moscow by the United States. As a result, Reagan announced on December 29 a whole package of sanctions on economic relations with the Soviet Union.[55] These wide ranging sanctions involved: the suspension of the issuance and renewed of all validated export licences; the suspension of all Aeroflot services; the postponement of negotiations on a new long term agreement; as well as various other measures including sanctions on oil and gas technology. The Soviet response to the line taken by Washington over Poland was one of utter dismay. The Soviet leader Brezhnev in a letter to Reagan on the situation in Poland accused America of interference in the internal Affairs of Poland and alleged that "the present US administration had done a lot ..... to undermine everything positive that had been achieved .... in relations between the two countries...", and that the further erosion of Soviet-American relations would be the sole responsibility of Washington.[56] On the question of sanctions imposed by the United States, the Soviet trade minister Nikolai Patolichev said that "the US administration has again resorted to an unlawful play .... and is trying to use trade and economic relations with the USSR and other socialist countries to bring pressure to bear on them".[57]

The sharp verbal exchanges between the superpowers were reminiscent of the cold war climate created in the aftermath of Afghanistan. Thus it was becoming increasingly evident in early 1982 that Soviet-American relations were settling down into their now customary adverse state.

Another area of Soviet-American conflict, in addition to the Polish crisis, which arose in early 1982 was the construction of a natural gas pipeline from Siberia to Western Europe (an East-West project between the Soviet Union and Western Europe). The United States was highly critical of its Western allies in Europe for the close economic cooperation that the pipeline project would entail. Many in the US administration were beginning to feel a sense of betrayal on the part of allies who were cooperating far too intimately with Moscow on economic matters. A major objection voiced by America was that "the natural gas pipeline would make Western Europe overly dependent on the Soviet Union for energy supplies and would provide billions of dollars in hard currency to prop up the ailing Soviet economy"[58] which Reagan argued was already heavily militarized and which would thus threaten a principal objective of his administration, to check and contain the growth in Soviet military power. Reagan deliberately made an effort to prevent completion of the pipeline, and this opportunity conveniently arose over the events in Poland which prompted Reagan to announce sanctions against Moscow which included "a prohibition on U.S. exports of equipment for construction of a natural gas pipeline from Siberia to Western Europe".[59] This led to a certain amount of friction between the United States and its European allies many of whom believed that economic detente was a useful way of easing East-West tensions and who also had strong commercial and economic links with the Soviet Union.

The Soviet reaction was one of total fury at Reagan's 'discriminatory measures' and attempts by the United States ".... to wreck East-West economic links-links which are mutually beneficial".[60] Moscow was also quick to highlight the critical reaction of America's European allies, claiming that Washington was trying "to deprive them of the undoubted advantages which they obtain from economic cooperation with socialist countries". The USSR was quite clearly infuriated by Reagan's attempts to sabotage the completion of the pipeline particularly as it was on the verge of finalising arrangements concerning the pipeline project.[61]

Preoccupation with the events in Poland and the pipeline fiasco meant that other issues had been largely forced into the background during the first few months of 1982.

In a key speech on March 16, 1982[62] widely regarded as having the makings of a peace initiative, Brezhnev declared a unilateral moratorium on the deployment of intermediate range nuclear weapons in European Russia, and a halt in the replacement of the old SS-4 and SS-5 missiles with the more modern SS-20 missiles. This moratorium was to remain in effect until an agreement had been reached on the reduction of intermediate weapons or until the deployment of the American Pershing 11 and cruise missiles in Europe would begin. Brezhnev's proposals helped further buttress the already growing peace movement in Europe.

The USSR, although critical of the Reagan administration's decision to abandon detente, urged the need for dialogue. At the 26th party congress the Soviet leader Brezhnev suggested a possible summit meeting in the autumn with Reagan while speaking "about the usefulness of an active dialogue with the United States on all levels".[63] While attracting much favourable commentary from the foreign media, Brezhnev's comments produced only a lukewarm response from Washington.

It seemed at last that there would be some scope for the positive development of Soviet-American relations. This was given a boost by Reagan's address on East-West relations delivered at Eureka College, Illinois[64] on May 9 during which he announced the resumption of the strategic arms reduction talks or START to culminate later in a joint US-Soviet statement announcing the beginning of such talks on June 29. More importantly Reagan during his speech at Eureka College pledged efforts to reduce the nuclear arsenals of both superpowers, providing further encouragement for the impending arms talks. In another important point Reagan stressed the necessity of dialogue in East-West relations remarking "that peoples' problems can be solved when people talk to each other instead of about each other", a significant statement when one considers that in cold war rhetoric the latter tended to predominate.

Reagan put forward further positive overtures during the summer of 1982 when during a speech delivered to the West German Bundestag[65] he announced a NATO initiative to be put forward at the Vienna talks, with the objective of reducing the ground forces in Central Europe in stages.

Despite the positive signals which had been evident from both Washington and Moscow concerning arms control, it was becoming clear that Moscow at least was still not fully convinced of the Reagan administration's wholesale commitment to substantive progress on arms limitations. The Soviets were wary of Reagan's latest arms proposals, and the Soviet press accused the United States of seeking unilateral advantages for itself and unilateral disarmament for the USSR.[66] Moreover Reagan's new proposals were seen as a ploy timed as a response to the "widening anti-nuclear movement in the United States, as well as the growth of anti-nuclear, pacifistic sentiments in Western Europe" thus raising once again the question of Reagan's sincerity. Most political commentators saw echoes of Reagan's zero option in his latest proposals. Some in the Soviet Union acknowledged Reagan's efforts to move the arms control process forward but were not at all satisfied with the specific contents of his proposals. A prime condition which Moscow wanted met was that any talks on arms reductions should take account "of the legitimate interests of each side and the strict observance of the basic principles of equality and equal security",[67] an ingredient which they saw missing from Reagan's arms control and disarmament package.

Just two weeks before the resumption of the START talks in Geneva, the Soviet foreign minister Gromyko in a speech to the UN General Assembly read out a message from the Soviet leader Brezhnev stating that the USSR would not be the first to use nuclear weapons in Europe.[68] He reiterated this point at a later press conference in New York calling his country's renunciation of the first use of nuclear weapons an "historic decision".[69] During his visit to America Gromyko held discussions with his U.S. counterpart Alexander Haig.[70] The meetings were not particularly productive, achieved no pre-Geneva boost and merely provided a stage on which both sides could set out their stall for the oncoming START talks.

US-Allied wrangling over the question of economic cooperation with the Soviet Union had not wholly subsided, and it resurfaced in June when Reagan expanded the sanctions he had imposed on the Soviet Union in December 1981 to include exports of pipeline equipment by foreign subsidiaries of U.S. firms or by foreign firms holding American licences. This move enraged America's allies who saw it as an encroachment upon their sovereignty and ignored Reagan's new stricter sanctions, instead ordering their firms to continue fulfilling contracts made with the Soviets. "American sanctions a flop" was the heading in one Soviet newspaper, commenting on the 'economic war' which it argued Reagan had declared on the Soviet Union, and which it stressed actually amounted to a trade war against its own allies.[71] U.S Secretary of State Alexander Haig resigned over his "disagreement with Reagan's economic sanctions against the Soviet Union".[72] His departure just days before the START talks attracted expressions of concern from Moscow who feared that his replacement by George Shultz raised the possibility that U.S. foreign policy might become more confrontational.

Three days after the death of Soviet President Leonid Brezhnev on 10th November 1982, Reagan announced that he was lifting sanctions imposed on the Soviet Union for its alleged complicity in the imposition of martial law in Poland. However Reagan's decision did not represent a sweeping reversal of the initial sanctions imposed in December 1981 and later added to in June 1982. Instead a number of measures were to remain in force because according to the State Department they had "a heavier short term economic effect on the Soviet Union" than the mainly pipeline related sanctions which were the subject of removal.[73] In reality, Reagan's decision to remove some of the sanctions represented the administration's realisation of the failure of such a policy, the unnecessary strains which it led to with America's NATO allies, and all this quite apart from the considerable damage to the U.S. economy itself. Thus the whole sanctions issue signalled a defeat for Reagan who was able "to reverse his policy on the sanctions with only a minimum of embarrassment"[74], thanks mainly to the quiet diplomacy of Secretary of State Shultz with America's European allies[75] which allowed Reagan a face saving formula. Reagan announced that he was able to lift the sanctions in return for allied assurances that they would be extra vigilant in the future when engaging in trade with the Soviet Union which contributed "... to the military or strategic advantage of the USSR....."

Despite the fact that a new leader, Yuri Andropov, was now at the helm in the Kremlin, U.S.-Soviet relations showed no sign of improvement towards the end of 1982. None of the major underlying problems which had soured relations between the two sides ever since the start of the 1980s looked any nearer resolution.

On November 22 Reagan announced his 'dense pack' plan for deployment of the new MX intercontinental ballistic missile which was likely to add further tensions to the superpower relationship.[76] The plan was part of a speech televised nationally with the intention of bolstering "support in the United States for his nuclear weapons policies and for his approach to arms control negotiations with the Soviet Union". During this speech Reagan emphasised the need to restore the military balance which he argued was heavily weighted in favour of Moscow. The Soviet Union quickly denounced Reagan's adoption of the 'dense pack' mode of basing for the MX missile as a serious violation of both the SALT 1 and SALT 11 treaties and later announced itself that the USSR would match the MX missile.[77]

The new general secretary Yuri Andropov raised hopes of a fresh injection of life into Soviet foreign policy.[78] Andropov reaffirmed the Soviet Union's rejection of the U.S. policy of linkage and at the same time expressed the importance of peace and reaching agreements based on support for detente. Andropov did nevertheless make a new offer on missile cuts in Europe on December 21 at a meeting commemorating the 60th anniversary of the Soviet Union.[79] This was seen as a modification of earlier Soviet positions. Among the major elements in the arms proposals were that the USSR would be prepared to reduce its strategic arms by more than 25%, propose a substantial cutback in the number of nuclear warheads and the greatest possible restrictions on the improvement of nuclear weapons.

1983 began as a year of hopeful expectation with arms control talks set to resume in late January. These expectations were somewhat blunted by Reagan's state of the Union address[80] during which he once again announced his administration's defence programme aimed at rectifying "the neglect of the past decade". Talk of major defence systems needing modernisation was hardly the most appropriate rhetoric at a time of important arms control talks. Reagan's address did not indicate any softening of the U.S. line towards Moscow.

In its analysis of the speech, the Soviet newspaper *Pravda* described it as a disappointing restatement of old positions and noted that the Reagan administration had "not learned from the sad experience of the past two years and intends to persist in its bankrupt policy of increasing military expenditures as much as possible".[81] It seems evident from Reagan's state of the Union address that his administration did not detect any change for the better in Soviet policy towards the United States, as exemplified in the new Soviet leader, Andropov's first few speeches, to warrant any significant change in its own policy towards the Soviet Union. Even Andropov's new arms proposals were more or less rejected by the U.S. as a mere propaganda manoeuvre. This prompted charges from the Soviet Union that the United States had caused a deadlock at the Geneva arms talks.[82] Moscow accused the Americans of dragging their feet and avoiding proposals on the issue of arms reductions. Later in February it was the turn of Andropov to reject Reagan's missile scrapping plan which Moscow said amounted to unilateral disarmament on the part of the Soviet Union, a concept which it would never accept.[83] Reagan's 'unrealistic proposal' was viewed by the USSR as a perfect example showing that Washington did not want to "find a mutually acceptable accord with the Soviet Union".

By late February it was becoming increasingly apparent that any upturn in Soviet-American relations was not forthcoming for the time being at least. The Geneva arms talks had been a total failure with both sides having made proposals unacceptable to the other. The major bones of contention centred on the planned deployment of missiles scheduled to begin at the end of the year, the U.S. zero option which would halt the proposed deployment but which was unacceptable to the Soviet side, and the question of Soviet SS-20 rockets aimed at Western Europe and which the Soviets were refusing to dismantle.

During the course of March Ronald Reagan made a number of speeches which resulted only in souring relations with Moscow. One of those speeches saw Reagan make particularly inflammatory references to the Soviet Union. This speech was delivered on March 8 to the U.S. National Association of Evangelicals, and in it Reagan depicted the leaders of the Soviet Union as 'evil' and the country itself an "evil empire".[84] Another speech made by Reagan on March 23 cast doubt on the future conduct of the already fledgling arms control and disarmament process.[85] This was the so called 'Star Wars' speech during which Reagan challenged the American scientific and strategic community to develop means of intercepting and destroying ballistic missiles before they reached the territory of the United States or its allies. This speech served as the foundation from which later emerged Reagan's Strategic Defense Initiative (SDI).[86] The Soviet response was predictable. The 'Star Wars' programme symbolised to them an attempt by the United States to attain a position of superiority over them. The programme also added a whole new dimension to the concept of nuclear deterrence by implying with its defensive nature the capacity to survive a first strike and itself sense the possibility of victory with a more effective retaliatory strike, or even be induced into a first strike with the added assurance of an adequate defensive cover that such a programme would entail. Thus the whole idea of such an Anti-Ballistic Missile System (ABM) would serve only to dangerously destabilise the concept of deterrence.

On May 17 the fourth round of Geneva talks began with the outlook very bleak. Ahead of the talks the Soviets had already rejected an American proposal concerning the limitation of nuclear weapons in Europe as a prelude towards the eventual elimination of medium range missiles from the continent, on the grounds that it was yet another attempt to impose unilateral reductions on the USSR.[87] In late May Moscow toughened its own stance by indicating that the USSR would respond to the proposed NATO deployment scheduled for the end of the year with new weapons of its own in Europe to counterbalance what it saw as the threat posed by the new U.S. missiles.

The persistent climate of suspicion and distrust in Soviet-American relations fuelled largely by poor progress at the talks on arms reductions continued throughout the summer, and to an extent was illustrated by a statement made by Secretary of State Shultz titled "Soviet-American relations in the context of U.S. foreign policy" delivered before the Senate foreign relations committee on June 15, 1983.[88] During this statement Shultz acknowledged that "we and the Soviets have sharply divergent goals and philosophies of political and moral order" and stressed the now familiar line of US policy "that peace must be based on strength" while committing the US to a 'constructive dialogue' with Moscow based on this premise. The statement was largely one of pessimism, underlining U.S.-Soviet differences, and went on to criticise Soviet behaviour over the past decade which had come into conflict (said Shultz) "with many of our objectives". Shultz then proceeded to review what he called the Soviet challenge citing various developments such as the "Soviet quest for military superiority" and the "unconstructive Soviet involvement in the third world" as indicators which had caused America most concern, and used this to justify the U.S. programme to boost its defences. Signs that the United States was not altogether optimistic about a successful outcome to the present negotiations with the Soviet Union were highlighted by Shultz's comment that "we have not staked so much on the prospect of a successful negotiating outcome that we have neglected to secure ourselves against the possibility of failure".

Shultz's statement came under intense criticism in the Soviet press.[89] The USSR saw it as evidence "that one should not look for results as long as President Reagan remains in the White House, a view given further credence by Shultz's own comment that one should not "expect any agreement to be achieved in the near future" in any of the Soviet-American negotiations at that time underway in the area of arms control. This gave support to the Soviet view that the Reagan administration would continue to rely on military strength and would sabotage efforts to limit nuclear weapons and curb the arms race.

Sporadic rumours of a possible U.S.-Soviet Summit reported to have originated in the West were dismissed as premature by Andrei Gromyko, speaking in June.[90] Gromyko emphasised that whilst the Soviet Union had always expressed its interest in the desirability of a Soviet-American summit meeting, American talk of such a meeting had to be backed up by American policy which exhibited "real signs of a willingness to conduct business in a serious and constructive manner" before it could be considered a reality.

The faltering Soviet-American relationship was put under strain once again following the shooting down of an unarmed South Korean airliner by Soviet warplanes on September 1.[91] The airliner had strayed into Soviet airspace and the ensuing incident led to an exchange of harsh accusations between Moscow and Washington. At a meeting of his National Security Council Reagan said the Soviets had carried out a 'barbaric act' that caused him "anger disbelief and profound sadness".[92] For its part the Soviet Union insisted that it did not know that the airliner was a civilian plane and maintained that the plane was spying on sensitive military installations on Sakhalin island. It also accused Washington of using the incident to whip up anti-Soviet propaganda, and called the presence of the South Korean airliner in Soviet airspace a deliberate provocation, planned in advance and which only Washington knew about.[93]

News of the downing of the airliner had provoked massive indignation in America's highest political circles. Both the Senate and House of Representatives voted unanimously to condemn the Soviet action.[94] Despite Reagan's tough verbal response there was much dissatisfaction among hardline conservatives who urged the President to take sterner action. The incident had made clear, yet again, the extreme fragility of Soviet-American's relations.

As the political wrangling generated by the incident petered out there was a return to the issue of arms control and disarmament which had dominated Soviet-American relations throughout the year. In late October Andropov made a new offer of missile cuts in order to relieve the impasse at the Geneva talks which he alleged had resulted from American inflexibility.[95] As the date for the deployment of new U.S. missiles approached Andropov stated that the USSR would pull out of the Geneva talks if the proposed deployment took place. The American response was a negative one, and appeared to indicate that with the date for the arrival of the 'Euromissiles' moving ever nearer, Washington had lost its zeal to negotiate a last ditch agreement.

The final blow to the fate of the already beleaguered arms talks came in Geneva on November 23 when the Soviet delegation announced that it was pulling out of the talks in response to the arrival of the new American missiles in Europe.[96] In a statement on November 25 Andropov listed steps[97] he said the Soviet Union would take in order to counter the 'Euromissile' deployment including no further participation in the talks on the nuclear arms limitations in Europe. Andropov expressed his concern at the deployment of the missiles which he envisaged as increasing "the real danger that the U.S. may bring a catastrophe on the peoples of Europe". The START talks were adjourned without a resumption date, thus signalling the total collapse of the Soviet-American arms negotiating process.[98]

3. Towards Conciliation (1984 - March 1985)

During Reagan's first three years in office, US-Soviet relations had been characterised by mutual hostility with regard to most issues enhanced by the confrontational stance adhered to by the new U.S. administration towards Moscow. In view of this, and the deteriorating climate of Soviet-American relations at the end of 1983, Reagan's final year of his first term in office began in sharp contrast to his previous three. In his annual state of the Union address, the President appeared to have remarkably softened his tone towards the USSR.[99] In the part of the speech addressed to the Soviet Union he spoke of the danger of a nuclear war and stressed that the onus was on both superpowers to avoid such a conflict, and urged the need for both countries to come together "to build a safer and far better world" with peace being his central theme. The degree of moderation detected in this Reagan address was a welcome relief from the problems which had dogged Soviet-American relations since the beginning of the 1980s, and it came just two weeks after Andropov restated Moscow's terms for resuming arms talks.[100] Thus both leaders appeared to indicate at the start of 1984 a willingness to resume some sort of dialogue which looked to have been shattered by the decision to proceed with the deployment of the new American missiles in Europe. The Soviet Union's willingness to resume talks with the United States however was conditional on the NATO countries displaying a readiness "to return to the situation that existed before the deployment of the American medium range missiles in Europe began ....."[101] Later Andropov once again reiterated calls for dialogue with the United States but only on the basis of what he called "an equal footing, and not from a position of strength as R. Reagan proposes".

After Andropov's death on February 9 1984 the new Soviet leader Konstantin Chernenko continued his predecessor's policy of open dialogue with the U.S. Chernenko's accession to power provided the impetus for fresh hopes of a possible return to detente since he was seen as a past advocate of it.[102]

This euphoria over a possible turn for the better in Soviet-American relations was not sustained chiefly because of the lack of any substantive progress on the most important determinants of the superpower relationship. Soviet policy towards the U.S. began to settle down into its familiar pattern of combining peace overtures with criticisms of U.S. foreign policy. Answering questions from the Soviet press in April, Chernenko expressed his concern at the deteriorating international situation which he said was the result of the dangerous policy pursued by the U.S. administration which relied on military force.[103] He held the view that there had been "no real changes in U.S. policy" and any peace-loving rhetoric heard from Washington was never backed up by 'practical deeds'.

In May 1984 the USSR decided to boycott the Los Angeles Olympics.[104] This was probably in retaliation for America's boycott of the Moscow Olympics in 1980, and represented a random action unconditional on the state of Soviet-American relations at the time. The explanation offered by the Soviet Union through its Olympic Committee was that participation in the games was impossible on the grounds of lax security, and fear for the safety of its athletes.

As the U.S. presidential elections approached, Moscow was in no mood to assist Reagan in his bid to win a second term. Most Reagan statements on relations with the Soviet Union were closely scrutinized to establish whether they were "purely tactical moves in the interest of the election campaign" and intended to mask the still relatively belligerent American policy towards Moscow. This was indeed how the USSR viewed the remarks by Reagan on a possible Soviet-U.S. summit in June. *Pravda* labelled the American president's talk of a summit meeting as 'frivolous' and intended to bolster his re-election chances.[105]

A major impediment in Soviet-American relations had emerged during 1984. This was the question of an arms race in space or the militarisation of space, a product of Reagan's 'Star Wars speech' of March 1983. Moscow, which could ill afford an escalation of the arms race into space quite apart from the serious strategic-military implication that space - based weapons would entail, pushed the question of space weapons near the top of its arms negotiating agenda. To the USSR Reagan's plan for outer space was yet another example of his administration's desire to continue the arms race and thwart any chance of serious negotiations.[106]

The upgrading of the U.S.- USSR hotline indicated a minor lull in the growing differences between Washington and Moscow. Senior Soviet academician Georgi Arbatov attacked Reagan's policy as still blatantly anti-Soviet, with its central goal being military superiority over the USSR allowing it to "wage any type of nuclear war and win it".[107]

The first meeting in a long time between Gromyko and U.S. Secretary of State Shultz took place in late September[108] on the occasion of the 39th Session of the UN General Assembly. In his meeting with Shultz, Gromyko blamed the U.S for "soured relations", and at the address to the Assembly[109] repeated this hard line on the United States that he had constantly deployed throughout 1984, accusing Washington of blocking arms stock and calling for action against the militarisation of space. Gromyko also met Reagan on September 28, and like his previous meeting with Shultz, this produced rather meagre results with Gromyko envisaging no positive changes in

American policy.[110]

By October it was becoming increasingly obvious that Reagan was going to be re-elected, and with this in mind Moscow was keen to improve relations with Washington knowing that it would be better to work with Reagan on a more conciliatory basis rather that risk renewed confrontation which would jeopardise the chance of an arms control agreement badly needed by Moscow. This cause was helped by the fact that in Reagan's re-election campaign "confrontational and anti-Soviet rhetoric was far less common than in his early years in office".[111]

A positive restructuring of Soviet-American relations began to take shape in the last few months of the year. For a start, Secretary of State Shultz, speaking in late October, appeared to indicate if not an end but a substantial phasing down of the policy of linkage[112] so abhorred by Moscow, and which had been a part of U.S negotiating strategy with regard to the Soviet Union at different times and under various American Presidents including Reagan. In a speech in Los Angeles Shultz was quoted as saying that "on the whole ...... linkage as a policy has its limitations".[113] Shultz's apparent renunciation of linkage could only help to improve the climate of bilateral relations.

Furthermore the Soviet leader Chernenko answering questions from the NBC Television Company[114] was reported as saying that better U.S-USSR relations were possible if the spirit of detente returned in Washington. Clearly by the end of the year Chernenko was offering the U.S an olive branch in the hope of engaging Washington in constructive dialogue. On November 23 it was announced in the Soviet press[115] that "the Soviet Union and the United States of America have agreed to enter into new talks with a view to reaching mutually acceptable accords on the entire range of questions relating to nuclear and space arms" with Gromyko and Shultz to meet on January 7-8 1985 in Geneva to set a precise agenda for the talks. In this way U.S. - Soviet relations ended on a high note and prospects for the new year appeared very much brighter.

On January, Gromyko and Shultz met as planned and announced[116] that the two countries would at the proposed resumption of talks on March 12 negotiate about three weapons: strategic nuclear weapons/bombers, intermediate range nuclear forces (INF) in Europe, and space weaponry. In a press conference held on January 9, Reagan pledged his commitment to a positive dialogue with Moscow by stating that he would be "flexible, patient and determined" in order to keep that dialogue alive. Nevertheless the U.S-Soviet arms talks to be held were in danger of being destroyed by the issue of space arms. In the weeks leading up to the talks statements from Moscow attacked the American 'Star Wars' programme[117] and Reagan's determined and defiant commitment to it was seen as causing a shadow over the impending Geneva talks.[118] Just two days before opening the talks the Soviet leader Chernenko died. He was replaced by Mikhail Gorbachev under whose leadership the Soviet Union embarked on the path to arguably its warmest relations with Washington since the heyday of detente.

Conclusions

It can be concluded that Soviet-American relations were in a state of adversity for the most part of 1980 through to March 1985. Even though there were momentary hopes of an upturn these were often unrealized. The lack of measurable progress is particularly evident from the fact that between 1980 and 1984 only five bilateral documents were signed by the USSR with the USA, with none at all in 1980 and 1983.[119] This was a low figure in comparison to the previous five year period when 17 bilateral documents were signed. The low figure for 1980 to 1984 is not unusual in view of the deterioration in superpower relations which occurred at this time. The depression in relations began in late December 1979 with the Soviet invasion of Afghanistan, which provoked a response of outrage from Washington. This led Carter to adopt a more confrontational policy towards Moscow which contrasted sharply with his previous three years in office and was an approach dictated by Soviet international behaviour, putting the USSR largely on the defensive.

In the wake of a wave of anti-Soviet sentiment Ronald Reagan, a hardline proponent of anti-communism, was elected. Reagan's foreign policy was based on an attempt to compensate for, and to a large extent, rectify the loss of U.S power and prestige which has occurred during the 1970s. Reagan's presidency injected a new intensity in its confrontational posture towards Moscow. It became rapidly apparent that Reagan and the Soviet Union were incompatible. In contrast to Carter, Reagan's approach to Moscow was dictated not primarily by world events or Soviet international behaviour as such but was part of a deliberate strategy to put into practice his anti communist credentials. The Reagan administration decided to challenge what it saw as the Soviet threat to American interests, a view perpetuated by alleged Soviet military superiority.

Soviet policy towards the U.S was a combination of calls for a return to detente and outright criticism of the tough militaristic course undertaken by Washington. To Moscow, Reagan was questioning as well as threatening the legitimacy of the Soviet Union as a superpower. Reagan's swift renunciation of detente implied immediately that he was not about to embark on a policy of rapprochement with the Soviet Union, not at least until he had restored U.S pride and prestige.

With regard to most bilateral issues Washington and Moscow were between 1980 and 1984 on a collision course. The U.S fostered a policy of containment concerning regional conflicts in order to deter or check the increasing Soviet influence in the third world. Reagan's assured support for any government or guerilla movement that could prove itself anti-communist often left him open to the charge from Moscow that America was aiding authoritarian and corrupt regimes known for their human rights abuses, for example the right wing government in El Salvador, and also supporting right wing guerilla groups responsible for the indiscriminate killing of civilians. The superpowers intervened indirectly around the globe in various regional flashpoints through economic, military and humanitarian assistance to governments and rebel movements of their respective inclinations.

There was no progress on arms control and disarmament despite numerous proposals and counterproposals, largely because of what appeared to be on the surface intractable obstacles such as the NATO decision to deploy new U.S. missiles in Europe, Reagan's plans for an Anti-Ballistic Missile system (ABM) in space, and the general American policy of accelerated rearmament.

1984 proved to be a more positive year, and although such hopes were dented during the middle of the year, they were revived towards the end with Moscow and Washington building some sort of rapprochement which was later substantially enhanced with Gorbachev and Reagan.

Notes

1. David W. Hunter, *Western Trade Pressure on the Soviet Union* (Macmillan 1991), p.83.
2. Michael Mastanduno, *Economic Containment* (Cornell University Press 1992), p.67.
3. See *Ibid* p.39.
4. See *Ibid* chapter 3.
5. See *Ibid* pp.93-98.
6. See *Ibid* p.109.
7. On Soviet-American relations since 1945, see D. McDougall, *Soviet-American Relations since the 1940s*, 2nd edition (Melbourne: Arnold 1990); Chris Jones, *Superpowers: Relations between the Soviet Union and the USA since 1945* (Melbourne: Longmans 1988); Richard Crockatt, *The Fifty Years War, The United States, and the Soviet Union in World Politics, 1941-1991* (Routledge 1994); see also A Horelick (ed), *US-Soviet Relations: The Next Phase* (Cornell

UP 1986); S. Bialer and M Mandelbaum, *The Global Rivals* (NY Knopf 1988); Raymond Garthoff, *Detente and Confrontation: American-Soviet relations from Nixon to Reagan* (Brookings Institution 1985); R.S.Ovinnikov, *Zigzagi Vneshnei Politiki SShA* (Moscow IPL 1986); G.A.Trofimenko (ed) *Sovetsko-Amerikanskie Otnosheniya V Sovremennom Mire* (Moscow Nauka 1987); P.T.Podlesnyi, *SSSR I SShA: 50 let diplomaticheskikh otnoshenii* (M.Mezh. Otnosheniya 1983); see further Peter E. Boyle, *American-Soviet relations: From the Russian Revolution to the fall of communism* (London, New York 1993) for an historical analysis of the U.S.-Soviet relationship since 1918 and for the origins of the Cold War.

8. For a detailed analysis of the concept of detente see Garthoff, *Detente and Confrontation.*
9. On the deterioration of Soviet-American relations at the start of 1980 and the return of the Cold War see Garthoff, *Detente and Confrontation*, pp.887-1009; see also Strobe Talbott, 'US-Soviet relations from bad to worse', *Foreign Affairs*, Volume 58, No. 3 (1980), pp.515-539.
10. *Congressional Quarterly Almanac 1979*, p.98.
11. Carter's state of the Union address *in Congressional Quarterly Almanac*, p.30-E, 1980.
12. See Congressional Research Service, *An Assessment of the Afghanistan Sanctions: Implications for trade and diplomacy in the 1980s*. Report prepared for the subcommittee on Europe and the Middle East of the Committee on Foreign Affairs, US House of Representatives (Washington D.C. US Government 75-985, 1981).
13. Carter's state of the Union address in *Congressional Quarterly Almanac*, 1980, p.30-E.
14. See *Mirovaya Ekonomika I Mezhdunarodnye Otnosheniya* No.3, 1980, pp.17-28 in which the Carter Doctrine is heavily criticised and viewed as an attempt by the US to substantiate American hegemonism and pursue the path of increased militarism, undermining detente and relations with the USSR on the way.
15. See Louisa S. Hulett, *From Cold Wars to Star Wars: Debates over defence and detente,* Chapter IV (University Press of America, 1988).
16. See Jimmy Carter, *Keeping Faith* (Collins, London 1982), p.473 and 475 where Carter's support for the treaty is clearly evident in his statement that "the worst disappointment to me personally was the immediate and automatic loss of any chance for early ratification of the SALT II treaty". He also goes on to say that "scuttling the SALT II treaty" was among those things he didn't want to do.
17. *Congressional Quarterly Almanac 1980*, p.5-E.
18. Carter stresses this very point that the treaty would have been easily defeated in Carter, *Keeping Faith*, p.475.
19. L.I.Brezhnev, *Leninskim Kursom* Vol. 8, (Moscow: Politizdat 1981), pp. 276-286.
20. *Pravda,* January 5, 1980, p.5.
21. *Extracts from Central Committee Plenum of 23 June 1980* (Centre for the Conservation of Contemporary Documentation, Moscow).
22. Nikolai Inozemtsev vice chairman of the Soviet State planning committee answering questions from a Novosti correspondent - printed in *Soviet News* Tuesday February 26, 1980, p.67.
23. *Pravda*, January 5, 1980, p.5.
24. *Ibid,* January 13, 1980, p.1.

25. *Congressional Quarterly Almanac 1980*, p.37.
26. Editorial in *Pravda*, January 29, 1980, p.4.
27. *Ibid,* p.6.
28. This speech was reviewed in *Ibid* May 11, 1980, p.5.
29. *Extracts from Central Committee Plenum of 23 June 1980* (Centre for the Conservation of Contemporary Documentation, Moscow).
30. *Pravda,* August 7, 1980, p.5.
31. *Ibid,* October 15, 1980, p.1.
32. *Ibid*, February 28, 1980, p.1.
33. *Congressional Quarterly Almanac 1980*, p.309.
34. Unpublished data from *Soviet Treaties Project*, Department of Politics, University of Glasgow.
35. *Congressional Quarterly Almanac 1980*, p.309.
36. *Izvestia* November 6, 1980, p.4.
37. See R. G. Kaiser, 'US - Soviet relations: goodbye to détente', *Foreign Affairs,* Volume 59, No. 3, (1981), pp. 500-521.
38. See Hulett: *from Cold Wars to Star Wars,* Chapter III.
39. On Reagan's approach towards the Soviet Union and on an intensification of the new Cold War during Reagan's first term see: Strobe Talbott, *The Russians and Reagan* (New York, Vintage books 1984); R. Garthoff, *The Great Transition: American - Soviet relations and the end of the Cold War* (Brookings Institution, 1994), Chapter 1; S.Bialer and J. Afferica, 'Reagan and Russia', *Foreign Affairs,* Volume 61, (Winter 82/83), pp. 249-271.
40. See *Weekly Compilation of Presidential Documents*, Volume 17 (February 2, 1981), p.66 on Reagan's remark that detente was a one way street.
41. Remarks from Reagan's Press Conference in: *Weekly Compilation of Presidential Documents*, Vol 17 (February 2 1981) pp. 66-67.
42. *Pravda*, February 1, 1981, p.5.
43. *Ibid,* March 25, 1981, p.4.
44. *Izvestia* April 23, 1981, pp.1-2.
45. *Pravda* August 14, 1981, p.4; In an article in *Mirovaya Ekonomika I Mezhdunarodnye Otnosheniya* No.11, 1982, pp.52-65, America's production of the neutron weapon is heavily criticised.
46. This was actually known as 'Peace through Strength' and became one of the mottoes of the Reagan administration as highlighted by Reagan himself in: Reagan, *An American Life*, (New York, Simon and Schuster 1990), pp.549-564.
47. For this Reagan address see *Weekly Compilation of Presidental Documents*, Vol. 17 (October 5 1981), pp.1074-75.
48. See *SshA*, January 1982, No. 1, pp. 80-83.
49. *Congressional Quarterly Almanac 1981*, p.126.
50. This Reagan address in *Congressional Quarterly Almanac 1981*, p.27 - E - 29 -E.
51. See footnote 47 as to why the Soviets rejected it outright.
52. *Izvestia*, November 20, 1981, p.6.
53. *Pravda*, May 9 1982, p.4 - Reagan's new arms proposals were seen as embodying the same ideas as his earlier zero option proposal. These new proposals made in spring 1982 were dubbed along with the zero-option as "zero options again" for the USSR.
54. See the memoir of Paul Nitze, *From Hiroshima to Glasnost* (New York, Grove,

Wiedenfeld 1989), pp. 363-411 where he recalls the major developments behind the Soviet-American arms negotiations during the years 1981-1985 at a time when he was the US Chief negotiator at arms talks with the Soviets.

55. See for more details on these sanctions: US Senate, 97th Congress 2nd session, *Soviet Economy in the 1980s: Problems and Prospects - Part 2,* selected papers submitted to the joint economic committee Congress of the United States, December 31, 1982 (US GPO Washington D.C. 1983), pp. 438-441.
56. *Izvestia,* January 9, 1982, p.4.
57. *Pravda*, January 9, 1982, p.4; see also *SShA*, April 1982, No.4, pp.55-62.
58. *Congressional Quarterly Almanac 1982*, p.163.
59. *Ibid,* p.130.
60. *Pravda*, January 10, 1982, p.4.
61. On the Soviet view about Washington's opposition to the pipeline see *SShA*, December 1982, No. 12, pp. 46-55.
62. L.I. Brezhnev, *Leniniskim Kursom* Volume 9 (Moscow: Politizdat 1983), pp.387 - 402.
63. *Izvestia* April 19, 1982, p.1.
64. The text of this Reagan speech is in *Congressional Quarterly Almanac 1982*, p.21 - E - p.24 - E.
65. For the text of Reagan speech to West German Parliament see: *New York Times*, July 10, 1982, p.16.
66. *Pravda* May 9, 1982, p.4.
67. *Ibid,* May 29, p.4.
68. The full text of Brezhnev's letter can be found in L.I.Brezhnev, *Leninskim Kursom*, Vol 9, pp.505-508, (Moscow 1983); Brezhnev's letter read out by Gromyko to the UN General Assembly - *Izvestia* June 16 1982, p.1.
69. *Pravda*, June 23, 1982, p.5.
70. Report on these talks is in *New York Times*, June 19 1982, p.6; see also Haig's comments on the talks at a news conference in *New York Times*, June 20, 1982, p.1.
71. *Sotsialisticheskaya industriya*, August 13, 1982, p.5.
72. *Congressional Quarterly Almanac 1982*, p.128; see also Alexander M Haig, *Caveat: Realism, Reagan and foreign policy* (New York, Macmillan, 1984), pp.312-316, where Haig outlines the background of events leading to his resignation. It also contains excerpts from his letter of resignation to Reagan.
73. *Ibid*, p.165.
74. *Ibid*, p.128.
75. See Shultz, *Turmoil and Triumph: My Years as Secretary of State* (Charles Scribner's Sons 1993), pp.142-143.
76. This plan is reviewed in *Ibid*, p.120.
77. *Izvestia*, December 8, 1982, p.4.
78. Yu.V.Andropov, *Izbrannye rechi i stat'i,* (Moscow: Politizdat 1983), pp.209-219.
79. *Izvestia,* December 22 1982, p.3.
80. Reagan's state of the Union address is in *Congressional Quarterly Almanac 1983*, p.4 - E.
81. *Pravda,* January 27, 1983, p.5.
82. *Ibid*, January 2, 1983, p.4.
83. *Vneshnyaya Politika Sovetskogo Soyuza*,1983, pp. 25-26.

84. *Weekly compilation of Presidential documents*, Vol.19 (March 14 1983), p.369.
85. *Ibid*, Volume 19 (March 28, 1983), pp. 442-448.
86. See Reagan, *An American Life* pp. 547-548 and 574-575 where Reagan outlines what the SDI was; see also Paul Nitze, 'SDI: its nature and rationale', *Atlantic Community Quarterly*, No. 23 (Fall 1983), pp.263-267.
87. *Pravda*, May 13, 1983, p.4.
88. This statement by George Shultz is in: *Department of State Bulletin*, Vol. 83, No.2076 (July 1983), pp.65-72.
89. *Pravda*, June 17, 1983, p.5.
90. *Ibid*, June 22, 1983, p.4.
91. See Alexander Dallin, *Black Box KALOO7 and the Superpowers* (University of California Press 1985) for a comprehensive analysis of the crisis created by the Korean Airliner incident.
92. *Congressional Quarterly Almanac 1983*, p.136.
93. *Pravda*, September 8, 1983, p.5.
94. *Congressional Quarterly Almanac 1983*, p.136.
95. *Vneshnyaya Politika Sovetskogo Soyuza, 1983*, pp.209-212.
96. *Izvestia*, November 24, 1983, p.4.
97. Statement by Andropov in *Pravda*, November 25, 1983, p.1.
98. The Soviets heavily criticised the US for the collapse of the arms negotiations and claimed that it was America's negative stand throughout 1983, which included total disregard for legitimate Soviet interests, that was responsible for the failure of the arms talks see: *Mirovaya Ekonomika I Mezhdunarodnye Otnosheniya* No. 12, 1983, pp.3-31.
99. Reagan state of the Union address in *Congressional Quarterly Almanac 1984* p5 - E - 8 - E.
100. *Izvestia*, January 13, 1984, p.1.
101. *Pravda*, January 25, 1984, p.1.
102. Indeed in his first major address since taking power Chernenko called for constructive dialogue with all countries, and restated Soviet dedication to peaceful coexistence. See *Pravda*, February 14, 1984, pp.1-2.
103. *Izvestia*, April 9, 1984, p.1.
104. Pravda, May 9, 1984, p.6.
105. *Ibid*, June 22, 1984, p.5.
106. *Ibid*, July 2, 1984, p.4.
107. *Ibid*, August 13, 1984, p.6.
108. *Izvestia*, September 28, 1984, p.4; Gromyko met Shultz while on a visit to the U.S. where he was due to address the UN General Assembly.
109. *Vneshnyaya Politika Sovetskogo Soyuza*, 1984, pp.113-125.
110. Gromyko recalls this meeting with Reagan and other conversations with American leaders during his visit, in A. A. Gromyko, *Pamyatnoe*, book two (Moscow: Politizdat 1988), pp.255-259/346-347.
111. *Congressional Quarterly Almanac 1985*, p.118.
112. Shultz writing in *Foreign Affairs*, Spring edition 1985, pp.705-721; see also George P. Shultz, Turmoil and Triumph pp.487-490, where Shultz outlines his views on the question of linkage.
113. This speech was reported in *New York Times*, October 19 1984, p.1.
114. *Vneshnyaya Politika Sovetskogo Soyuza*, 1984, pp.166-168.

115. *Izvestia*, November 24, p.5, 1984.
116. Reported in *Congressional Quarterly Almanac 1985*, p.175; see also *Za Mir i Bezopasnost' Narodov*, Dokumenty Vneshnei Politiki SSSR, 1985, Book One, pp.11-12.
117. *Izvestia*, February 14, 1985, p.4.
118. *Pravda*, February 20, 1985, p.2.
119. Unpublished data from *Soviet Treaties Project*, Department of Politics, University of Glasgow.

2 Soviet-American Relations: Reagan, Gorbachev and Summit Diplomacy

Introduction

Soviet-American relations had began to show signs of improvement during the thirteenth month or so leadership of Konstantin Chernenko but this was yet to be translated into practical results. When Mikhail Gorbachev assumed the leadership of the Soviet Union upon Chernenko's death on March 10, 1985, he inherited a number of problems which were impeding the attainment of practical goals in areas of the Soviet-American relationship. The arms negotiations at Geneva were in deadlock and their resumption on March 12 gave little cause for optimism. The latest stalemate at the arms talks was primarily due to the inability of both sides to resolve the issue of anti missile defence systems in space. Regional conflicts in the horn of Africa, Central America, and Afghanistan were fuelling much discord between Moscow and Washington. Soviet internal policies particularly on the issue of human rights were attracting Western criticism, and at the same time had led to the USSR's near ostracism from participation in the international economy.

The new Soviet leader however sparked fresh cause for optimism. Gorbachev like his predecessor was in favour of relaxing East-West tension.[1] He showed a willingness to go much further by revealing a desire to back up increased dialogue with Washington with deeds, and during the course of 1985-1988 made some startling proposals in the field of arms control and disarmament. On top of this, President Reagan's more conciliatory posture towards Moscow during his second term allowed the two countries to embark upon an unprecedented road to high level diplomacy characterised by a wave of high level meetings between American and Soviet leaders.[2]

What probably contributed in a major way to the improvement in American-Soviet relations was the changing Soviet approach to international relations which became known as the 'new political thinking'.[3] Gorbachev outlined this 'new thinking' in pronouncements he made even before he assumed the leadership, and then throughout the years that followed including in his book: *Perestroika*.[4] The 'new thinking' was linked to Gorbachev's agenda for domestic restructuring. Gorbachev saw a radical reappraisal of the Soviet approach to foreign relations as one answer to the Soviet Union's social and economic ills.

The evolution of the 'new thinking' was perhaps most clearly set out in Gorbachev's address to the United Nations General Assembly on 7 December 1988,[5] and saw the abandonment of some of the traditional premises of Soviet foreign policy. The 'new thinking' envisaged a future based on cooperation of all countries, even those on opposing sides. The essential features of this 'new thinking' in international relations were[6]: the United Nations should play a wider global role, particularly with regard to ecological and environmental issues, and in aiding third world development; the attainment of comprehensive security through nuclear disarmament and political decisions rather than by military means emphasising that a nuclear war could not be won, and that the arms build up had put the survival of mankind in danger; that there was a growing interdependence between the nations of the world; and the principle of reasonable sufficiency for defence.

The implications of the new thinking for US-Soviet relations were that it played a large part in the improvement of superpower relations, as seen during the year 1985-88, by helping to put cooperation and dialogue, instead of confrontation, at the top of the agenda, with results on issues such as arms control and regional conflicts (e.g. The INF Treaty, peace settlement in Afghanistan, and the Angola Peace Accords), that had embittered relations in the past.

This chapter will analyse the state of Soviet-American relations beginning from March 1985 to the end of Ronald Reagan's presidency.[7] It will show a slow but steady improvement in superpower relations in 1985 and 1986 which gathered pace in 1987 and 1988, and was marked by substantial progress, the high point coming with the signing of the INF treaty at the Washington Summit.

1. Soviet-American Relations Under Gorbachev and Reagan: The First Two Years (1985 and 1986)

On March 11 1985 a meeting of the Communist party of the Soviet Union (CPSU) Central Committee appointed Mikhail Gorbachev as its new General Secretary following the death of Konstantin Chernenko. Gorbachev's appointment as Soviet leader did not attract any immediate optimistic commentary in the United States. President Reagan for one admitted[8] that he did not believe from the start that Gorbachev was going to be different from previous Soviet leaders whom he had never held in particularly high regard, and the American ambassador to the Soviet Union, Art Hartmann confirmed Reagan's belief that Gorbachev would be as tough as any previous Soviet leaders.[9]

Nevertheless the initial communication between Gorbachev and Reagan was positive. Reagan had sent in the hands of vice-president George Bush an invitation to Gorbachev for a Summit meeting during the vice-president's visit to Moscow to attend the funeral of Chernenko, and at the same time emphasised his commitment to working with the new Soviet leader ".... and the rest of the Soviet leadership in serious negotiations".[10] Gorbachev's reply[11] was equally encouraging, indicating his own inclination towards the idea of a Summit.

Despite the initial positive exchanges between Gorbachev and Reagan, Soviet-American relations under the new Soviet leader got off to a rather shaky start. On March 18 1985 Reagan delivered a tough anti-Soviet speech in the Canadian province of Quebec where he criticised the Soviet record on compliance with international agreements and attacked the foreign policy of the Soviet Union.[12] The speech came under considerable criticism in the Soviet press. One leading Soviet newspaper, *Pravda*, depicted it as "blind anti-communism", aimed at dampening hopes "... for a normalization of Soviet-American relations".[13] To add to this, in late March 1985 an American army officer based in East Germany - Major Arthur Nicholson Jr. was shot and killed by a Soviet border guard. In a letter to Gorbachev, Reagan protested about the killing of Major Nicholson.[14]

Putting aside these negative developments at the start of Gorbachev's leadership, the Soviet leader made it abundantly clear that he wished to build on the improvement in superpower relations which had begun to emerge under Chernenko.[15] In an interview published in the Soviet press Gorbachev asked for better US-Soviet relations and "honest dialogue" to ease tension and expressed what he saw as the urgent "need to end the arms race".[16] He backed his words with deeds and announced that the Soviet Union was introducing a unilateral freeze, until November 1985, on the deployment of Euromissiles, and at the same time stated that he was ready to meet Reagan.[17]

Later in April 1985 Moscow expressed its regret at what it saw as the hasty dismissal by Washington of Gorbachev's decision to impose a moratorium on the deployment of its medium range missiles in Europe, and the West's unwillingness to reciprocate by ceasing deployment of Pershing II and cruise missiles in Western Europe.[18] The United States had dismissed

Gorbachev's missile moratorium as a "propaganda gesture".[19]

On May 8 1985 President Reagan delivered an address to the European Parliament in Strasbourg, France, on the occasion of the 40th anniversary of the end of World War II.[20] During this speech Reagan made mixed references to the Soviet Union, citing on one hand Soviet aggression and adventurism in the third world, and on the other, embracing dialogue and "fruitful cooperation with the Soviet Union" backed up with a whole-hearted commitment to the process of arms control. This Reagan address was now becoming typical of his remarks towards the USSR which tended to combine the usual criticism of Moscow with proposals to ease East-West tension.

The arms talks in Geneva, which had resumed in March 1985, were yielding few results with the now familiar uncompromising stances of both sides leading to a deadlock situation once again.[21] The Soviet Union blamed Washington for the latest failure of the talks, accusing the United States of persisting in plans for what it called an "unlawful" space-based missile defence, a reference to Reagan's strategic defence initiative or by critics as 'Star Wars'.[22] The Soviet newspaper *Pravda* said that the American position at Geneva "was devoid of any elements of constructiveness ..... and ran counter to the meaning of the January accord on the objectives and subject of the talks".[23]

It was becoming increasingly apparent that while the Soviet Union and the United States had both shown a genuine desire to substantially improve their relationship, this was not being realised in terms of concrete results. Differences between the two sides on a whole host of issues meant that the generally developing dialogue which had been steadily emerging since Gorbachev's arrival on the scene would not be easily translated into major accords.

Also in May 1985 the SALT II treaty re-emerged as a potential obstacle to an improvement in Soviet-American relations. The treaty had become a victim of the Soviet invasion of Afghanistan[24] in late December 1979, preventing its ratification by the U.S. Senate. Nevertheless the two countries had been voluntarily adhering to the treaty which was due to expire in December 1985. Reagan had always been wary of the treaty[25] and his central reservation against the treaty now was whether the United States should continue to abide by the SALT treaty's limits amidst growing concern over Soviet violations of arms control agreements. The SALT II issue was made more contentious by the fact that the United States was to launch its first new trident missile-firing submarine later in 1985, and if Washington was to remain within the limits of the treaty it would have to scrap the older Poseidon submarines. The Soviet press immediately attacked the United States saying that "the situation is such that only one trident submarine separates the United States from an open pointed violation" of the SALT II treaty.[26] It accused America of a deliberate bid to sabotage agreements on arms limitation and reduction.

At the same time members of the Reagan administration, most noticeably Casper Weinberger, encouraged the President to go ahead with the deployment of the trident submarines but not remove the older Poseidon Submarines. Their argument was that it made no sense to continue observing the treaty limits in the face of clear Soviet cheating, and "that denouncing the treaty would highlight alleged Soviet violations .....".[27] Reagan made his decision on the question of SALT 11 on June 6 1985, two days after a meeting with his National Security Council.[28] He decided "on a policy of guarded and cautious restraint" indicating that "restraint will keep us generally within the framework of the SALT II but only commensurate with the Soviet observance of the SALT II restraints and for only as long as the Soviets abide by SALT II restraints".[29] On June 10 1985 Reagan announced his decision in a formal statement.[30] During this statement he severely criticised the Soviet Union for failing to comply with several provisions of the SALT II treaty and expressed "serious concerns regarding their compliance with the provision of other accords". At the same time he reiterated the decision of the United States to continue abiding by the SALT limitations. But there was one important qualification in the U.S. decision to continue observance of the treaty: this was that the United States reserved the right to change its mind if it became further convinced of Soviet violations. For their part, the Soviets voiced anger over Reagan's remarks concerning the treaty. Gorbachev sent a tough letter to Reagan attacking U.S. criticism of what he called "imaginary Soviet violations of the SALT agreement ....".[31] His letter was reminiscent of the many sharp exchanges which took place between the two countries, particularly in the early 1980s.

On July 3 1985 the United States and the Soviet Union formally announced that Reagan and Gorbachev would meet in Geneva, Switzerland, on November 19 and 20 1985.[32] Thus, the long awaited date for a summit meeting had now been set. At a press conference in the White House, US Secretary of State Shultz remarked that President Reagan saw the planned meeting with Gorbachev "as an opportunity to expand the dialogue between the US and the USSR and to lay the foundation for practical steps to improve Soviet-American relations".[33] It was becoming clear from the comments emerging from both countries that the summit would be nothing more than a trial run, a kind of getting to know each other meeting for the two leaders that would vastly advance the cause of bilateral relations. Indeed U.S. officials said that they did not expect any important agreements to be reached at the November event.

Shortly afterwards, a new Soviet foreign minister Eduard Shevardnadze was appointed[34], replacing Andrei Gromyko who was promoted to the purely ceremonial position of head of State of the USSR having held the position of foreign minister for twenty-eight years. Shevardnadze's appointment appeared to breathe new life into Soviet foreign policy. Past Soviet policy under Gromyko had been largely characterised by hostility and inflexibility particularly regarding relations with the United States. Indeed Shevardnadze made a favourable impression immediately upon Shultz who had flown to Finland to meet the new foreign minister, and make arrangements for the forthcoming summit.[35]

Towards the end of July 1985, the Soviet Union announced a unilateral moratorium on all nuclear explosions to take effect from August 6 1985 and to be valid until the end of the year.[36] Gorbachev said later that this was an example of the USSR paving the way "by creating a more favourable climate" in preparation for the summit.[37] The Soviet moratorium on nuclear testing was just one of a number of arms initiatives announced by Moscow in the months preceding the Geneva summit in what was widely seen as an attempt to attain the propaganda high ground. On September 30 1985 the Soviets made what appeared on the surface a spectacular new arms negotiating offer: a fifty per cent cut in strategic nuclear weapons.[38] A month later the United States put forward a counter offer which included as one of its elements Gorbachev's idea of a fifty per cent reduction in nuclear weapons.[39]

However, what appeared to be a convergence of the American and Soviet position on arms reductions actually masked the deep rift between the two countries over the Strategic Defence Initiative (SDI). In the run up to the summit in Geneva, the Soviet Union attacked the Reagan administration's refusal to negotiate on 'Star Wars' and limit research on the SDI programme, and by doing so increased its propaganda offensive against SDI prior to the summit.[40] It had become evident that the pre-summit arms proposals made by the Soviet Union were actually conditional on deep restrictions on the American SDI programme, a trade-off that Reagan unequivocally rejected. SDI, which had been a major irritant in Soviet-American relations since 1983, was proving just that once again. In a meeting preparatory to the summit Shultz met Gorbachev in Moscow[41] in early November 1985 to go over the issues that were to be considered at Geneva. It turned out to be a rather fruitless exercise, and Shultz later commented that there was not going to be much hope of progress at Geneva since "Gorbachev is adamant we must cave in on SDI".[42]

Since September 1985 both superpowers had been engaged in a

substantial pre-summit jockeying for positions aimed at gaining some political advantage. The Soviets had made various arms proposals and had escalated their propaganda war against SDI hoping to show the world that the U.S. space programme was the only major obstacle to far-reaching arms accords at Geneva. The Americans for their part had made it clear that their agenda for the summit would be a broad one touching on a range of subjects such as the Soviet intervention in Afghanistan and human rights in the USSR, thus hoping to put Moscow on the defensive.[43]

The first Soviet-American Summit in six years got underway on November 19 1985 in Geneva. Apart from the two leaders both sides had brought an experienced team of officials, indicating the importance of the meeting and the wide range of topics to be discussed. On arrival at the airport Gorbachev said he and Reagan would see what they could do "to halt the unprecedented arms race .... to stop it from spreading to new spheres, to avert the threat of nuclear war..... and to ensure peace and continued fruitful cooperation among peoples".[44] He went further and affirmed that both leaders would be seeking a positive outcome from the meeting. Therefore the Soviet leader had set an optimistic tone for the summit.

The opening session of the summit began with a short private meeting between Gorbachev and Reagan at which only their interpreters were present. They then joined their respective officials[45] for a two hour session at which each gave his own view of the current state of U.S-Soviet relations and the problems that divided their countries. The key session of the summit dealing with arms control and disarmament was to take place in the afternoon. American officials had earlier emphasised that the President was not prepared to bargain away his Strategic Defence Initiative in exchange for cuts in Soviet offensive weapons. Gorbachev for his part was expected to repeat his insistence that there could be no progress on reducing strategic weapons until the US abandoned 'Star Wars'. As the two countries' arms control experts were given the floor for the afternoon session Reagan suggested to Gorbachev that they go for a walk, an offer the Soviet leader accepted without hesitation. Both then walked down to the boat house where they had a fireside chat beside a glowing hearth. A unique sight it was indeed, not to mention unimaginable not so long ago for the leaders of the two countries to be in such a position.

The second day of day of talks began on November 20 with firstly a private conservation between the two leaders and then a continuation of the session, with the participation of both delegations during which some strong words were exchanged on SDI.

At the concluding session both leaders summed up the results of their meeting in Geneva over the two days to be made known in the form of a joint Soviet-American statement released later. The two sides had discussed regional conflicts, human rights, arms control and bilateral issues.

On November 21 both delegations left for the International Press Centre to attend the closing ceremony hosted by the President of Switzerland Furgler. At the ceremony both Gorbachev and Reagan made speeches. The Soviet leader spoke first and said that while the talks had been useful it had not proved possible "to find solutions to the most important issues connected with the task of halting the arms race and strengthening peace, and there remain major disagreements on fundamental issues between us". But he vowed that the USSR would continue working together with the United States to find solutions to these problems.[46] Reagan's utterance was not much different. He too expressed the usefulness of the Summit talks saying that they had injected a certain amount of momentum "into our work on the issues between us - a momentum we can continue" at future meetings, and viewing the Summit as a "fresh start" he asked Gorbachev to join him in the hard work which lay ahead.[47]

The full extent of the agreements reached at Geneva became apparent with the release of the joint Soviet-American Summit statement.[48] This communique pointed out that "serious differences remain on a number of critical issues" but that the two leaders had agreed "about the need to improve US-Soviet relations and the international situation as a whole". Among the most important areas of agreement reached were the following: that "nuclear war cannot be won and must never be fought", emphasising "the importance of preventing any war between the two countries whether nuclear or conventional"; early progress on the principle of a 50 per cent reduction in nuclear weapons "as well as the idea of an interim agreement on medium range missiles in Europe"; the two countries reaffirmed their commitment to the nuclear no-proliferation treaty (NPT); emphasised the importance of the Vienna negotiations on the reduction of armed forces in Central Europe, and on accelerating a new round of arms talks; and "on the need to place on a regular basis and intensify dialogue at various levels" including most importantly an agreement to hold follow-up Summits in 1986 and 1987. The Summit also yielded a number of accords on less controversial issues such as cultural, educational and scientific - technical exchanges.

At a post-summit press conference Gorbachev stated that he was hopeful about the start of a US-Soviet dialogue but blamed Reagan's intransigence on 'Star Wars' for the lack of progress on arms reduction.[49] After the Summit both leaders briefed their respective allies in Europe.

Reagan addressed NATO ministers in Brussels, while Gorbachev reported to Warsaw Pact leaders who approved his performance expressing their "full support for the constructive position set forth" by Gorbachev at the talks with President Reagan.[50] Back in their own countries the two leaders also addressed their domestic audiences. On November 21 1985, Reagan delivered his remarks on the Summit to a joint session of Congress,[51] describing his meeting with Gorbachev as "constructive". He praised the Soviet leader for being "an eloquent speaker and a good listener" and said that the best part of the Summit for him was what he called the "fireside Summit" during which he spent hours in private conversation with Gorbachev. In his report to the fourth session of the 11th USSR Supreme Soviet, Gorbachev indicated that the results of the Summit had been positive and that there was now a growing basis for trust between the two countries. But as before he once again slammed US inflexibility on SDI, arguing that this had prevented accords on nuclear and space arms.[52]

A closer analysis of the Summit makes clear that the two superpowers were still profoundly divided over the American Space defence programme, and that it had produced little concrete progress on other important issues such as regional flashpoints and the question of the missile balance in Europe. If one were to evaluate the Summit in terms of winners and losers then Reagan probably came out ahead on points. He made no concessions on SDI and resisted intense Soviet pressure to do so. Gorbachev may be regarded as having come out second best on the grounds that he failed to achieve any substantial progress on the issue of major importance to Moscow - arms control.

However such an evaluation would be misleading on the grounds that it was the first Summit, both sides were always likely to be cautious and resistant to compromise.

Despite the general lack of progress both leaders were relatively satisfied with the outcome, and in particular with the knowledge that there would be more opportunities. Also the optimism expressed by Gorbachev and Reagan stemmed from the fact that both leaders got on really well together, and indeed this was probably the most talked about aspect of the Summit. A vivid indication of how well the leaders had got on was represented by the fact that they spent more than two hours in private conversation on the first day, eight times longer than planned - in a move clearly intended to inject a personal dimension into the superpower relationship. Their talks had been more cordial and constructive than expected. American officials pointed out that there would probably not even have been a joint statement but for the rapport built up between the two leaders. This relationship which they developed[53] was seen as the most positive achievement of the Geneva Summit. The Soviet newspaper *Pravda* claimed that the Reagan-Gorbachev private sessions had created a "new psychological climate".[54]

The Summit also attracted considerable favourable commentary from both the Soviet and Western press, despite the lack of major agreements. Part of the reason was that no one really expected major breakthroughs, and proof that this was the case was provided by a commentary in the Soviet newspaper *Izvestia* which said that only those who expected a miracle could be disappointed in "modest" results.[55]

Indeed what the Summit certainly did was to lay the foundation for a fresh dialogue, and a basis for trust between the two sides which was to bode well for the future. Evidence that Geneva had boosted Soviet-American relations towards the end of 1985 was exemplified by the fact that the superpowers agreed on an unprecedented exchange of new year's greetings. It was announced that Reagan would speak to the people of the Soviet Union via radio and television, and that Gorbachev would deliver a similar message to the American people. As a result 1986 got off to a hopeful start from the viewpoint of Soviet-American relations. Further cause for optimism was provided by the announcement on 15 January 1986 by the Soviet Union of a far-reaching Nuclear Disarmament programme,[56] which Gorbachev later said provided a "unique opportunity to fundamentally improve Soviet-American relations". The Soviet proposals involved a plan to eliminate all nuclear weapons by the year 2000; a plan to eliminate all U.S. and Soviet intermediate nuclear forces (INF) in Europe over a five to seven year period, in effect accepting Reagan's 1982 zero option proposal but publicising it as a Soviet idea; and an extension for another three months of the USSR's unilateral moratorium on nuclear testing, calling on the United States to follow suit. What was more, Moscow appeared to have dropped its long time insistence that both British and French nuclear systems be counted in the overall Western tally of forces. But there was one major sticking point which meant that any euphoria which the proposals might have created was short lived: Gorbachev said that the United States must renounce "the development, testing and deployment of space - strike weapons", a reference to SDI.[57] As a result the USSR's disarmament programme was dismissed by the United States as a propaganda move, even though Reagan agreed with the goals outlined by Gorbachev. Reagan also emphasised the enormous problems which would have to be overcome before any agreement could be reached such as the issue of effective verification, Warsaw Pact superiority in conventional forces, and the threat posed to Europe by the presence of Soviet missiles in Asia.

On February 4 1986 Reagan delivered his annual state of the Union address to Congress.[58] Commenting on relations with the Soviet Union he stressed the American desire for a more peaceful world, and an arms control agreement if the Soviet government truly wanted one. He couldn't help but have an indirect jibe at the Soviet Union accusing the communist system of exporting its ideology by force, and of commanding people's lives.

Also in February 1986 Gorbachev received US Senator Edward Kennedy at the Kremlin.[59] During his conversation with the Senator, the Soviet leader pointed out that the next US-Soviet Summit would be pointless without practical results. He argued that although the Geneva Summit had created "the prerequisites for an improvement in relations between our two countries ...mere lip service .... is not enough". He pointed out that the Soviet Union had already paved the way for achieving practical results at a new Summit with its announcement on January 15 1986 of a Disarmament Programme.[60] It appears as though the urgency expressed by Gorbachev regarding an agreement on arms reductions indicated Moscow's desperation, given the further deterioration of the Soviet economy. An arms control agreement with the United States would remove future overwhelming strains on Soviet resources, and allow resources to be deployed for civilian needs.

On March 13 1986 Gorbachev once again extended the Soviet Union's moratorium on nuclear testing.[61] Much to Moscow's dismay the United States did not follow the Soviet example with Reagan actually ordering a continuation of nuclear testing. This prompted charges from Moscow that Washington was not committed to peace. In a letter to Reagan in early April, Gorbachev conveyed his disillusionment with the American policy on nuclear testing and proposed that the two should meet in Europe to discuss specifically this issue.[62] Also in April 1986 the USSR cancelled a meeting which was to take place between Shevardnadze and Shultz to discuss a possible date for a future summit, to protest at the American bombing of Libya. This was followed a few weeks later by the Chernobyl disaster, regarded by many as the worst public relations setback for Moscow since the Korean airliner incident in 1983.[63]

What was by now becoming a sore point in Soviet-American relations ever since Afghanistan was rekindled towards the end of May 1986. This was the SALT II Treaty on which both sides traded bitter words in 1985. The United States had constantly accused Moscow of violating the provisions of the treaty, while the Soviet Union sensed a conspiracy in Washington to sabotage and then scrap the treaty altogether. On May 27 1986 Reagan made a statement during which he announced that the United States would no longer observe the terms of the SALT II Treaty.[64] This decision ended a six-year policy of informal compliance with the agreement. Reagan said that he was taking this step "because the Soviets had repeatedly violated the terms of the treaty".[65] In the statement Reagan reiterated that the United States had "fully kept its part of the bargain" while the Soviets had not, noting that a country "cannot be serious about effective arms control unless it is equally serious about compliance". He outlined the Soviet pattern of non-compliance with both the SALT and ABM agreements. The Reagan statement came only days after Soviet officials reiterated support for the SALT II Treaty claiming that it remained "an effective document that embodied the results of many years of cooperation between the USSR and the U.S. during the 1970s to halt the nuclear missile arms race and strengthen strategic stability".[66] Clearly Reagan was not convinced and his decision cast doubt on any future arms control agreement with the Soviet Union, for the time being at least. The fear now was that it might trigger off a new arms race with both sides less inhibited by a treaty, and would also weaken their desire to conclude a new treaty. A Soviet government statement attacked Reagan's announcement with the now familiar charge that the United States was pursuing a militaristic foreign policy.[67] Moscow viewed Reagan's abandonment of SALT II as an attempt to free the U.S. of restraints that the treaty imposed on Washington's bid to implement its comprehensive strategic nuclear programme, and therefore came to them as no surprise.

Reagan's May 27 announcement attracted considerable criticism from Congress as well. Arms control advocates in Congress were highly critical of the President while other critics warned that "abrogation of the treaty limits will allow Moscow to expand its nuclear force far more rapidly than the United States".[68]

Towards the end of July 1986, Reagan proved that he was still serious about arms control when in a letter to Gorbachev he made sweeping new arms reduction proposals.[69] This new arms initiative called for both sides to scrap all ballistic missiles while research on missile defence systems (SDI) would continue. In the event that such a defence proved feasible it would be shared with all nations. However, Gorbachev appeared less than convinced about this latest U.S. offer and in his reply to Reagan showed little interest.[70]

What didn't help the chances of a positive Soviet response to the Reagan arms offer was that, in between, a Moscow correspondent Nicholas Daniloff, was arrested by Soviet officials and accused of spying for the United States on August 30 1986. The arrest of Daniloff, an American journalist of Russian origin, came just days after KGB agents were arrested in the United States on espionage charges. The whole affair threatened to undermine U.S.-Soviet relations and destroy the progress made in superpower relations between Reagan and Gorbachev. The incident highlighted yet again the great sensitivity to which American-Soviet relations were prone when confronted by adverse developments. There was total fury at the arrest of Daniloff from Washington. The seriousness of the situation became quickly apparent when the U.S. administration "insisted that there could be no progress toward the INF reduction agreement nor towards scheduling the Summit until Daniloff was freed".[71] The Soviet Union insisted that Daniloff was a spy, and detailed charges against him.[72] After intense negotiations including a number of meetings between Shultz and Shevardnadze, and a Reagan-Shevardnadze meeting on September 19 the two sides agreed to a settlement on September 29 whereby the charges against Daniloff were dropped and a prominent Soviet employee of the United Nations, Gennadi Zakharov - who had been arrested a week before Daniloff - was sentenced to five years probation providing that he left the country and never returned.[73] The whole fiasco was prevented from inflicting serious damage to U.S.-Soviet relations by the politically skilful manoeuvring of both superpowers. The result was that on September 30 1986 Reagan announced that he would meet Gorbachev in Iceland on the following October 11 and 12.

Soviet-American relations experienced a rough ride in the months leading up to the Reykjavik Summit, with the Daniloff affair casting a shadow at one stage over a future summit, and with Gorbachev's insistence that a summit must lead to results. Added to this, there had been little progress at the arms negotiations in Geneva.[74]

Nevertheless, the summit went ahead as planned. On October 10 1986 Gorbachev arrived in Reykjavik for his meeting with Reagan. On arrival at the airport Gorbachev made a short statement for the press during which he stressed that the dominant topic at the summit meetings should be nuclear disarmament.[75] On October 11, the two leaders held their first conversations during which they discussed the state of the international situation, Soviet-American relations, and problems of ending the arms race. As expected Gorbachev was keen to limit discussions to arms control. But in accordance with American plans Reagan broadened the agenda to include regional conflicts - in particular the Soviet occupation of Afghanistan, and human rights, during which he emphasised the question of emigration saying "Soviet human rights policies were impeding the improvement of our relationship".[76] After these early exchanges on a number of issues the rest of the day, indeed the remainder of the summit talks concentrated solely on arms control.

The remaining one and half days saw the two countries make

considerable progress on arms reductions, along the following lines: Gorbachev accepted in principle Reagan's zero-zero proposal for the elimination of intermediate nuclear forces in Europe (INF) including the proposals made by the U.S. President in July 1986, calling for the elimination of all ballistic missiles over a 10 year period. He also agreed to scrap 50% of the USSR's arsenal of nuclear weapons on a reciprocal basis, in the course of five years; and the Soviet Union agreed in principle to the U.S. verification approach with Gorbachev pledging his commitment to strong and mutually acceptable procedures. The two sides also agreed to freeze shorter range missiles; in addition Gorbachev accepted a 10 instead of 15 year period for observance of the ABM treaty. The two countries in fact ignored their noon deadline on October 12 and continued working until the evening. The superpowers appeared to have "negotiated the most massive weapons reductions in history".[77] So it seemed at the time, than Gorbachev dropped a bombshell. He stated that the agreements negotiated were conditional on stringent limits to the strategic defence initiative. To put it precisely, the Soviet leader demanded that SDI be limited to laboratory research during the 10 years observance of the ABM treaty. At this point Reagan could not hide his anger and the talks broke down immediately with the U.S. President making it plain that his SDI was not negotiable.

The post-summit comments summed up the mood in both camps. Shultz said that the United States was "deeply disappointed" at the outcome.[78] At a press conference, Gorbachev for his part blamed Reagan's insistence on SDI for thwarting accords on eliminating strategic nuclear arms and Euromissiles saying that an "historic chance" had been missed.[79]

Back in the United States Reagan addressed the nation on October 13 on the Iceland Summit.[80] During this speech he gave details of his various meetings with Gorbachev insisting that he placed on the agenda issues which America believed were at the heart of the differences between the United States and the Soviet Union, namely human rights and regional flashpoints including Soviet military actions around the world. Then he went on to explain the importance of SDI and why the United States refused to bargain it away. He argued that SDI was America's insurance policy and "security guarantee" against Soviet cheating and believed that it was the "key to a world without nuclear weapons".

Like Reagan, Gorbachev also addressed his nation on television on two occasions. His first televised speech [81] to the Soviet people on October 14, 1986 was similar to his past summit press conference during which he was highly critical of American intransigence on SDI testing, and argued that this had prevented the taking of historic steps in the field of arms control and disarmament. He also gave a brief rundown on developments as they had unfolded in Reykjavik, outlining a whole package of measures which he said the Soviet Union had put on the negotiating table while arguing that "the Americans had come to Reykjavik with nothing at all" (this clearly contradicted Reagan's comment on American television that the United States "proposed the most sweeping and generous arms control proposal in history").

In the second speech on Soviet television on October 22, 1986[82] Gorbachev accused the United States of distorting the true outcome of the Reykjavik summit and claimed that the American administration had misled the American public by telling it that Moscow blocked potential accords by setting a trap on 'Star Wars' and went on to insist that the strategic defence initiative was the "....chief obstacle on the path to a nuclear weapon free world".

From an overall perspective the summit ended in deadlock after Reagan refused to accept any limitation on his SDI research programme. The two leaders had communicated quite well together as they had done in Geneva. In fact they spent far longer together arguing over the details of arms control than either had expected.

However, despite their rigorous negotiations, and what appeared for a moment substantial agreements everything more or less fell apart over SDI. Both leaders were disappointed, and this was plain to see at the end of the summit. The two sides departed with a rather bitter taste in their mouths and at that point the outlook for a future summit seemed bleak to say the least. The general opinion then was that the summit had been a failure. This view was echoed by both the U.S. and the USSR who blamed each other for the negative outcome. The United States argued that Gorbachev did not understand the importance of "Star Wars" as a defensive shield against devastating ballistic missiles, while the Soviet leader launched scathing attacks against SDI, explaining that he did not see the need for it when both sides had agreed that their goal would be the ultimate eradication of nuclear weapons.

Since the Reykjavik summit was initially billed as 'pre-summit' talks preparatory to a formal summit to be held in the United States, the superpowers did not regard the outcome as a total disaster but merely as a setback, and believed as they had done in the aftermath of the Geneva summit that they could build in the future on areas where they shared common ground.

The summit at Reykjavik did nothing positive for the state of Soviet-American relations, and developments in the final two months of 1986 did not augur well for the superpower relationship. First there was the

Iran/Contra affair which arose in November 1986, and concerned revelations that the United States had been secretly selling arms to Iran and diverting the funds to the Contra rebels in Nicaragua. After initially denying reports about the arms sales Reagan eventually acknowledged that he had allowed transfers to Iran of what he labelled as "defensive" weapons.[83] Not only did it undermine Reagan's credibility, the Iran-Contra affair threatened to endanger any chances of progress on arms control and disarmament because it weakened Reagan's position at home and made it questionable whether a 'lame duck' President could get the Senate to ratify any treaty reached with the Soviets. Secondly, in November 1986 the Geneva arms talks were dogged once again by the question of arms in space. A statement by Karpov, the head of the USSR delegation to the Soviet-American talks, criticised the American plan for space which he said would send arms into space and said that it was the chief obstacle in the way of nuclear disarmament. He further attacked the overall stance of the American delegation at the talks, which he said was aimed at blocking work that would lead to mutually acceptable agreements.[84]

In December 1986 Moscow condemned the United States for exceeding the limits set by the SALT II treaty by adding another bomber to its strategic arsenal. A Soviet government statement denounced Washington's repudiation of the treaty and said that the Soviet Union would continue to observe the treaty "for the time being".[85] Since the Soviets already knew that the United States had expressed its rejection of SALT II earlier in the year, this latest criticism from Moscow was nothing more than an attempt to score a public relations victory by drawing world attention to the fact that Washington was actually putting its earlier rejection of the SALT II treaty into practice.

On December 17 1986 the Soviets hardened their position on a moratorium on nuclear testing by announcing that its unilateral halt to tests would continue in 1987 only if the U.S. refrained from further tests.[86]

2. Soviet-American Relations Under Reagan and Gorbachev - The Last Two Years

1987 began in a rather gloomy fashion from the viewpoint of Soviet-American relations. On January 27 Reagan delivered a tough state of the union address[87] which was reminiscent of some of his earlier ones. He attacked Soviet expansionism, and at the same time, the colossal Soviet military budgets since the 1970s. The President also staunchly defended SDI calling it "the most positive and promising defence programme we have undertaken". Reagan pointed out that while the United States remained open to "more constructive relations with the Soviet Union" this depended largely upon more responsible Soviet conduct around the world and progress in other areas such as human rights. It was clear that the Reykjavik Summit had led to a certain amount of mutual bitterness between the USSR and the United States, and to an extent this was reflected in Reagan's address to Congress when he remarked that "In Iceland last October, we had one moment of opportunity that the Soviets dashed because they sought to cripple our strategic defence initiative".

A statement by Gorbachev on February 28 1987 encouraged hopes that an agreement on the elimination of medium range missiles in Europe would be forthcoming very shortly.[88] This new Soviet offer saw Gorbachev propose the formula adopted at Reykjavik whereby both sides had agreed on eliminating all their medium range missiles within five years, except this time the USSR appeared to have removed a major obstacle by dropping its insistence that any such agreement be linked to settlement of the anti-missile defence issue which had provoked much squabbling at Reykjavik. This paved the way for the signing of a treaty eliminating intermediate nuclear forces (INF) possibly at the next summit.

In mid-April 1987 the superpowers resumed their high level dialogue when Shultz travelled to Moscow for three days of meetings with Soviet leaders, seen as the most important East-West talks since the Reykjavik Summit. The aim of the talks was largely to achieve progress toward an agreement on abolishing Intermediate Nuclear Forces (INF) in Europe, and to discuss prospects for a Reagan-Gorbachev summit in Washington. During the conversation between Gorbachev and Shultz[89] it became clear that although both countries expressed their readiness to conclude an agreement on the question of medium range missiles (or INF) in Europe, there was one major sticking point: this was the question of how to address Soviet superiority in short range nuclear missiles which could circumvent any benefit of an INF agreement. Despite Gorbachev's proposal to abolish all Soviet shorter range missiles in Europe if the West agreed not to build its own, Shultz relayed the American position which was that the United States had the right to build such weapons and deploy them in amounts approximately equal to those that the USSR would have remained after it eliminated its shorter range missiles in Europe. This American position was criticised by the Soviets, who also attacked what they saw as a departure by the United States from the positions which the two countries had adopted at Reykjavik accusing Washington of adding "other pretexts" to complicate matters.[90]

Nevertheless, according to the Soviet press "a greater understanding of each other's position showed up in the course of a thorough exchange of opinions".[91] A Soviet spokesman characterised the atmosphere as favourable. Gorbachev also stated that he was ready to meet Reagan.

It was becoming evident by the middle of 1987 that Soviet-American relations were gradually warming up after being slightly cool following the Reykjavik summit. This was picked up by various Soviet newspapers. In late May 1987, *Izvestia* claimed that the "winds of change for the better in Soviet-American relations are gaining strength in the United States". It also went on to say that a growing number of Americans were answering the question "can the Russians be trusted"? with the answer yes, with a growing number of them showing greater interest in establishing normal Soviet-American relations than ever before.[92] A *Tass* statement issued in early July 1987 claimed that an "historic opportunity" existed for better US-Soviet relations and that the two countries should take advantage of this chance. It went further and declared that the "necessary prerequisites now existed for carrying out the understandings reached in Reykjavik", particularly an agreement to eliminate INF in Europe the conclusion of which would "help bring about a substantial improvement in Soviet-American and international relations".[93]

In mid-September 1987, Soviet foreign minister Shevardnadze arrived in Washington continuing the now familiar regular high level American - Soviet meetings, for more discussions on removing the obstacles to a positive INF treaty. When Reagan met Shevardnadze he reiterated that he was not going to cave in on SDI.[94] The meetings were generally described as making a favourable contribution to Soviet-American relations and Reagan commented that "they were good meetings, free of the hostility we used to see even if we were disagreeing on some things".[95] Shultz and Shevardnadze also signed an agreement establishing crisis centres in each country, the aim of which was to reduce the threat of an accidental war between the superpowers.[96] Before leaving, Shevardnadze gave a upbeat press conference in Washington on the completion of the Soviet-American talks.[97] He announced that the two countries were completely confident that an INF treaty would be signed before the end of the year. Just two weeks later a final problem pivotal to reaching agreement on the INF treaty was resolved. This was the question of West Germany's older Pershing missiles. Under a compromise reached these missiles were excluded from the U.S.-Soviet agreement, but the Germans agreed to remove them once the agreement took effect.

In late October 1987, it was the turn of U.S. Secretary of State Shultz to travel to Moscow where he met Soviet leaders.[98] Welcoming Shultz at the Kremlin Gorbachev pointed out "the positive significance of the .....

contacts and talks between the representatives of the governments" which were now regularly taking place.[99] However commenting on a possible summit meeting Gorbachev sounded rather cautious and stated that the possible signing of an INF treaty itself would not be enough to justify coming to Washington, and that some work still had to be done over the next month or so before a firm date could be set for a summit with Reagan.

Less than a week later, in early November 1987, Shevardnadze was back in Washington for more meetings on INF and plans for the summit. He brought with him a letter from Gorbachev in which the Soviet leader stated he wanted to discuss the SDI at the next summit but dropped his insistence that limits on SDI development be accepted by the Americans as a prerequisite to signing the INF treaty. In their talks in Washington, Shevardnadze and Reagan managed to set a date for the summit - to be held in Washington on December 7 1987. So after initial doubts about the next meeting between Gorbachev and Reagan, summit diplomacy was back on track.

From December 8-10 1987 Reagan and Gorbachev held their third summit meeting, this time in Washington. On arrival at Andrews air force base near Washington on December 7 Gorbachev was greeted by Shultz. The Soviet leader made a brief statement in which he said that the purpose of his visit was to sign a treaty eliminating intermediate and short-range missiles. He added that at the heart of his discussions with Reagan would be questions concerning strategic arms reductions which he described as "the pivotal problem of Soviet-American relations".[100] On December 8, after the customary welcoming ceremony on Gorbachev's arrival at the White House, the Soviet leader and President Reagan held a meeting where they exchanged differences of opinion on human rights and on their respective systems - Capitalism and Communism. It was more of an informal debate and chat than anything else. Then it was time for the serious business of the day, and both Gorbachev and Reagan made brief remarks before they signed the historic Intermediate Nuclear Forces (INF) treaty. This treaty provided for the elimination of all missiles with ranges between 500 and 5000 miles together with their launching and support facilities. The final stumbling block was eliminated when the two sides agreed to unprecedented verification procedures under which each would be able to send inspection teams to the other's missile sites.

After signing the treaty both leaders delivered speeches to the Soviet and American peoples. In his address, Reagan said that the countries had made history because they had signed "the first agreement over to eliminate an entire class of U.S. and Soviet nuclear weapons". He added that discussions would continue at the summit on further arms reductions and other issues, and stressed that as with the INF treaty "it will take time and patience to reach agreements".[101] In his speech, the Soviet leader also viewed the signing of the INF Treaty as an historic step, but stressed that it was only a first step toward nuclear disarmament and "moving ahead will require further intensive intellectual endeavour and honest effort....".[102]

On December 9, the summit continued with both sides now concentrating largely on their next aim: to achieve a fifty per cent reduction in the strategic missile stocks of both sides. Indeed the remainder of the summit centred mainly on discussions on this issue.

At the end of the summit a joint Soviet-American summit statement on the outcome of the summit was issued.[103] The document revealed that the leaders of the two countries had held "comprehensive and detailed discussions" on a broad range of issues. These were primarily arms reductions, human rights, settlement of regional conflicts and bilateral relations. Both sides agreed that "official contacts at all levels should be further expanded and intensified...". The joint statement also revealed the matters on which there was mutual understanding and also those on which big differences still remained, emphasising that the talks which had been "candid and constructive" had led to an understanding that areas of differences would not be barriers to agreement on areas of mutual interest.

The post - summit reaction of both leaders was extremely positive. In a television speech to the Soviet people on December 14 1987, Gorbachev told them that relations with the United States were now better, and the signing of the INF treaty represented "a victory for new political thinking" and was only the prelude "toward the actual destruction of the nuclear arsenal".[104] Reagan's address to the nation, at the conclusion of the summit on December 10, was similar in tone to Gorbachev's. He said that the INF treaty represented a landmark in postwar history as it abolished an "entire class of U.S. and Soviet nuclear missiles", and called the summit a "clear success", saying that there was reason for "both hope and optimism".[105]

Overall the Washington summit had been a resounding success and arguably the most productive American-Soviet summit to this date. Most progress was made on arms control, although the two countries were unable to make any headway on other contentious issues such as human rights and regional conflicts. Both Reagan and Gorbachev were clearly in buoyant mood after their talks, and the personal rapport which the two had developed since the Geneva summit in 1985 had contributed greatly to the positive movements in the superpower relationship. Reagan summed up this fact when he said that "Mr. Gorbachev and I continued to build a foundation for better relations between our governments and our peoples".[106]

Fresh from the success of the Washington summit, Reagan delivered an upbeat state of the union address on January 25 1988.[107] Remarking on arms reduction he hailed the historic INF agreement and urged the Senate to ratify it. He expressed optimism on the possibility of an even more significant agreement which would reduce U.S. and Soviet long range (strategic) missiles by 50%, but yet again stressed what he saw as the importance of his Strategic Defence Initiative as a programme which "supports the same goals of arms reduction .... and reduces the risk of war".

On the same day as Reagan's annual state of the union address, the Senate began its hearings on the INF treaty.[108] Reagan had campaigned vigorously for its approval by the Senate, and the general view was that the treaty would not encounter any serious difficulties since it appeared to have widespread support across the country and across the political spectrum, with large numbers of both Democrats and Republicans expressing their unreserved support for it.

Nevertheless, as with any agreement involving the Soviet Union, the treaty did have its critics - mainly conservatives. As a result the debate on the INF Treaty which started on January 25 pitted these critics against the vast number who supported the treaty, including the administration which emphasised the treaty as a "substantive and tactical triumph". The danger was that if the opponents of the treaty succeeded in fatally wounding it, the implications of that could be serious for Soviet - American relations given the widespread euphoria that this historic agreement had attracted at the last superpower summit. The arguments put forward by opponents of the treaty were essentially that the treaty could not be verified and that the Soviets could not be trusted. According to Senator Helms the USSR had already begun cheating by concealing hundreds of missiles that should have been scrapped.[109] They also argued that the agreement undermined an important part of the nuclear arsenal "upon which the NATO alliance relied to offset the numerically superior conventional forces of the Soviet-led Warsaw pact".[110] Other critics were less hardline in their opposition to the treaty. They were merely looking for loopholes which would allow them to argue for modifications or amendments to the INF pact "without making the kind of sweeping changes that would send it back to the drawing board".[111]

Proponents of the treaty including those in the administration contended that "it served the U.S. interest since it required the Soviets to remove from service substantially more nuclear firepower than the United States".[112] The INF treaty was very important to Reagan as it gave him a major arms accord in the final year of his Presidency, and allowed him to argue that his policy of peace through strength had paid dividends.

One area of Soviet-American relations on which there had been scant progress was the issue of regional conflicts. Both superpowers had been either directly or indirectly involved in various regions of the world providing economic, military, and humanitarian aid to guerilla movements and governments of their respective political persuasion. On 2nd February 1988 Reagan delivered a speech on television to lobby for new aid for the Contra rebels fighting the Moscow-backed left wing Sandinista government in Nicaragua.[113] The address highlighted the intensity of the differences which existed between Moscow and Washington on regional flashpoints. Concentrating on Central America, Reagan claimed that the Sandinista regime was a threat to democracy in the region and to the security of other states in the area. He accused the government of Nicaragua of flouting its promises to embrace democracy, respect human rights, and adopt a non-aligned foreign policy. Despite the recent upward trend in Soviet-American relations, Reagan did not hesitate to criticise the Soviet backing for the Sandinistas, and questioned the logic behind the substantial military and economic aid the Soviet Union was providing its ally. Reagan made a determined appeal for aid to the Contras, even overplaying the extent of the Soviet backed Communist threat in order to make a stronger case. In reality however, Congress was not really convinced by Reagan's at times impassioned arguments, and on the following day, the House of Representatives rejected the President's request for $36.75 million in combined humanitarian and military aid. Nevertheless Reagan had proved with this speech that despite the recent rapprochement with Moscow he was more than willing to speak out in defence of his political beliefs.

The spring of 1988 saw a number of top level meetings between American and Soviet leaders the contents of which included preparations for the impending summit in Moscow, a review of the state of Soviet-American relations, and intensive efforts by both sides to conclude a draft treaty on a 50% reduction of strategic offensive weapons which could then be signed at the next summit. It was obvious that the superpowers were keen to complete a START treaty but much work remained to be done since negotiations were more complicated, in particular there were technical problems especially on verification with regard to sea-launched nuclear cruise missiles - these, as Reagan put it, "were the hardest to count and verify",[114] and even from space it was virtually impossible with the aid of satellites to tell whether such missiles could fire nuclear or conventional warheads.

The final set of meetings between the two countries prior to the Moscow summit took place in late April 1988 when Shultz revisited Moscow where he held talks with Soviet leaders including Gorbachev.[115] During their discussion Gorbachev complained to the U.S. Secretary of

State about recent Reagan speeches which he said cast Soviet foreign policy in a negative light, and he ridiculed Reagan for implying that the achievements being made in Soviet-American relations were the result of America's pressure, which had influenced Soviet behaviour. But Gorbachev and Shultz did agree on a draft agenda for the upcoming summit and expressed optimism that concrete and major results would be achieved.

The long-awaited breakthrough on regional flashpoints came when on April 14 1988 a United Nations - brokered agreement providing for the withdrawal of Soviet troops from Afghanistan was reached in Geneva.[116] A Soviet government statement issued in Moscow on April 26 announced that the withdrawal of Soviet troops would begin on May 15 and be completed not later than February 15 1989. At the same time the statement hailed the Geneva accords "as an event of exceptional importance .... creating the external conditions required to settle the Afghanistan problem".

However, the Geneva agreement did not lead to a resolution of the Afghan problem and the war continued. The problem was that both Moscow and Washington disputed the details of how the agreement reached would be carried out. Washington complained that Moscow was continuing to arm the government of Afghanistan, and said it too would continue to aid the Mujahideen rebels fighting the Moscow-backed Kabul regime. The Soviets for their part accused outside forces - by inference Pakistan and the United States - of violating the Geneva agreement by sending supplies to the rebels. Indeed on November 4 1988 the Soviet Union announced a delay to further withdrawals because of concern that the anti-Soviet guerillas were being supplied with more Western military aid. Furthermore the Afghan guerillas had no formal role in the Geneva accords and said that they would ignore it and fight on. The Geneva agreement provoked indignation in the United States. Some Conservatives charged that "the administration was overly eager to get the agreement .... prior to the summit" and accused it of a "sellout".[117] They argued that the USSR would continue to aid the Kabul regime while Pakistan would face international pressure to shut down the major arms routes to the rebels.

By agreeing to leave Afghanistan the Soviets made clear they were serious about concentrating on internal reforms, and the decision to withdraw would "reduce a significant drain on their sagging economy".[118] It would also help to facilitate an improvement in Soviet-American relations since it illustrated that the two superpowers were capable of meaningful cooperation on issues other than arms control, and coming not long before the Moscow summit, it was seen as a major boost to the prospects for an agreement.

A further boost to the forthcoming summit came when on May 27 the

U.S. Senate overwhelmingly ratified the INF treaty by a 93-5 vote.[119] This paved the way for the treaty to be formally ratified by Reagan and Gorbachev at the next summit.

This summit was to be the fourth in less than four years. It began on May 29 1988. The first two days of the summit, May 29 and May 30, were dominated largely by Reagan's outspoken criticism of the Soviet record on human rights, in particular on the issue of emigration. On May 30 Reagan caused a stir when he held a meeting with a number of well known 'refuseniks' and 'dissidents' who wanted to emigrate from the Soviet Union. They asked the President to keep up pressure on the USSR to improve its behaviour on human rights. The meeting was quickly slammed by the Soviet press as a propaganda stunt, and after Gorbachev appeared to express annoyance and irritation, Reagan toned down his criticism during the remainder of his visit and accused the Soviet bureaucracy rather than the leaders of the USSR as being responsible for human rights abuses.

On June 1 came the high point of the summit when the two leaders exchanged the ratification documents of the INF treaty.[120] During the ceremony Gorbachev made a speech in which he said that the exchange of the instruments of ratification meant that "the era of nuclear disarmament has begun".[121] In his speech Reagan argued that the treaty had made possible "a new dimension of cooperation between us" but that much remained to be accomplished and that the two countries must not stop at this point.[122]

In their final meeting, Reagan and Gorbachev concluded their discussion of what was a broad agenda encompassing disarmament, regional conflicts, bilateral relations, and humanitarian issues. The results of the summit were summed up in a joint U.S.-Soviet summit statement.[123] The two sides signed two minor arms control agreements. One required each side to give the other 24 hours notice of a ballistic missile test, whether over land or sea, and the other set up procedures for joint experiments to test techniques to measure nuclear explosions. The two sides also signed seven other bilateral agreements ranging from an expansion of cultural exchanges to cooperation on atomic energy and space research. An agreement in principle emerged in discussions on regional issues, specifically with respect to the withdrawal of Cuban troops from Angola, that in the long term proved to be very significant. Among the major achievements was the exchange of INF ratification instruments. At a press conference, Gorbachev argued that there now existed a new realism in U.S-USSR relations, although he regretted the "missed opportunities" in the summit and expressed dismay with Reagan's performance on human rights.[124]

All in all the summit was a success in its promotion of a better understanding between the U.S. and the USSR even although the practical achievements were modest. The expectations on both sides were limited and so were the results. Most disappointingly there was no real progress on the goal of concluding a treaty which would reduce the strategic nuclear arsenals of the superpowers by half. As with previous summits the two leaders communicated remarkably well, considering some of the tough exchanges which had taken place on the issue of human rights. On the third day of the summit Gorbachev and Reagan took an historic 20 minute stroll through Red Square bringing the American President close to the Soviet people through television. Afterwards, Reagan said it was wonderful and agreed that he and Gorbachev had become old friends after so many meetings. One Soviet political commentator said that the Moscow summit marked a new "normalcy, stability, and constructiveness" in Soviet-American relations, and saw this improvement in relations as the direct fruit of the USSR's domestic and foreign policy restructuring.[125]

The period from May to August 1988 saw a critical review of past Soviet foreign policy, in the Soviet Union. In an article published in the Soviet press a scholar blamed Brezhnev for initiating a new arms race which had proved very costly for the USSR, by his decision to involve the Soviet Union in Afghanistan. He added that "errors and the incompetent approach of the Brezhnev leadership to the accomplishment of foreign policy talks" had created a crisis characterised by an exacerbation of tension in the USSR's relations with the West. He went on to remark that the realities of the nuclear age and advancements in science and technology made it imperative that "a new thinking and new approaches" to the attainment of foreign policy tasks be developed.[126]

Addressing a foreign ministry conference which opened on July 25 1988, the Soviet foreign minister Shevardnadze took the debate a step further when he outlined Soviet foreign policy's new look.[127] During the conference Shervardnadze discussed the possibility of involving elected bodies and the public in the decision making process of foreign policy. He also pointed out that the world was no longer characterised by a clash or struggle between the two opposing systems of Communism and Capitalism. In his report the Soviet foreign minister severely criticised the old style of confrontation and inflexibility which had been a hallmark of Soviet foreign policy under his predecessor Andrei Gromyko. He also blamed problems in domestic policy or wrong turns in domestic policy as having "exerted a serious negative impact on Soviet diplomacy" and remarked that positive changes had occurred in Soviet foreign policy over the past three years through considerable restructuring. This restructuring had already began to pay dividends, particularly with regard to relations with the United States, an example of how the new thinking was making headway. The years since Gorbachev became Soviet leader had seen growing progress in relations between America and the Soviet Union and a movement away from the confrontational cold war thinking which had been the predominant feature of East-West relations since 1945.

In late September 1988 Shevardnadze visited Washington for yet another round of Soviet-American talks. But by now it was becoming increasingly obvious that despite extensive work on the START treaty there were still a number of problems which were not going to be resolved before Reagan left office.[128] The two major hurdles were how to verify cut-backs in sea launch and other missiles, and the continuing refusal of the Soviet Union to destroy the huge radar station it was constructing at Krasnoyarsk, which according to Washington was in violation of the ABM treaty.

In what was seen by many as an attempt to influence the incoming President George Bush to sustain the momentous progress made in Soviet-American relations during Reagan's second term of office, Gorbachev came to New York to make a speech on December 7 to the United Nations where he announced a major package of proposals which included substantial unilateral cuts in the conventional forces of the Warsaw Pact.[129] According to Gorbachev's plan, in the two following years the number of troops would be decreased by 500,000 men. There would also be a substantial reduction in conventional weapons; the withdrawals of six tank divisions from the GDR, Czechoslovakia and Hungary by 1991 and their disbandment; a reduction in Soviet troops in these countries by 50,000 men and a cut in armaments of 5000 tanks; and a major reorganisation of the remaining Soviet divisions in Eastern Europe, assigning them a new "strictly defensive" role. Although Gorbachev stated "these reductions will be conducted unilaterally with no connection to the talks on the mandate of the Vienna meeting"[130] he stressed however that he hoped the West would "also take some steps".

Further evidence that Gorbachev was attempting to create a favourable atmosphere in preparation for dealing with the new US President was provided by his proposals on the issue of human rights which went some way to addressing American concerns at the dismal Soviet record on human rights.[131] Gorbachev pledged that no persons would be refused emigration or persecuted in the USSR because of their political or religious beliefs. Furthermore he accepted the rulings of the world court regarding international agreements on human rights.

The Western reaction to Gorbachev's unilateral arms cutbacks was generally full of praise.[132] However, reservations were expressed: Chairman of the joint chiefs of staff, Admiral W.J.Crowe, argued that Gorbachev's plan "falls far short of redressing the conventional balance" between the Warsaw Pact and NATO.[133] NATO responded on December 8, 1988 with its own proposals for sweeping arms cutbacks which would limit both the Warsaw Pact and NATO to no more than 20,000 tanks with the further stipulation that no one country could deploy more than 30 per cent of the tanks in its alliance.[134]

Gorbachev's military cuts announced at the UN, although largely supported by the Soviet military,[135] did attract an element of dissension from some in the military. A senior Soviet military officer, Marshal Akhromeyev, who had argued against any unilateral reduction, unexpectedly retired just hours before Gorbachev's UN address, fuelling speculation that the military would oppose the arms cutbacks. Also a Soviet Lieutenant Colonel complained that the troop cuts were hard to come to terms with, and cited the grievances of many officers who were concerned at the loss of housing since many military compounds housed the families of many officers, and the problems in adjusting to civilian life.[136]

Soviet-American relations under Reagan were ending on a high note, and in a farewell address reviewing U.S. foreign policy during his tenure Reagan spoke about the improvement in relations with the Soviet Union. Although he acknowledged that differences remained, he stressed that the relationship "once marked by sterility and confrontation .... is now characterised by dialogue - realistic candid dialogue - serious diplomatic dialogue..." and personally praised Gorbachev, who, he said had taken "some daring steps" and deserved credit.[137]

Conclusions

Overall then the story of Soviet-American relations in the period 1985-1988 revolves largely around Gorbachev, Reagan and summit diplomacy. The leaders of two superpowers developed a noticeable rapport which allowed the Soviet-American relationship to flourish with diplomatic dialogue replacing the wrangling of the early 1980s. This was most evident in a series of summit meetings between the two leaders held from 1985 to 1988. During these summits Reagan and Gorbachev displayed their ability to have a frank or candid dialogue allowing them to absorb more easily any criticism which each threw at the other. At these summit meetings there were detailed discussions on a variety of major issues which had a bearing on the superpower relationship. More dialogue meant more opportunities for resolving differences.

As a result the years from 1985 through to 1988 saw a remarkable improvement in Soviet-American relations. In comparison to the period 1981-1984 (when only 5 bilateral documents were signed)[138] 19 bilateral documents were signed in the period from 1985 to 1988, the most in any four year period since 1973-76. Also in 1988, 12 documents were signed, the most in any single year since 1973.[139] The two countries were more willing to sign accords after having done much under Gorbachev and Reagan to remove the climate of suspicion and fear. 1985 and 1986 witnessed slow but continuous progress. There were shaky or difficult moments such as the Daniloff incident which threatened to undermine relations, and the abrupt break-up of the Reykjavik Summit. There was also the Strategic Defence Initiative (SDI) which remained a bone of contention in relations between the two countries, and which was responsible for jeopardizing progress in 1985 and 1986.

However, Soviet insistence that SDI be linked to progress on arms control issues had been dropped by 1987 allowing the superpowers to make historic headway on arms control and disarmament culminating in the INF treaty. Furthermore in 1988 the conflict in Afghanistan which had been responsible for sparking off the 'new cold war' in 1980 moved a step nearer resolution with the signing of the Geneva peace agreement on April 14. Throughout the 1980s Afghanistan had long highlighted the intense differences which existed between Moscow and Washington on the question of regional conflicts. As a result 1987 and 1988 saw the upward trend in Soviet-American relations gather increasing momentum.

While both Reagan and Gorbachev were quite rightly accorded much credit for pursuing the path to cooperation it is important to keep in mind that the USSR's internal problems, especially the dire state of the economy, made Moscow conscious of the fact that competition and confrontation with Washington was not profitable. This was especially so since Reagan had demonstrated between 1981-85 that he would deal very strictly with the USSR and threatened to engage Moscow in a new arms race which it could ill afford. A top Soviet priority was to achieve substantial arms reduction agreements with Washington that would release much-needed resources for civilian purposes. Gorbachev's 'new thinking' in line with his programmes of Perestroika and Glasnost involved a considerable restructuring of Moscow's foreign policy and contributed a sharp reduction in East-west tension. Gorbachev's internal reforms saw him take steps to improve human rights particularly on emigration, and on the international scene he showed a willingness to disengage Moscow from third world 'adventurism'. All this helped to enhance his stature in the West and meant that previous objections to Soviet behaviour voiced by the West were no longer wholly applicable.

If there was a scene which symbolised more than anything else the new level of understanding which had been established between the U.S and the USSR, it was when Gorbachev and Reagan, at the Moscow summit, put their arms around each other's waist almost as if posing for a photograph. When Reagan departed from office he and Gorbachev had reached agreement in principle on a number of issue areas which was to bode well for the future.

Notes

1. A good biography of Gorbachev is *Gorbachev* by Zhores Medvedev (Oxford and New York, Revised Edition 1988).
2. On American-Soviet relations under Reagan and Gorbachev see the following: Michael Mandelbaum and Strobe Talbott, *Reagan and Gorbachev* (New York, Vintage Books 1987); Seweryn Bialer and Michael Mandelbaum (eds), *Gorbachev's Russia and American Foreign Policy* (Boulder Westview Press, 1988); E.E Grigoriev and T.A. Kolesnichenko, *Vashington, Moskva, Chto Dal'she?* (Moscow: Mezhdunarodnye Otnosheniya 1988); See also Eduard Shevardnadze, *Moi Vybor V Zashchitu Demokratii I Svobody* (Moscow: Novosti 1991).
3. On the new political thinking, see: Margot Light, *The Soviet Theory of International Relations* (Wheatsheaf Books Brighton 1988); David Holloway, 'Gorbachev's new thinking', *Foreign Affairs*, Vol. 68, No.1 (1989) pp.66-81; Seweryn Bialer, 'New thinking and Soviet foreign policy', *Survival*, Vol. 30, No. 4, (July/August 1988) pp.291-310; Peter Shearman, 'The new Political thinking reassessed', *Review of International Studies*, Vol. 19, No.2 (April 1993) pp.139-158; M.S.Gorbachev, *Perestroika I Novoye Myshlenie Dlya Nashey Strani I Dlya Vsego Mira* (Moscow: Politizdat 1987), particularly Part 2.
4. Gorbachev, *Perestroika I Novoye Myshlenie......*
5. *Pravda*, December 8, 1988, pp.1-2.
6. See Eduard Shevardnadze, *Moi Vybor V Zashchitu Demokratii I Svobody*, p.99.
7. See Mandelbaum and Talbott, Reagan and Gorbachev; Bialer and Mandelbaum, *Gorbachev's Russia and American Foreign Policy*; Kolesnichenko, *Vashington, Moskva, Chto Dal' She?* See also for a briefer account of Soviet-American relations 1985-88, Peter E Boyle, *American-Soviet relations from the Russian revolution to the fall of communism* (London, New York, 1993) Chapter 15.
8. Ronald Reagan, *An American Life* (New York, Simon and Schuster, 1990), p.614.
9. *Ibid* p.615.
10. *Ibid* p.612.
11. *Ibid* pp.613-614 (text of Gorbachev's letter).
12. See *New York Times* March 19, 1985, p.1
13. *Pravda,* March 25, 1985, p.5.
14. See Reagan, *An American Life*, pp.615-616.
15. See *chapter 2*, section 3.
16. *Pravda*, April 8, 1985, p.1.
17. *Ibid.*

18. *Ibid*, April 13, 1985, p.5.
19. *Congressional Quarterly Almanac 1985*, p.176.
20. *Ibid*, p.16-D.
21. See Thomas Schelling, 'What Went Wrong With Arms Control'? *Foreign Affairs*, Vol. 64 (Winter 1985/86), pp.219-233, in which Schelling looks at what had become the customary failure of US-Soviet arms control negotiations at the time.
22. See Paul H Nitze, *From Hiroshima to Glasnost* (New York, Grove, Wiedenfeld 1989), pp.410-411, where he stresses the fact that during the Geneva negotiations the Russians were concerned above all about the SDI Programme; see also *Mirovaya Ekonomika I Mezhdunarodnye Otnosheniya*, No. 11, 1985, pp.14-24. The Soviets actually viewed Reagan's SDI Programme as an attempt by America to attain military superiority over the USSR, calling it a "programme of aggression in space".
23. *Pravda*, May 27, 1985, p.4.
24. See *chapter 2*, section 1.
25. See Reagan, *An American Life*, p.620.
26. *Pravda*, May 28, 1985, p.5.
27. *Congressional Quarterly Almanac 1985* p.176.
28. See Reagan, *An American Life*, p.620.
29. *Ibid.*
30. *Congressional Quarterly Almanac 1985*, p.22-D.
31. See Reagan, *An American Life*, pp.621-622.
32. *Izvestia* July 4, 1985, p.1.
33. *Pravda*, July 5, 1985, p.5.
34. See Shevardnadze, *Moi Vybor V Zashchitu Demokratii I Svobody*, pp.79-82, where he recalls his feelings about his appointment to the post of minister for foreign affairs.
35. On Shultz's trip to Finland and his feelings about Shevardnadze as the new Soviet Foreign Minister, see George P Shultz, *Turmoil and Triumph: My Years as Secretary of State* (Charles Scribner's Sons 1993) pp.571-576.
36. See *Za mir i bezopasnost' narodov, dokumenty vneshnei politiki SSSR* 1985 Book one pp.430-431
37. Gorbachev, *Perestroika I Novoye Myshlenie....*, p.238.
38. *Congressional Quarterly Almanac 1985*, p.178.
39. This counter offer was put forward at an address before the 40th session of the UN General Assembly on October 24 1984 by Reagan. This address is in: *Weekly Compilation of Presidential Documents*, Vol. 21 (October 28 1985) pp.1291-1296; See also Reagan's letter to Gorbachev, outlining American proposals in Reagan, *An American Life*, pp.629-631.
40. Izvestia, October 9, 1985, p.5.
41. See *Za mir i bezopasnost' narodov, Dokumenty Vneshnei Politiki SSSR*, 1985, Book Two, pp.233-234.
42. See Reagan, *An American Life*, p.631. See also Shultz, *Turmoil and Triumph*, where he recalls Gorbachev's insistence that SDI must be abandoned.
43. Reagan set out this agenda at a speech to the United Nations on October 24, 1985 - See *Congressional Quarterly Almanac 1985*, p.32-D for the text of this speech.
44. *Pravda*, November 19, 1985, p.1.
45. For a full list of officials from both sides, see *Sovetsko-Amerikanskaya Vstrecha*

na Vysshem Urovne, Zheneva 19-21 noyabrya 1985 goda: Dokumenty i materialy (Moscow 1985) p.13.

46. *Ibid*, pp.18-19.
47. *Ibid*, pp.19-20.
48. *Ibid*, pp.13-17.
49. *Ibid*, pp.21-42.
50. *Ibid*, pp.43-46.
51. This address is in *Department of State Bulletin*, Vol. 86 (January 19 1986), pp.13-14.
52. *Sovetsko-Amerikanskaya Vstrecha na Vysshem Urovne, Zheneva 19-21, noyabrya*, pp.51-76.
53. Shultz noted the friendship which the two had developed in his recollection of the summit in Shultz's *Turmoil & Triumph*, pp.586-607.
54. *Pravda*, November 23, 1985, p.4.
55. *Izvestia*, November 22, 1985, p.5.
56. M.S.Gorbachev, *Izbrannye rechi i stat'i*, vol. 3 (Moscow: Politizdat 1987) pp.133-144; see also Gorbachev, *Perestroika i novoye myshlenie* pp.242-246.
57. See Reagan, *An American Life*, p.650.
58. *Congressional Quarterly Almanac 1986*, p.3-D.
59. *Pravda*, February 7, 1986, p.1.
60. See p.18.
61. M.S.Gorbachev, *Izbrannye rechi i stat'i*, vol. 3 pp.289-291.
62. See Reagan, *An American Life*, pp.662-664.
63. See *chapter 2*, pp.35-36.
64. *Congressional Quarterly Almanac 1986*, p.19-D.
65. *Ibid.* p.462.
66. *Pravda*, May 24, 1985, p.5.
67. *Izvestia*, June 1, 1985, p.1.
68. *Congressional Quarterly Almanac 1986*, p.463.
69. See Reagan, *An American Life*, p.665.
70. *Ibid.* pp.669-672.
71. *Congressional Quarterly Almanac 1986*, p.460.
72. *Izvestia*, September 9, 1986, p.6.
73. *Congressional Quarterly Almanac 1986*, p.460.
74. See *Pravda*, August 6, 1986, p.4.
75. *Ibid*, October 11, 1986, p.1.
76. Reagan, *An American Life*, p.675.
77. *Ibid*, p.677.
78. Although disappointed at the outcome of the summit Shultz in his memoirs argues that more was achieved at the Reykjavik Summit than was generally believed. See Shultz, *Turmoil and Triumph*, pp.776-780.
79. *Sovetsko-Amerikanskaya Vstrecha na Vysshem Urovne, Reyk'yavik, 11-12, oktyabrya 1986 goda*, Dokumenty i materialy (Moscow 1986) p.8.
80. *Congressional Quarterly Almanac 1986*, p.30-D.
81. *Sovetsko-Amerikanskaya Vstrecha na Vysshem Uorovne, Reyk'yavik, 11-12, oktyabrya* p.34.
82. *Ibid*, p.50.
83. *Congressional Quarterly Almanac 1986*, p.355.
84. *Pravda*, November 15 1986, p.5.
85. *Za Mir I Bezopasnost Narodov*, 1986 Book two, p.431.
86. *Pravda*, December 19, 1986, p.1.
87. *Congressional Quarterly Almanac 1987*, p.6-D.
88. M.S.Gorbachev, *Izbrannye rechi i stat'i*, vol 4, (Moscow: Politizdat 1987), pp.444-446.
89. *Pravda*, April 15, 1987, pp.1-3.
90. *Ibid.*

91. *Ibid.*
92. *Izvestia,* May 26, 1987, p.5.
93. *Pravda*, July 9, 1987, p.5.
94. See Reagan, *An American Life*, p.691.
95. *Ibid.*
96. For the text of this agreement signed on September 15 1987, see *Department of State Bulletin*, Vol. 87, (November 1987), pp.34-37.
97. *Pravda,* September 19, 1987, p.4.
98. *Ibid,* October 23, 1987, p.4.
99. *Ibid*, October 24, 1987, p.1.
100. *Izvestia,* December 9, 1987, p.1.
101. *Vizit general'nogo sekretarya Tsk Kpss M.S. Gorbacheva V SSh.A 7-10 dekabrya 1987 goda*, Dokumenty materialy (Moscow 1987), p.61.
102. *Ibid,* p.63.
103. *Ibid*, p.141.
104. *Pravda,* December 15, 1987, p.1.
105. *Congressional Quarterly Almanac 1987*, p.31-D.
106. *Ibid.*
107. *Ibid,* 1988, p.3-C.
108. US Senate, 100th Congress 2nd Session. *The INF Treaty: Hearings before the committee on foreign relations 1988* (US GPO Washington DC 1988).
109. *Congressional Quarterly Almanac 1988*, p.380.
110. *Ibid,* 1987, p.137.
111. *Ibid,* 1988, p.387.
112. *Ibid,* 1988, p.382.
113. *Ibid*, 1988, p.7-C.
114. Reagan, *An American Life,* p.701.
115. *Pravda*, April 23, 1988, pp.1-3.
116. *Congressional Quarterly Almanac 1988*, p.467; see also *Department of State Bulletin* Vol. 88 (June 1988) pp.56-60, for the texts on the agreements signed.
117. *Congressional Quarterly Almanac 1988*, p.467.
118. *Ibid.*
119. *Ibid,* p.379.
120. *Sovetsko-Amerikanskaya Vstrecha na Visshem Urovne, Moskva, 29-Maya-2iyuni, 1988 goda* Dokumenty i Materialy (Moscow 1988) pp.126-127.
121. *Ibid,* p.127.
122. *Ibid,* p.129.
123. *Ibid*, p.185.
124. *Ibid,* p.112.
125. *Izvestia,* June 4 1988, p.4; see also *Mirovaya Ekonomika I Mezhunarodnye Otnosheniya*, No. 9, 1988, pp.24-35.
126. *Literaturnaya gazeta,* May 18, 1988, p.14.
127. *Pravda*, July 26, 1988, p.4.
128. See Nitze, *From Hiroshima to Glasnost*, pp.456-457.
129. *Pravda* December 8, 1988, pp.1-2.
130. *Ibid.*
131. *Ibid.*
132. Reaction to Gorbachev's arms cuts is in: *NATO Review* No. 6, December 1988, p.25.
133. *Congressional Quarterly Almanac 1988*, p.465.
134. NATO's own proposals announced on December 8, 1988, are in *NATO Review* No. 6 December 1988, p.25.
135. *Pravda,* December 17, 1988, p.4.
136. *Krasnaya Zvezda,* December 15, 1988, p.2.
137. *Congressional Quarterly Almanac 1988,* p.28-C.
138. See *Chapter 1*, p.43.
139. *Soviet Treaties Project*, Department of Politics, University of Glasgow.

3 The Impact of American Trade Pressure on the Soviet Union: 1-The Question of Non-Strategic Trade

Introduction

There has always been a strong interrelationship between Soviet-American political and economic relations (with trade forming the key component of economic relations). It is clear that superpower economic relations have been governed by a different set of rules and principles, dictated more by political considerations than the economic benefits that either side might have derived.[1] This is particularly true of the United States, which has sought to use its powerful economic position in relation to the Soviet Union to exert a degree of trade pressure[2] on the USSR for the attainment of political objectives.[3]

The instruments of trade pressure used by the United States have ranged from comprehensive economic sanctions and embargoes of particular goods to the denial of most favoured nations status, credit and export controls. These have been used at various times, though not always simultaneously. The various political goals have included: to punish Soviet International behaviour; to impose economic leverage or influence in the hope of altering particular Soviet policies - domestic and foreign; and to maintain American military superiority through the denial of Western technology and know-how to Moscow.[4]

The debate over how to conduct trade with the Soviet Union, the aggregate level and composition of which has been the subject of much scrutiny and controversy in America, heightened with the onset of the 'new cold war' at the beginning of 1980, and trade pressure became a central plank of America's trade policy towards Moscow when Reagan was elected to the Presidency.[5] The political 'Cold War' was thus supplemented by an economic 'Cold War'.

It is true that the United States also used trade as a political weapon during the 1970s but in a more positive sense. In other words increased trade and economic ties were used in order to bolster detente and provide an incentive for the Soviets to improve their international behaviour and some areas of domestic policy. Trade was offered as more of a 'carrot' rather than as a 'stick' for the most part of the 1970s.[6]

However with the renewal of cold war rivalry and increased tension at the start of the 1980s, the Carter and then the Reagan administration adopted a policy of comprehensive trade pressure against the Soviet Union which it put into practice throughout the 1980s. Trade was now being used as a 'stick' rather than as a 'carrot'.

The aim of this chapter is basically twofold. One is to provide an analysis of the impact of US trade pressure on the total level of Soviet-American trade. The second, and perhaps more important task is to look at the economic impact of trade pressure on the target country - the USSR - and assess the extent to which it was punished. The chapter is divided into two sections.

Section one will analyze the impact of American trade pressure on the aggregate level of trade flows, and on the direction of trade between the two superpowers. The second section will look more specifically at the economic impact on the USSR of selective commodity sanctions, denial or limits on particular goods to the USSR (excluding technology and other strategic items which are the subject of the next chapter), and boycotts of various Soviet exports. In this section the following questions will need to be addressed: were American sanctions and restrictions on particular exports to the Soviet Union successful or was Moscow able to circumvent the U.S. measures by finding alternative suppliers? And what about Soviet exports? How much did American limits, and boycott of Soviet exports harm the USSR's hard currency earnings, or did Moscow find alternative buyers for its goods? The answers to these questions will allow us to determine the extent to which the USSR was punished and if indeed the U.S. measures had the intended negative economic impact.

1. Impact of U.S. Trade Pressure on the Aggregate Level of U.S. - USSR Trade and on the Pattern of Trade

The Scale of American - Soviet Economic Activity

A look at any Soviet-American trade figures since 1945 will reveal that bilateral trade amounted to a very insignificant proportion of the overall trade conducted by each side, and hence the level of economic activity has been very small. This can be explained by a number of factors.

The autarkic nature of the communist bloc led by the Soviet Union meant that trade with the world was minute, let alone with the principal adversary, the United States of America. Only the need for the most essential commodities saw the Soviet bloc break out of its shell. Even though the scale of Soviet trade with the capitalist countries did increase since the 1960s most of the upward trend was confined to Western Europe rather than the United States.

Other problems associated with communist countries such as the non-convertibility of their currencies, and the production of often low quality and shoddy goods coupled with a lack of variety did not make these countries an appealing proposition for the non-communist world.

Not least, Cold war rivalry also played a major part in the small-scale economic activity generated between the two superpowers. As two superpowers confronting each other on a global scale their mutual mistrust spilled over into the economic sphere. In the early days of the Cold War economic ties were almost unthinkable. Trade ties began to emerge on a measurable scale by the 1960s, and benefited greatly from detente during the 1970s. The renewed period of conflict in the early 1980s characterised by major world events, and the election of Ronald Reagan, a fervent anti-communist, proved a disaster for Soviet - American economic relations. As part of Reagan's overall strategy toward Moscow, the President made clear his desire to deny the USSR advanced Western technology and punish it economically through the use of American trade and economic coercion. That Reagan's policy was indeed to punish Moscow economically was picked up by Soviet Foreign Trade Minister Nikolai Patolichev who noted what he saw as US attempts to try "to eliminate trade and economic relations with the Soviet Union ...." by the use of discriminatory economic measures.[7]

Appendix Table 3.1 illustrates how little bilateral trade amounts to as a proportion of the overall foreign trade conducted by both countries. In the case of the United States, the USSR has never accounted for more than 1% of overall American foreign trade with the exception of 1979 (in the period 1979-88). Throughout the 1980s trade with Moscow consistently amounted to less than 1% of the total value of American foreign trade (see Appendix Table 3.1).

If we look at the proportion of Soviet trade conducted with the United States the figure is only slightly higher (see Appendix Table 3.1). America accounted for over 3% of Soviet foreign trade in 1979 but this figure fell dramatically to less than 2% and never rose above 2% again during the 1980s. In 1987 it even dropped to less than 1% (0.9%).

The Impact of American Trade Pressure on the Aggregate Volume and Pattern of Superpower Trade 1979-88

Aggregate Volume of Soviet-American Trade (1979-88)

The evidence of any substantial impact of American trade pressure on the total volume of superpower trade during the course of the period 1979-88 is not easily determinable by simple observation of the total volume of superpower trade. As Appendix Table 3.2 reveals the volume of superpower trade fell by a massive amount (47%) in 1980, the result largely of the comprehensive package of economic sanctions imposed by President Carter following the Soviet invasion of Afghanistan[8] (see chapter two). Thereafter, during the remainder of the period 1981-88 the volume of trade between the two countries followed a fluctuating path, with trade turnover increasing in 1981, 1982 and 1984 but falling in 1983, 1985, 1986 and 1987. American trade measures designed to punish the USSR had no uniform visible impact on the aggregate volume of Soviet-American trade, with the exception of 1980. Caution must be taken when attempting to explain the depression in various years of Soviet-American trade since the downward trend may be the result of economic factors and cannot be attributed solely to American trade pressure applied for political purposes.

Pattern of Soviet-American Trade

The story is much the same when we analyze the volume of Soviet imports from the United States, and the volume of Soviet exports to the United States during the period 1979-1988. The year 1980 stands out once again as the exception to the rule largely because American trade pressure was targeted on the commodities which made up the bulk of Soviet-American trade (see section 2). This is represented by a decrease of 46% in goods imported from the United States, and a fall of 56% in Soviet exports to the United States. Despite further American sanctions in late 1981 and in 1982, Soviet imports from the U.S. actually rose in both these years. As with the total volume of Soviet-American trade, Soviet exports and imports to and from the United States followed no obvious pattern. Appendix Figures 3.1 and 3.2 illustrate the fluctuating path followed by Soviet imports and exports.

2. Economic Impact on the Soviet Union as a Result of U.S. Trade Pressure on the Commodity Composition of Superpower Trade 1979-88

The Structure of Soviet-American Trade

Structure of Soviet Imports from the United States A look at the commodity composition of Soviet imports from the United States (Appendix Tables 3.3 (a) and 3.3 (b)) will show that they can be divided into two categories: selected agricultural products and selected non-agricultural products. Of the first category the most important of those imported were grain, wheat, maize and soyabeans; while machinery equipment and means of transport, chemical products and superphosphoric acid represented the most important non-agricultural imports, in terms of volume.

i) Soviet Imports of Agricultural Products and American Trade Pressure

After 1950 North America emerged as the undisputed bread-basket of the world (the USA and Canada being the largest net exporters of grain), with the USSR and Eastern Europe emerging as the leading importers after Africa. For the Soviet Union, the United States became a particularly important source for agricultural products due largely to poor Soviet grain harvests and generally poor agricultural performance which yielded less output in the late 1970s and early 1980s. In 1979, grain, maize and wheat were by far the largest Soviet imports from the United States. In fact America took well over half the Soviet market for these products in 1979. This seemingly apparent dependence of the Soviet Union on America for major agricultural commodities came to the forefront in 1980 when in response to the events in Afghanistan President Carter announced a wide ranging package of economic sanctions[9] which included an embargo on future grain exports,[10] leading to a cancellation of an offer of 17 million metric tonnes of wheat and corn. This had a dramatic domestic effect on the volume of these goods imported by the Soviet Union (as can be seen in Appendix Tables 3.3 (a) and 3.3 (b)). Imports of each of the four main agricultural products from the United States plummeted by massive amounts. Grain fell by 51.6%, maize by 46.4%, wheat imports plunged 59.3%, while soya beans were drastically reduced by 80%.

What about the economic effect on the Soviet Union or the economic impact of the denial of all or a substantial quantity of such important food products from an important source? Clearly the aim of the United States government was to impose the maximum economic cost (punishment) on the Soviet Union by drastically cutting back on its exports of agricultural goods.

However, the American move backfired. Such an approach could only be effective if it were backed up by all leading exporters of the same commodities, who were willing to bear the substantial economic cost themselves by undergoing a simultaneous reduction or total embargo of these goods to the USSR for an unlimited period.[11] But the other leading exporters were not willing to follow the U.S. In other words the USSR had available alternative supplier countries who were more than willing to meet the Soviet demand for agricultural products.[12] As a result, the United States share of agricultural exports to the USSR fell while other countries, most notably Argentina, Australia and Canada increased their share (see Appendix Table 3.4 (a)). In 1981, despite the lifting of the grain and agricultural embargo by President Reagan, Argentina and Canada surpassed the United States as the leading exporters of grain to the Soviet Union. Likewise, Argentina which on July 10 1980 had signed an agreement to provide the Soviet Union with 22.5 mmt of soyabeans, corn (maize) and sorghum during the five years beginning January 1, 1981, became the top exporter of maize moving ahead of America, while Canada became the leading exporter of wheat. It appeared as though despite assurances later in 1982 from Reagan that agricultural exports would never again be subject to restrictive trade measures for political reasons, the Soviet government saw America as a unreliable source for important products and opted for more politically risk free countries such as Argentina and Canada. The Soviet Union was in fact able to increase its imports of grain, wheat and soyabeans in 1980 and 1981.[13] The United States did gradually recover between 1982 and 1987 the ground it had lost to other countries by re-establishing its share of the Soviet market particularly in regard to maize and grain. But it was not until 1988 that America regained the position of leading exporter of agricultural commodities to the Soviet Union (see Appendix Table 3.4 (b)).

The fall in the U.S. share of agricultural exports to the USSR during the 1980s was the result of a self-inflicted policy started in 1980 which put political goals before economic gain. This coupled with increasing competition from other nations meant that for the most part of the 1980s America was no longer the dominant supplier to the USSR. The analysis has shown that American trade pressure on the Soviet Union with regard to agricultural products was unsuccessful on the whole, and the USSR encountered no difficulty in diversifying the source of its imports. Alternative suppliers were available and Moscow was able to import as much during the 1980s as it did before 1980, despite U.S. trade pressure.

ii) Soviet Imports of Non-Agricultural Products and American Trade Pressure

Soviet imports from the United States of non-agricultural goods consisted largely of industrial items (see Appendix Table 3.3 (a)) such as machinery equipment, chemical products, and superphosphoric acid. Other items imported but on a much smaller scale included energy equipment, agriculture equipment and metal working machines.[14] These non-agricultural items were also subject to American trade pressure. Appendix Tables 3.3 (a) and 3.3 (b) will show that imports of machinery equipment and transport means fell in each year from 1979 to 1988 with the exception of 1986. This category not surprisingly came under close scrutiny during the 1980s because many of the items in this category constituted what were termed as dual use items. These were civilian items with potential military applications whose transfer to the Soviet Union America was keen to prevent, particularly at a time of heightened political tensions (see the next chapter for a more detailed study of U.S. and Western control of modern and sophisticated technology to the USSR). As a result such items became a major part of American trade controls and embargoes.

The West had become an important source for modern technology for the Soviet Union which was lagging behind the West in industrial development due to the very nature of the command economy system. Problems such as outdated technology and lack of incentives for innovation meant that the USSR would be to some degree dependent on Western imports of machinery and technology in order to modernize and renovate its industrial base.

The United States' use of trade pressure in this area was more successful in its goal of attempting to punish the Soviet Union. The USSR was unable to compensate for the fall in American imports of machinery equipment by turning to other major Western nations. Imports of machinery equipment from Britain, France and West Germany saw a largely downward trend in the period 1979-88.[15] The consequences of this were serious for the already ailing Soviet economy. The improvement in Soviet-American relations which began to take shape in 1985 (see chapter 3) did not rectify the Soviet position, and machinery imports from the West continued to fall. The Soviet Union was able to increase its overall volume of imports of this category but had to settle for Eastern Europe as the source.[16] Moscow's East European allies, most notably Hungary, Poland, Bulgaria, GDR and Czechoslovakia, were already the largest suppliers of machinery to the Soviet Union. In other words the USSR was unable to find other countries which were alternative and acceptable sources of supply.

Soviet imports of chemical products and superphosphoric acid were heavily hit by U.S. trade pressure in 1980. On February 25, 1980 the United States embargoed exports of phosphoric acid and phosphate fertilizers to the USSR.[17] This followed an effective suspension in early February 1980[18] when the Commerce Department required validated licences, and suspended issuance of such licences. However, restrictions on the export of these products were greatly eased, and Soviet imports of these products from the United States actually rose for the most part of the 1980s (see Appendix Tables 3.3 (a) and 3.3 (b)).

It is very important to consider the availability of alternative supplier countries to the Soviet Union for any major commodity it is denied or the supply of which is severely curtailed by America.[19] As seen, American attempts to punish the USSR economically by restricting or denying various agricultural products were generally a failure. This was because substitute countries - namely Argentina, Canada, and Australia - were available to meet the amount of the products demanded by the USSR. Therefore the intended negative economic impact on the target country - the USSR - did not materialise to the desired extent. In this case American trade pressure ended up being nothing more than a gesture having no more than a symbolic effect, rather than any intended economic effect. In some ways the United States contributed to its own failure in instituting effective agricultural trade pressure on the USSR. For a start the American agricultural embargo of 1980 was beset with problems. It failed to take into account the availability of other exporters to the USSR and underestimated their ability to meet the level of Soviet demand. To add to this, the embargo was short lived with Reagan lifting it in April 1981. To have any chance of success the embargo had to be sustained over a longer period of time. The United States ended up suffering considerable economic costs.[20] There was considerable domestic opposition from farm lobby groups whose members' incomes were significantly reduced, and the loss of a major Soviet market.

The key problem, however, for the United States was the lack of market power it had over the trade in agricultural commodities. A market structure known as perfect competition prevailed in international agricultural trade, with a large number of suppliers such that no one supplier country was able to exercise exclusive control over the market for agricultural goods. Only in a situation where a country exercises considerable monopoly power (cases where it is the sole producer and supplier of a commodity) can unilateral trade measures such as embargoes or sanctions be expected to work. Even then the target country may overcome the problem if the commodities denied to it have a close substitute which can be attained elsewhere. In the absence of such monopoly power the formation of an international cartel by the leading suppliers of the commodity in question can sometimes be effective.[21]

U.S. attempts to deny or curtail other exports to the Soviet Union, particularly machinery equipment and means of transport, met with more success. This was because the Soviet Union had no other sources available from which to obtain Western technology since America's allies in Europe also tightened their exports of this item to the East because of its possible strategic and military applications. In short there was no substitute for Western technology and its particular qualities. The USSR was forced to turn inward to Eastern Europe to meet its demand for machinery equipment not attainable from the West.

Soviet Exports to the United States

Soviet-American bilateral trade amounted to a very insignificant proportion of the overall trade conducted by each side, and trade was dominated mostly by Soviet imports from America. Nevertheless the Soviet Union did export a number of goods to the United States, the most important of which are illustrated in Appendix Table 3.5 (a).

U.S. Trade Pressure on Soviet Exports American imports from the USSR comprised such as small amount that they appeared to be no more than a symbolic gesture on part of the United States that trade should be conducted on a mutual basis. Therefore it was not surprising why many political analysts argue that American-Soviet trade was a 'one-way street' with trade flowing principally from the United States to the Soviet Union. America was not dependent on the Soviet Union for its most important imports. It was either self-sufficient in these or could attain them from other countries. The United States had always been anxious to avoid purchasing large volumes of goods from the Soviet Union which could contribute significantly to the Soviet's stock of hard currency earnings. This anxiety was demonstrated by Defence Secretary Casper Weinberger when commenting on America's dispute with its Western European allies over what was the most desirable level of trade with the Soviet Union. In a statement the Defence Secretary spoke of Soviet earnings from gas sales as providing the hard currency to obtain militarily useful technology from the West thus threatening one of the principal objectives of the Reagan administrative to check and contain Soviet military power.

A look at Appendix Figure 3.3, which shows the percentage change from 1979 to 1980 in selected American imports from the Soviet Union, will reveal evidence that the United States took measures to restrict purchases of certain Soviet exports. Out of the six major Soviet exports to the United States, four suffered from the American policy of trade pressure. Imports of oil and oil products fell by a huge 91.7% in 1980. Imports of machinery equipment went down by 56.2%, vodka by 12.3% while consumer goods were reduced by 45.4%. In contrast there were increases of 96% and 105% respectively in Soviet exports of ammonia and chemical products to the United States. Even by the end of 1988 Soviet exports of machinery equipment, oil and oil products and consumer goods were significantly down on their 1979 level (see Appendix Tables 3.5 (a) and 3.5 (b)), while chemical products and ammonia exports only increased slightly in 1988 in comparison to their 1979 level. 1979 was the last year before the deterioration in Soviet-American relations was to begin and which was to be accompanied with U.S. trade pressure which was to hit superpower trade very hard during the course of the 1980s. The improvement in Soviet-American relations in the post-1985 period failed to increase trade ties by any significant level and in many years during the 1980s Soviet exports continued to suffer from a restrictive U.S. trading policy.

What about the economic impact on the Soviet Union of the American policy of curtailing purchases of Soviet goods or boycotting Soviet exports? It is doubtful whether the Soviet Union suffered very badly since Soviet exports to the United States formed a very small proportion of overall Soviet exports of these products to all countries. The United States never accounted for more than 1% of Soviet exports of consumer goods throughout the entire period 1980-88. The same can be said of machinery equipment, and oil and oil products (up until 1986). Only in chemical products, ammonia and vodka did the United States account for more than 5% of Soviet exports during the period 1980-88, and coincidentally these were the very products which suffered least from U.S. trade pressure.

In addition the USSR's leading exports - energy and arms - were not exported to the United States, meaning that its most important or leading export sectors back home were fairly secure.

As far as the effect on the USSR's hard currency export earnings is concerned it is not likely to have been particularly disastrous. While a reduction or boycott by the United States of various Soviet exports would certainly have depleted Soviet hard currency earnings, Moscow was able to compensate for this by increasing its volume or maintaining the same volume of its overall exports of the goods in question to the rest of the world.[22] As a result the Soviet Union managed to offset any negative impact resulting from the U.S. measures by either finding alternative export markets or by increasing its exports to existing markets, thus preventing any serious erosion of its hard currency earnings. Of course there would be some depletion of hard currency earnings, since increased sales to the rest of the world aimed at offsetting reduced sales generated from the United States need not mean increased exports to hard currency countries. This is because not all countries have convertible currencies and are not therefore able to meet payment in hard currency, as in the case of many developing countries. A substantial fall in hard currency earnings can be more serious as it reduces the ability to purchase hard currency imports and a country may have to do without important imports. For the Soviet Union the situation was never that serious. The USSR was believed to have a substantial gold stock that acted as a guarantee that in any particular year the Soviet economy could absorb a fairly severe blow to its hard currency earnings (due to e.g. a fall in demand by the U.S. for certain Soviet goods) without having to seek new credits with which to pay for hard currency imports.

However, it was always questionable whether in fact the USSR could enter the gold market with large amounts of gold without pushing down the price of gold which would be of no use to it, and indeed whether the Soviet Union had enough freedom to manoeuvre with regard to gold that would allow it to attain hard currency imports.

With trade playing a very little role in Soviet-American relations, and with the USSR managing to sustain to a large extent its export volume to the world - even though exports of some products to America drastically fell, there was very little chance of U.S. economic measures against Soviet exports causing any significant damage economically. Only a large scale boycott of Soviet exports by the United States and its Western allies on a multilateral basis could seriously be expected to have damaged the Soviet Union by eroding its export base and depleting its hard currency earnings.

However, in a world of diverse political views and alignments coupled with the availability and opportunity to find and exploit new export markets there are ways of circumventing trade pressure on one's exports. Moreover such a scenario where Western Europe supported a full scale boycott of Soviet exports was unlikely in view of the expanded economic contacts between the Soviet Union and Western Europe and the latter's degree of dependence on trade with Moscow, an issue which proved to be a major point of contention between United States and its European allies with the two sides differing on how trade with the USSR should be conducted (especially in the case of trade in technology: see the next chapter).

Another way in which the United States punished the Soviet Union through the use of trade pressure was by denying it most favoured nation status (MFN). As a result the high rate of tariffs on Soviet goods entering America meant that any prospect of new products successfully breaking into U.S. markets was greatly diminished. Furthermore existing Soviet exports to the United States became uncompetitive as the discriminatory measures imposed by America in the form of high tariff rates made it difficult for Soviet goods to compete in the U.S. market. The only option left to Moscow in order to counteract the high tariffs was to lower its export prices, something which the exporting nation would rather not do.

The effect on the target nation's employment, in this case, was likely to be negligible. This is because in the USSR (as in the other socialist countries of Eastern Europe) employment was determined by government economic planning (everyone was given a job) and not by external factors like international trade performance. The low levels of unemployment achieved by the USSR and its East European allies after the Second World War was something of which they were very proud and was not immediately prejudiced by external trade sanctions.

Conclusions

It can be concluded that American trade pressure on the Soviet Union during the period 1980-88 had only a very limited negative economic impact on the USSR. Indeed the United States suffered considerable economic costs itself, and in the case of the grain embargo in 1980-81 it arguably suffered more than the target country - the USSR.

The lack of overall success of the United States strategy of trade pressure adopted against the Soviet Union can be attributed to a number of factors. For a start the US policy was not universally supported, not even by its staunchest allies. The lack of allied support was noted by Soviet Foreign Trade Minister Patolichev in an interview he gave in 1981. Asked about how the other Western countries had reacted to the trade boycott imposed by the US against the USSR, the Minister replied "... the facts tell us that our Western partners in Europe were not influenced by this US policy directed against the USSR .....". He went on ".... the business circles in Western Europe in particular were keen to continue to broaden business links with the USSR ....".[23] More importantly America was unable to form any sort of cartel with major exporting nations in order to effectively curtail supplies of sanctioned commodities to the USSR. America was unable to exercise monopoly power due to the fact that markets of the commodities concerned exhibited a perfectly competitive structure, so it was not able to wield much market power. This meant that the Soviet Union was able to circumvent the denial of certain imports to it by a certain amount of trade diversion. Alternative suppliers were in most cases very easily found. To safeguard against overdependence on one nation for its most important imports (particularly agricultural products) the Soviet Union spread its share of such imports to a number of countries. In such a case the United States sanctions proved to be nothing more than a short term inconvenience quite easily overcome.

In the case of the boycott of Soviet exports and limits on Soviet goods entering America the results were mixed. Soviet exports were always on a small scale to the United States, and the denial of most-favoured nation status meant that there was little opportunity for existing and new Soviet products to make any significant impact in the U.S. market, with Soviet goods being priced out by foreign competitors who benefited from the granting of more preferential tariff rates against their countries.

There was also some limited effect on Soviet hard currency earnings, which fell during this period. However even in this case the USSR managed to cushion much of the adverse impact by finding alternative buyers for its goods, thus safeguarding its export earnings.

There was no particular pattern in the figures for total trade and in the volume of Soviet exports and imports to and from the United States to suggest any major impact of U.S. trade pressure on the aggregate flow of American-Soviet trade, with the exception of 1980 when trade pressure was most marked. After 1980 American trade pressure became more of a selective policy with measures taken largely with regard to particular commodities rather than a whole package of general sanctions as in 1980. So it is trends in the commodity composition of superpower trade (particularly trends in the major commodities traded) which provide real evidence of US trade pressure.

Also it can be seen that American trade pressure during the 1980s, in particular its ferocity in the years 1980-84, was in line with the overall state of U.S.- Soviet relations which were tense during this period. However as relations improved after 1985 U.S. trade pressure did ease somewhat (with the exception of the transfer of strategic goods).[24] Nevertheless this slight relaxation of trade policy towards the USSR was not really reflected in the figures of the commodity composition of trade, partly because the USSR was no longer willing to engage in trade with the United States to the extent it had done prior to 1980, with America now seen as a unreliable trading partner and Moscow opting for politically safer markets.

The United States failed to punish the Soviet Union economically for the reasons mentioned.[25] A country of the size of the USSR was also an unsuitable target for economic sanctions. The USSR was not very dependent on trade, had a formidable reservoir of basic energy resources and raw materials, and was reasonably self-sufficient.

Notes

1. See *Pravda*, December 11, 1986 p.2 - in which there is a speech by Gorbachev in which the Soviet leader points out that the main obstacles to the development of Soviet-U.S. trade and economic ties are political and not economic in nature.
2. The term trade pressure has been used to define the use of economic measures such as sanctions, embargoes, denial of most favoured nations status etc., in order to punish the Soviet Union for its domestic and international behaviour, and to exert leverage on the USSR. The term closely coincides with Baldwin's comprehensive exposition of what he prefers to call 'economic statecraft'.
3. See David W. Hunter, *Western trade pressure on the Soviet Union* (Macmillan 1991); for a more general analysis of the use of economic sanctions for political purposes see Gary C. Hufbauer & Jeffery Schott, *Economic Sanctions in support of foreign policy goals* (Washington 1983); see also Gordon B. Smith (ed.), The politics of East-West trade (Westview Press 1984); For much earlier Western efforts at trade pressure against the Soviet pressure see Gunnar Adler-Karlsson, *Western Economic Warfare 1947-1967* (Stockholm: Almqvist and Wiksell 1968).
4. For a briefer account of the instruments of trade pressure used by the West and the various political objectives see Philip Hanson, *Western Economic Statecraft in East-West relations* (London: Routledge and Kegan Paul for the Royal Institute of International Affairs, Chatham House Papers no. 40 1988).
5. See *SSh.A* March 1986, No. 3, pp.16-26. In this article the Soviet viewpoint is outlined by the writer who argues that Reagan's coming to power led to a deterioration in political relations which contributed in turn to an adverse effect on economic relations, with Reagan using trade as an instrument of political pressure.
6. See Stephen Woolcock, *Western Policies on East-West Trade* (Routledge and Kegan Paul for The Royal Institute of International Affairs, Chatham House Papers 15, 1982), pp.10-14.
7. *Vneshnyaya Torgovlya*, 1982, No. 7, pp.2-5; See also *SSSR I Mezhdunarodnye Ekonomicheskie Otnosheniya*, Sbornik Dokumentov I Materialov, pp.197-199 (Moscow: Mezhdunarodnyye Otnosheniya 1985), where the USSR noted the imposition of restrictive trading measures such as sanctions and embargoes by capitalist countries like the USA for political aims.
8. See Congressional Research service, *An Assessment of the Afghanistan sanctions: Implications for Trade and Diplomacy in the 1980s*, report prepared for the subcommittee on Europe and the Middle East of the Committee on Foreign Affairs, US House of Representatives (Washington D.C. US government 75- 985, 1981), for a comprehensive analysis of these economic sanctions.
9. See Congressional Research Service, *An Assessment of the Afghanistan sanctions.*
10. See US Senate. 97th Congress 2nd session. *Soviet Economy in the 1980s: Problems and prospects - Part 2*. Selected papers submitted to the joint economic committee Congress of the United States, December 31, 1982 (US GPO Washington D.C. 1983), pp.124-141 for a case study of the US grain embargo of 1980-81.

11. See *Ibid* p.139 where the authors argue that only through co-operation from other grain exporters would the grain embargo have been effective. In addition they also set out in detail on pp.136-138 the conditions they believe were required for grain to be an effective lever.
12 See *Soviet Economy in the 1980s: Problems and prospects - part 2*, p.135 where it is noted that the effect of the grain embargo diminished very quickly as Canada and Australia joined Argentina in replacing most of the grain.
13. See figures in *Vneshnyaya Torgovlya SSSR*, Volumes for 1980 and 1982.
14. *Ibid* volumes for 1980, 1982, 1984, 1986 and 1988 for a detailed look at Soviet Imports from America.
15. *Ibid* volumes for 1980, 1982, 1984, 1986 and 1988.
16. *Ibid.*
17. See Congressional Research Service, *An Assessment of the Afghanistan sanctions* ...., p.53.
18. *Ibid.*
19. In a statement published in *Vneshnyaya Torgovlya SSSR* (1981 No. 1 pp.2-5) Brezhnev said "that the necessary quantity of goods on which the US imposed sanctions or embargoed were bought elsewhere". In other words Brezhnev here states clearly that Moscow diversified its sources and was able as a result to attain goods from elsewhere.
20. See Bruce Parrott (ed.), *Trade, Technology and Soviet-American relations* (Indiana University Press, 1985), especially Part 111 pp.324-351. On the impact of trade and trade denial on the US economy.
21. See *Ibid,* pp.327-334; Soviet Economy in the 1980s ......, pp.519-534.
22. See figures in *Vneshnyaya Torgovlya*, volumes for 1980, 1982, 1984, 1986 and 1988.
23. *Vneshnyaya Torgovlya*, 1981, no. 9, pp.2-5.
24. See *chapters 2 and 3.*
25. See David Baldwin, *Economic Statecraft* (Princeton University Press 1985), Chapter 8 on why sanctions are often seen as having failed to work.

Appendix

Appendix Table 3.1 Trade with the United States as a Proportion of Overall Soviet Foreign Trade and Trade with the Soviet Union as a Proportion of Overall United States Foreign Trade, 1979-88

Year	Trade with the United States as a proportion of overall Soviet Foreign Trade[a]	Trade with the Soviet Union as a proportion of overall American Foreign Trade[b]
1979	3.5%	1.1%
1980	1.6%	0.4%
1981	1.7%	0.5%
1982	1.9%	0.6%
1983	1.5%	0.5%
1984	2.2%	0.7%
1985	1.9%	0.5%
1986	1.1%	0.3%
1987	0.9%	0.2%
1988	1.6%	0.4%

[a] Derived from figures in the following volumes of *Vneshnyaya Torgovlya SSSR*: 1980, 1982, 1984, 1986 and 1988.
[b] Derived from figures in the *Statistical Abstract of the United States* for the following years: 1985, 1988, 1989, and 1991.

Appendix Table 3.2 Total Volume of Soviet-American Trade 1979-88 and % Change from Previous Year* (in millions of roubles)

Year	Total Volume of Trade	% change from previous year
1979	2837,1	+53
1980	1502,5	-47
1981	1845,4	+23
1982	2226,4	+21
1983	1900,5	-15
1984	3134,9	+65
1985	2703,1	-14
1986	1458,5	-46
1987	1198,5	-18
1988	2104,1	+76

Source: *Vneshnyaya Torgovlya*: Volumes for 1980, 1982, 1984, 1986 and 1988.
*According to figures in the Vienna Institute publication *Comecon Data* which have also been taken from *Vneshnyaya Torgovlya*, the figures for the total share of Soviet-American trade represents millions of foreign exchange roubles at current prices.

Appendix Table 3.3 (a) Volume of Selected Soviet Imports from the United States, 1979-83 (in thousands of roubles)

Imports	1979	1980	1981	1982	1983
Grain	1544615	746802	1103161	1399327	872029
Maize	968458	518248	594945	701109	333791
Wheat	556647	226084	508216	698218	538238
Soyabeans	318415	64518	6383	123355	98732
Machinery Equipment and Means of Transport	342236	311484	200707	169360	143877
Chemical Products	81544	28579	106491	185047	167586
Super phosphoric Acid	60541	11288	94146	170590	159067

Source: *Vneshnyaya Torgovlya SSSR*, Volumes for 1980, 1982 and 1984.

Appendix Table 3.3 (b) Volume of Selected Soviet Imports from the United States, 1984-88 (in thousands of roubles)

Imports	1984	1985	1986	1987	1988
Grain	2106920	1632204	318848	436170	1100459
Maize	1070277	1438672	318848	228643	592216
Wheat	1006638	193532	-	207527	508243
Soyabeans	33569	-	237226	7663	105850
Machinery Equipment and Means of Transport	137157	121447	153656	93144	89684
Chemical Products	174377	237457	244841	172436	136088
Super phosphoric Acid	160060	209998	222881	153146	128761

Source: *Vneshnyaya Torgovlya SSSR*, Volumes for 1984, 1986 and 1988.

Appendix Table 3.4 (a) Leading Exporters % Share of Soviet Imports of Grain, Wheat, Maize and Soyabeans, 1979-83

Imports	1979	1980	1981	1982	1983
Grain					
United States	68.5	23.5	22.9	33.1	24.0
Australia	7.1	16.8	5.4	6.2	3.6
Argentina	6.3	19.4	27.5	15.0	20.0
Canada	13.3	24.7	23.4	29.0	31.2
Maize					
United States	87.3	53.1	34.5	64.3	52.7
Argentina	11.7	30.3	51.3	28.6	31.0
Canada	0.4	5.65	7.18	5.3	3.8
Wheat					
USA	55.4	12.0	20.3	24.6	18.7
Argentina	1.34	16.8	17.1	11.5	18.5
Canada	21.5	32.2	28.0	31.1	36.0
Australia	13.3	23.2	9.03	9.03	4.61
Soyabeans					
USA	-	-	1.8	44.6	37.5
Argentina	-	-	52.8	38.9	52.7

Source: Derived from figures in *Vneshnyaya Torgovlya SSSR*, Volumes for 1980, 1982, and 1984. Dashes (-) represent instances where the relevant data was not available in the above source or cases where the particular commodity was not imported at all in a certain year.

Appendix Table 3.4 (b) Leading Exporters % Share of Soviet Imports of Grain, Wheat, Maize and Soyabeans, 1984-88

Imports	1984	1985	1986	1987	1988
Grain					
United States	39.2	33.7	15.8	28.0	46.6
Australia	5.24	3.5	15.1	-	-
Argentina	11.0	15.8	1.8	5.7	4.84
Canada	23.8	17.1	22.8	21.5	18.1
Maize					
United States	75.0	74.0	54.1	48.7	77.1
Argentina	15.4	11.1	5.83	13.2	9.86
Canada	3.17	0.64	1.19	-	0.4
Wheat					
USA	26.8	7.7	-	21.1	34.9
Argentina	9.8	21.8	0.25	2.76	2.38
Canada	31.8	32.0	29.2	30.7	29.0
Australia	7.09	7.6	24.5	4.6	1.35
Soyabeans					
USA	23.7	-	74.0	4.0	58.0
Argentina	21.1	48.7	-	35.5	-

Source: Derived from figures in *Vneshnyaya Torgovlya SSSR*, Volumes for 1984, 1986 and 1988. Dashes (-) represent instances where the relevant data was not available in the above source or cases where the particular commodity was not imported at all in a certain year.

Appendix Table 3.5 (a) Major Soviet Exports to the United States, 1979-83 (in thousands of roubles)

Imports	1979	1980	1981	1982	1983
Machinery Equipment and Means of Transport	10025	4385	5389	6361	8116
Oil and Oil Products	159749	13129	36	246	28225
Chemical Products	37526	73556	61053	56890	65893
Ammonia	34036	69900	58066	53742	60986
Vodka	5700	4995	1626	5213	5985
Consumer Goods	8380	4572	2574	2327	2287

Source: Vneshnyaya Torgovlya SSSR, Volumes for 1980, 1982, and 1984.

Appendix Table 3.5 (b) Major Soviet Exports to the United States, 1984-88 (in thousands of roubles)

Imports	1984	1985	1986	1987	1988
Machinery Equipment and Means of Transport	5517	7130	8545	5849	7499
Oil and Oil Products	9520	6762	18201	31653	57520
Chemical Products	114994	117511	59995	33014	40693
Ammonia	104631	95872	48710	26124	35594
Vodka	5431	9871	14622	11376	11347
Consumer Goods	2504	2465	1998	3351	3289

Source: Vneshnyaya Torgovlya SSSR, Volumes for 1984, 1986 and 1988.

(*Exact volume in brackets*) *In millions of foreign exchange roubles at current prices*

Appendix Figure 3.1

Volume of Soviet Imports from America

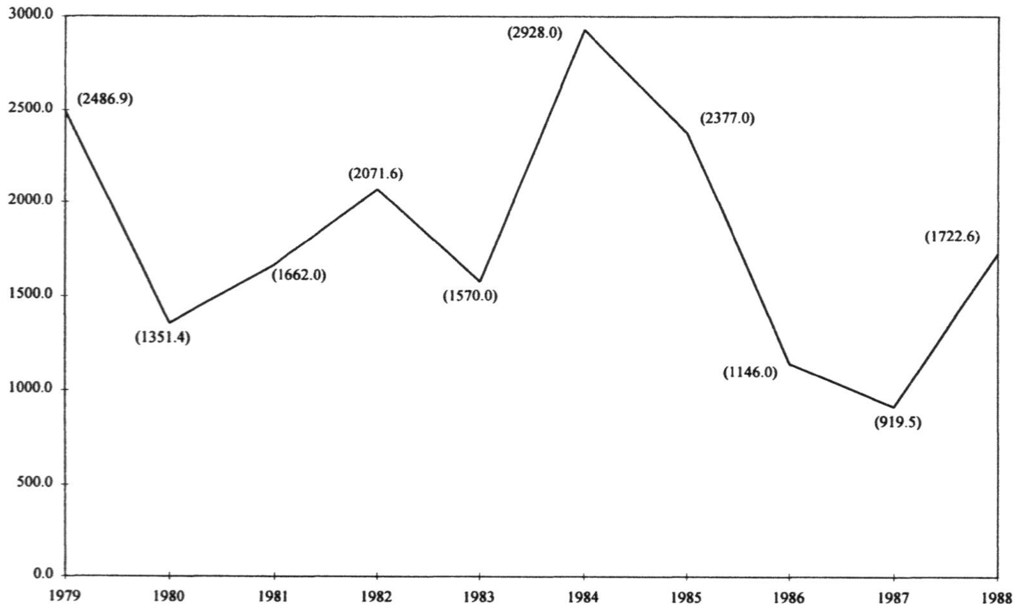

Source : The exact volume figures have been taken from Vneshnyaya Torgovlya Volumes (SSSR) 1980, 1982, 1984, 1986, 1988

(Exact volume in brackets) In millions of foreign exchange roubles at current prices

Appendix Figure 3.2
Volume of Soviet Exports to America

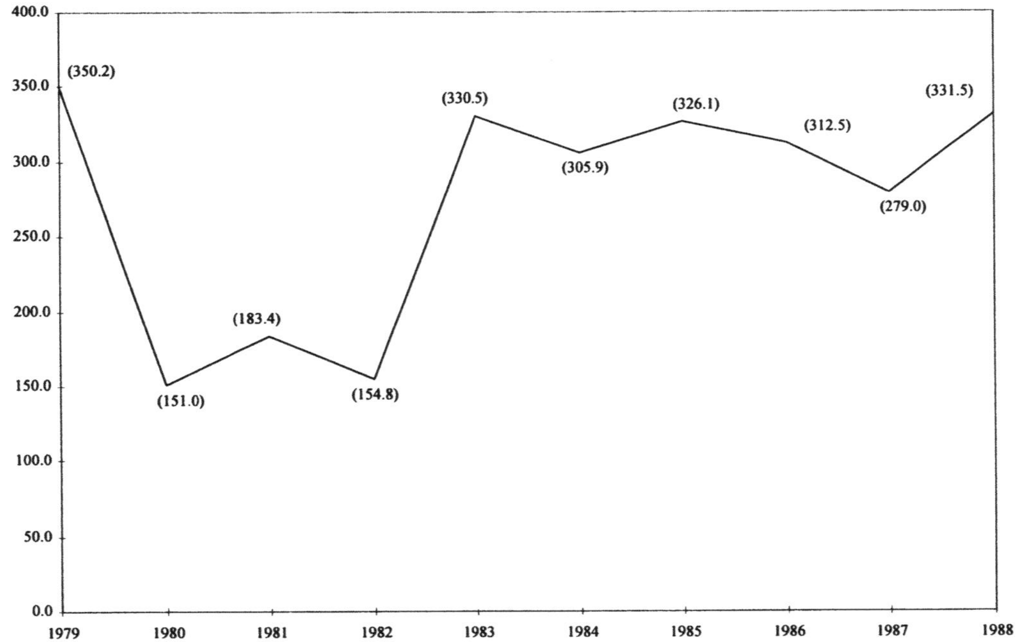

Source : The exact volume figures have been taken from Vneshnyaya Torgovlya Volumes (SSSR) 1980, 1982, 1984, 1986, 1988

Appendix Figure 3.3
% Change from 1979-80 in Major American Imports from the Soviet Union

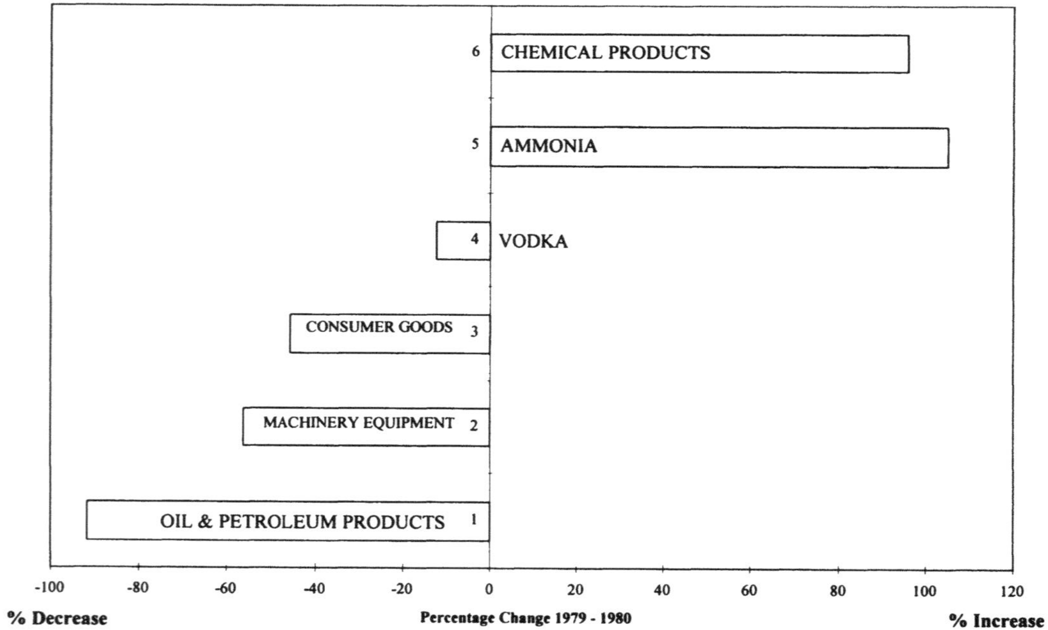

Source : Derived from figures in Vneshnyaya Torgovlya, SSSR, Volume 1980

Technical Note on Sources[a]

Soviet foreign trade statistics in this chapter have been taken from the official Soviet source: *Vneshnyaya Torgovlya*. This is an annual publication of the Soviet ministry for foreign trade.

However, because it is widely accepted that Soviet statistics, as they are presented, can be quite ambiguous, especially as there is no footnote explaining any technical points which may arise (an example of this can be seen in *Vneshnyaya Torgovlya* which gives no adequate information as to whether Soviet trade figures are based on current or constant prices), alternative sources have been referred to in order that one can make a comparison with the Soviet sources and/ or use them as a back up to the official Soviet sources. Furthermore alternative sources such as the *Statistical Yearbook of the United Nations* also provide Soviet foreign trade figures in their international denomination i.e. dollars.

The aim of this chapter is simply to get an indication of the volume and value of Soviet - American trade over a period of time in order to analyse trends and patterns in superpower trade. As a result whether the figures are expressed in roubles or dollars should not make a difference.

The figures provided by the Vienna Institute in its publication *Comecon Data* are more or less identical to the figures in this chapter since in both cases statistics have been derived from *Vneshnyaya Torgovlya*. But the publication *Comecon Data* provides more explanation as to the technical aspects.

In the case of Soviet imports of agricultural products one could refer to the *International Wheat Council Grain Market Reports*. An advantage of using these reports is that they provide figures for products in terms of their weight and not just their value in monetary terms. These reports can be used in conjunction with Appendix Tables 3.3 and 3.4 of this chapter.

Some of the shortcomings of the data on foreign trade as published in official Soviet sources like *Vneshnyaya Torgovlya* is highlighted by B.P.Pockney in his publication: *Soviet Statistics Since 1950* (New York: St. Martins 1991). See Section 5 on Foreign Trade.

The Vienna Institutes' publication, *Comecon Data*, provides conversion factors which allow the conversion of Soviet trade figures in roubles into dollars. This can be done by multiplying the conversion factor by the export/import figure.

Current and Constant Prices

Constant prices are a measure of an economic variable (in this case exports or imports) deflated to allow for price changes: thus the imports of a country at constant prices would show imports for a number of years at the price of one year. In contrast current prices are a measurement of an economic variable at the prices of the period at which data were collected, e.g. imports at current prices would show for years X,Y, and Z the actual cost of purchasing such goods at the prices ruling in years X, Y, and Z respectively.

Measurement of a country's trade can be provided in a number of ways. Two of these are the volume of trade and the value of trade. Although both the volume of trade and the value of trade are expressed in monetary terms, the volume of trade is a more accurate reflection of trade since it is an attempt at giving figures in real terms i.e. inflation is taken into account. It is similar to the idea of constant prices where the figures have also been deflated and are expressed in constant monetary units. In comparison the value of trade actually includes the inflationary element. In other words the value of trade represents what are in effect nominal figures, similar to the concept of current prices where the figures have been taken as they are. Even then we may see the use of value of trade despite the fact that volume of trade is a better measurement. This could be because the figures for the inflation rate may not be available.

a Full details of the sources referred to in this technical note can be found in the bibliography.

Glossary

The following short glossary will define some of the key economic terms used in this chapter, and with which the reader may be unfamiliar.

1. *Economic Sanctions*

   This is the economic boycott of a nation by another nation or a group of countries (e.g. the United Nations), as a protest against the policy that country is pursuing at home or abroad, and in order to make it change its policy.

2. *Embargo*

This is a ban on imports of certain goods coming from a particular country and / or a ban on exports to a particular country of a certain good usually for political reasons. The embargo may be imposed by either side and prevents the unloading or loading of certain goods.

3. *Most-Favoured Nation Status (MFN)*

The concept of MFN status embodies the idea of preferential or non-discriminatory treatment. It implies the same tariff rates as those extended to the most favoured nation, i.e. accorded the lowest rates.

4. *Tariffs*

This is the most used instrument of commercial policy. It involves the imposition of an indirect tax on imported goods (although it can also take the form of export tariff imposed on exported goods, but this is far less common).

5. *Market Power / Monopoly Power / Perfect Competition/Cartel*

We have seen that the degree of market power a country (in this case the United States) has in relation to a particular commodity or in the market for that commodity can be crucial in determining whether it can prevent the target country (in this case the USSR) from acquiring that commodity. In a situation where a country applying sanctions has monopoly power in the world market because it is the sole producer or supplier of a commodity then it can use this considerable market power to regulate output, and has a chance of preventing the target from obtaining that commodity.

However, as we have seen (for example in the case of the grain embargo) this is very rarely the case as there are usually more than producer or supplier countries of a commodity. This means that the target country has substitute countries available from which to purchase the commodity denied by its original supplier. In this situation a country like the U.S. would have little or no market power, and a situation similar to perfect competition (where there are a considerable number of supplier countries such that no one supplier nation can alone influence the market), or an oligopoly (where there are a few but more than one producers) would exist.

Nevertheless even in such a situation it is still possible for a nation to exercise monopoly power through some form of co-operative agreement with other nations or through the creation of a cartel with other major suppliers, allowing them as a group to restrict output. However such co-operation in reality is difficult to achieve especially since the different nations may have totally diverging political interests which may make effective co-operation impossible. Even if they are political allies economic interests may make co-operation unlikely.

It has to be stressed that the analysis here has deliberately been simplified and that in reality there are much more complex issues of costs and revenue involved in the formation of a cartel, or in any economic grouping of countries.

4 The Impact of American Trade Pressure on the Soviet Union: 2 - The Question of Strategic Trade

Introduction

The previous chapter was concerned with American trade pressure on the Soviet Union involving non-strategic goods. This chapter will look at United States unilateral and multilateral (in conjunction with its NATO allies) trade pressure concerning the export of strategic items, mainly the transfer of Western technology to the Soviet bloc[1], during the period 1980-88.

Different schools of thought emerged over the years on the idea of using technology denial as a form of trade pressure by the West against the Soviet Union. There were those such as Hanson[2], who argued that Western strategic trade pressure in the form of technology denial was "part of the necessary defensive arrangements" and that the 'strategic embargo' acted as an obstacle to the Soviet Union's bid to acquire Western technology.

On the other hand, another school of thought illustrated by Parrott[3] believed that United States economic measures against the USSR in the form of technology denial had not been very successful, as could be said of the general use of trade pressure by the US against the Soviet Union. Although they did not dismiss the idea of using economic sanctions as a "tool of diplomacy", they believed that the effect of such a policy on the Soviet Union was limited because "the USSR has achieved an impressive measure of success in the independent development of a wide range of military technologies"[4] and that American measures to greatly expand technology controls did not contribute "...to attempts to shift the military balance... in America's favour".[5]

Not surprisingly the issue of technology transfer (particularly militarily sensitive technology) to the communist countries was always an important topic of discussion for the United States and its NATO allies ever since the cold war began.[6] Indeed COCOM - the co-ordinating committee on multilateral export controls - was created in 1949 to regulate the export of technology to communist countries. On the unilateral front the United States passed legislation aimed at curbing the transfer of its own strategic exports to Soviet bloc nations.[7] The first American national controls on exports to the USSR and its allies were introduced in 1948, and formalised in the Export Control Act of 1949.[8] In 1969 this act was replaced by the Export Administration act.[9] To this day, the United States maintains a unilateral commodity control list which is somewhat wider in scope than the COCOM control lists. Controls on U.S. strategic exports to the USSR were somewhat relaxed during the period of detente in the 1970s.

However, with the deterioration in the Soviet-American relationship following the Soviet invasion of Afghanistan[10] the debate over technology transfer to the Soviet Union heightened. Soviet international behaviour coupled with reports that the USSR was ahead in the arms race made technology transfer a sensitive issue, and a major national security concern in America.[11] The formidable growth in Soviet military power which had occurred during the 1970s appeared to have given Moscow an edge entering the 1980s.

Therefore, it was hardly surprising that the Soviet-American trade relationship once again came under close review from the United States. The renewed tension in East-West relations (particularly in US-Soviet relations) led America to formulate a radical reappraisal of the conditions and procedures for the transfer of Western technology to the Soviet Union. Only by denying important technology and know-how to the USSR could America and its Western partners be sure of maintaining their qualitative edge over the Soviets, which would go some way to compensating for Moscow's apparent quantitative supremacy.

As in the case of non-strategic trade pressure, U.S. restrictions and bans on certain types of technology to the USSR were imposed chiefly for political reasons. But there was more to it than just the aim of illustrating American displeasure at Soviet international actions, and concern over Soviet internal policies in areas such as human rights. Reasons of national security and the state of the East-West military balance also played no small part in the hardening of American policy on technology. President Reagan, on taking office in 1981, was very keen to redress the military balance in favour of the United States, and realised that this could only be achieved by adopting a strict policy of technology denial, something that would have to be carried out with the effective co-operation of its West European allies. In other words, the tough American policy on technology transfer was part of the overall grand strategy of the Reagan administration when it assumed office, and a central premise of what later became known as the Reagan doctrine.

As mentioned, the objective of this chapter is similar to the previous one in that we are looking at United States efforts to punish the Soviet Union for political reasons (in this case for national security reasons as well) by applying trade pressure, in this case strategic trade pressure involving the denial and curtailment of advanced technology. The aim was to hurt Moscow in an area where it would be greatly affected. All this of course depended on the continuing assumption that the Soviet Union was still dependent to a degree on Western technology.[12] It was widely believed that this indeed was the case with Western technology being in great demand in the East, and many Soviet activities legal and illegal to acquire Western technology proved this fact. The Soviet interest in Western technology stemmed from the fact that there existed a gap between Soviet/East European and Western standards of technology and know-how with the former communist countries of Eastern Europe lagging quite a distance behind the West. The very nature of the Soviet-type system which inhibited individual initiative and provided few incentives for innovation meant that the results of practical scientific research were not able to be incorporated into the manufacturing process in a variety of different fields, leaving the Soviets behind the West in the technology race and in search of Western technology in order to bridge the gap, and at the same time help the cause of economic development. For the West, the danger was that Soviet acquisition of Western technology for potential use for military and strategic purposes would threaten their national security. The aim was therefore to deprive Moscow of advanced Western technology through trade pressure and policies symptomatic of economic warfare. In some cases even non-military technology was embargoed with the argument that the Soviets did not deserve to benefit from Western advances in technology until there were irreversible changes in Soviet policies.

The division of this chapter into three sections will allow an analysis of the following areas: Section one will give an outline of U.S. government policy on the issue of technology transfer to the Soviet bloc in Carter's final year in office and under the Reagan presidency, and the domestic political debate this policy generated. Having established American policy on the issue, section two will look at the measures-unilateral and multilateral - taken by the U.S. to implement this policy. The final section will examine the effectiveness of these measures in preventing the Soviet bloc nations from acquiring Western technology and know-how.

1. American Policy on Technology Transfer to the Soviet Bloc

Under Jimmy Carter's presidency U.S. policy on technology transfer to the Soviet Union and its allies had always been restrictive. However, by about 1979 amidst growing fears that the restriction of American exports was threatening to harm the balance of payments, and that the export sector needed a boost, Carter signed into law the new Export Administration Act [13] which was intended to minimise controls and facilitate the licensing of exports. These signs of optimism for a flourishing U.S.-Soviet trade relationship were short lived because of the rapid deterioration in superpower relations at the start of 1980 which brought to the forefront the "complicated and politically sensitive question of technology transfer to the Soviet Union".[14] Following the Soviet intervention in Afghanistan the administration of President Carter in its final year in office hardened its policy on technology exports to the Soviet Union. As part of his package of sanctions against Moscow the President suspended licensing for all high technology and other products requiring validated export licences pending review. This was followed shortly afterwards in March 1980 by a announcement from the Department of Commerce that the government would be further tightening controls on American exports of high technology products to the USSR[15] thus ending the administration's review of export control policy that had been prompted by the events in Afghanistan. In a statement, the Commerce Department said that the new guidelines adopted would impose tighter controls in various areas such as computers, software and manufacturing technology. So as Carter left office he left behind him a drastically hardened American attitude towards strategic trade with the Soviet Union.

When Reagan came to office in 1981 his administration voiced concern over its predecessor's policy on technology transfer. The new administration was unhappy that although Carter's policy was strict enough in theory it had not been effective in practice from the point of view of preventing the drain of military related technology to the USSR, and had not implemented effectively the various clauses of the Export Administration Act.

The Reagan administration had come to power in a context of a steadily deteriorating East-West climate. Therefore it was hardly surprising that Reagan, a fervent and committed anti-communist, adopted a tough approach towards the Soviets on issues such as East-West trade.[16] Reagan's policy on technology transfer to the Soviet bloc was simply that ".... the Soviets must not have access to Western technology with military applications". He made this clear at an address on East-West relations delivered at Eureka college in 1982.[17] Defence Secretary Caspar Weinberger had earlier reiterated this point in his annual report to Congress when he stated that the major aim of national strategy should be to cut off Western technology to the USSR.[18] It quickly became evident that the Reagan administration was ready to take steps to put into practice this policy which had begun to evolve in the administration's first two years in office. On October 1, 1982 the U.S. government was reported to be seeking to toughen the multilateral system (COCOM) that America and its allies used to control the flow of technology, and other strategic exports to communist nations.[19] because as Undersecretary of Defense for policy, Department of Defense, Richard Perle put it "the US government recognises a critical need to overhaul and modernise the existing system of controlling militarily relevant Western technology".[20]

Reagan's policy on technology transfer to the Soviet Union was the same as his overall approach to economic relations with the USSR namely that security and foreign policy concerns should normally take precedence over the economic interests and economic benefits that might be derived.

Many in American political circles recognised and acknowledged that the Reagan administration was truly committed to stemming the flow of Western technology to the East in a consistent and effective manner. At the 1982 Senate Hearings on the transfer of American technology to the Soviet Union and Soviet bloc nations, James Buckley - under secretary of state for security assistance, science and technology at the Department of State said that "this administration has placed a very high priority on improving the effectiveness of the executive branch in enforcing export controls".[21] He added further that the various initiatives launched by the Republican administration would be focused "on those elements of advanced technology ..... which are of the most critical importance to the Soviet bloc".[22] Others such as the Commissioner of the US Customs Service, William Von Raab, also noted the Reagan administration's efforts to thwart "the flow of high technology to the Soviet bloc and other unfriendly nations".[23]

The United States government was naturally keen to enlist the help of its major allies in Western Europe in curbing the transfer of technology to the communist bloc.[24] The co-operation of America's allies would be imperative in order to ensure success in the execution of U.S. policy on the issue. Reports that the leakage of American technology to the USSR had been damaging to U.S. national security[25] gave Washington's allies in Europe food for thought, after all the Soviet Union posed probably just as serious a threat to Western European Security as it arguably did to American national security.

In its attempt to execute its restrictive policy on technology transfer, the Reagan administration faced problems similar in nature to those confronted by Carter, which had forced the latter into a certain amount of liberalisation of export controls by the time the Export Administration Act came up for renewal in 1979. As well as facing intra-alliance problems which stemmed from the fact that many West European governments believed that America wanted to improve restrictions on the transfer of items to the Soviet bloc which had no relevance to the politico-strategic debate (see section 3 for a fuller discussion of U.S.-West European differences), and the fact that Western Europe had stronger commercial links with the Soviet Union and Eastern Europe which they saw being unnecessarily jeopardised in some cases, the Reagan administration faced domestic pressures over its policy as well.

These came to the forefront during the debate over the renewal of the Export Administration Act (EAA) which was set to expire on September 30, 1983.[26] The renewal of this act had always been a constant source of controversy in America even during the term of the previous Democrat administration. The whole affair turned out to be a highly politicised one, and the act which was set to expire on September 1983 was extended until 1985. The debate over the renewal of the act highlighted the dilemma facing the Reagan administration in its attempts to reconcile its free market orientations with its intention of more strictly curbing the transfer of strategic goods to the Soviet Union. The continued debates about the issues and the legislation required to update the act brought to the forefront differences between those who were worried about the discriminatory effect on U.S. exporters and who favoured relaxation of controls - the pro-traders, and those who believed in the continuing need to prevent the diffusion of strategic goods and technology and the need to toughen up the act. They were the so called anti-traders who were keen to promote the restrictive policies of the American government on all trade with the Soviet Union and not just on strategic trade. They pointed out that trade with the USSR was threatening to erode America's traditional technological superiority, and was therefore dealing a damaging blow to American attempts to check Soviet military growth. The fact was that the whole issue of strategic trade with the Soviet Union had ignited a debate over the overall conduct of U.S. economic policy towards Moscow with both pro-traders and anti-traders using the opportunity to make their respective cases.[27]

Table 4.1 Key United States Legislation Relating to the Control of Technology Transfer to the Soviet Union, 1979-88

Legislative Measure[a]	Year Passed/Amended
Export Administration Act[b]	1979 (Renewal)
Amendment to the Atomic Energy Act[c]	1981 (Amendment)
Executive Order 12356	1982
Defence Authorisation Act	1984
National Security Decision Directive 145	1984
National Security Decision Directive 189	1985
Invention Secrecy Act[d]	1988 (Amendment)

[a] These legislative measures are referred to in more detail in Section 2 of this Chapter.
[b] The Export Administration Act was first passed with this title in 1969. The 1979 version represented a renewal of this Act which was subsequently renewed again throughout the course of the 1980s.
[c] The Atomic Energy Act was originally passed in 1954, and in 1981 an amendment to this Act was passed.
[d] The Invention Secrecy Act, passed in 1951 was amended by Congress in 1988.

In addition, there was also a substantial and serious amount of dissension within the Reagan administration itself on the issue of strategic trade with the Soviet Union. In 1983 the director of the office of East-West trade, William Root, resigned[28] over technology export policy, saying that any further attempts to tighten controls on East West trade would lead to a major justified explosion of allied resentment. Earlier in June 1982 Secretary of State Alexander Haig had resigned[29] as a result of what many political commentators saw as being linked to the decision on June 18 of that year to widen the U.S. embargo on the export of technology and equipment to the USSR.

Despite the domestic and alliance repercussions of the Reagan administration's hard-line policy on strategic trade with the Soviet bloc, the established policy by and large remained in place for the remainder of the administration's term characterised by strict strategic export controls, and aided by unilateral and multilateral measures designed to promote this policy. Table 4.1 lists the key legislative measures, newly passed, renewed or amended by the American government during the period 1979-88, affecting the control of technology transfers to the Soviet Union.

2a. Unilateral American Measures to Control the Transfer of Technology to the Soviet Bloc

During the course of 1980-88 the United States took a number of unilateral measures to enforce the policy of controlling the transfer of technology to Soviet bloc nations.

Following the Soviet invasion of Afghanistan President Carter announced a package of economic sanctions against the USSR which included a review of American technology export policy towards Moscow during early 1980.[30] The steps taken included moves to tighten the unilateral commodity control list.[31] This list covered industrial items which might have potential military application. It is similar to the COCOM list but much wider in scope with many items appearing on this list which were not on the COCOM list. All technologies which appear on this list require a validated export licence and are "subject to a rigorous application process".[32] There would also be a revision of licensing policy. In a speech on January 4, 1980, Carter announced that "no high technology or other strategic items will be licensed for sale to the Soviet Union until further notice...."[33] In addition to the halting of new licences the Carter administration announced that it would be reviewing licences already issued with the possibility that some may be revoked. In March 1980 the debate over the export of high technology to the Soviet Union, which had been fuelled by the events in Afghanistan, finally ended with an announcement by the U.S. government that there would be a substantial tightening of controls on the transfer of high technology to Moscow with the areas most likely to be affected being computers, software and manufacturing technology.[34]

President Carter departed from office leaving behind him a tough American policy on exports of technology to the USSR, and his successor Ronald Reagan adopted a similar policy and gained the opportunity to put into practice this policy towards the end of December 1981 following the imposition of martial law in Poland. Citing Soviet complicity in the events in Poland, Reagan announced a list of sanctions against Moscow similar in nature to those imposed by Carter in January 1980.[35] Reagan effectively ordered a total ban on exports of high technology goods. In a speech in Los Angeles he announced that the United States would be suspending any further issuing or renewal of licences for high technology exports to the Soviet Union such as electronic equipment and computers.[36]

As part of its drive to stem the flow of sophisticated technology to the Soviet bloc, and to address increasing concerns about the illegal transfer of U.S. technology by American and foreign companies which were infringing U.S. export laws, the Reagan administration unveiled in January 1982 'Project Exodus' "a national enforcement program" integrating ".. the various operational units of the U.S. customs service".[37] The customs service which was to be the linchpin of this enforcement operation was to have the task of launching new initiatives "aimed at combating the trafficking in illegal exports".[38] Its activities would include intelligence, investigation and inspection in both America and abroad. The objectives of 'Project Exodus' were essentially threefold[39]: one was to stop the illegal flow of technology to the Soviet bloc and other "unfriendly nations". The second aim was to disrupt the flow of technology to the USSR. The third was to "intercept shipments" of goods being exported in violation of other U.S. sanctions and embargoes against nations like Libya and Cuba. William Von Raab, commissioner of the U.S. customs service, emphasised the importance of distinguishing between 'critical technology' which represented "technological advances to the Soviet bloc", the curtailment of which would be essential from the point of view of achieving and maintaining military parity with the Soviet Union, and 'high technology' which Moscow could manufacture itself but chose to obtain from the U.S. "in order to reduce costs and improve quality".[40] Disrupting the flow of this type of technology would go some way in adversely affecting the 'Soviet military complex'.[41] The objectives implicit in 'Operation Exodus' served to typify overall U.S. policy on technology transfer to the Soviet Union which was based on increasingly restrictive criteria.

It was becoming evident that the Reagan administration would not hesitate to take unilateral steps to stop the transfer of technology to the Soviet Union even if it led to disagreements and a conflict of interests with its West European allies.[42] This situation arose in June 1982 during the dispute over the construction of a gas pipeline from Siberia to Western Europe. The sanctions imposed by Reagan over the events in Poland in December 1981 which included a ban on U.S. exports of equipment for the pipeline did in a way set the scene for the full-blown crisis over the issue which culminated in 1982.[43] In June 1982 Reagan antagonised the allies by extending the pipeline sanctions to include exports of oil and gas equipment technology by foreign subsidiaries of U.S. firms or by foreign firms holding U.S. licences.[44] The Reagan administration made no secret of the fact that it was dedicated to preventing construction of the pipeline as Secretary of Commerce Lawrence Brady pointed out in early 1982.[45] American reservations about the proposed pipeline centred on the dangerous degree of dependence on the Soviet union that it would entail for Western Europe, and further when completed "would provide the Soviet Union with huge amounts of hard currency .... which in all likelihood will be used .... to acquire and exploit further Western technology for Soviet aims".[46]

United States legislation in the form of the Export Administration Act of 1979 was the basis by which the Americans sought to control technology exports to Soviet bloc and other 'unfriendly nations'.[47] Both U.S. unilateral and multilateral measures involved as their basis this Act which was renewed at various times throughout the 1980s amidst much domestic political debate. The primary aim of the act, which outlined the fundamental reasoning behind U.S. export policy, particularly towards the Soviet bloc nations, was to restrict the export of commodities and technology which make a significant contribution to the military capabilities of a country or countries which would prove harmful to American national security. Various sections of the act outlined measures which the President could take to curtail the export of technology. The Export Administration act (EA) as it stood in 1979 did not adequately reflect the Reagan administration's policy on technology transfer since it appeared to be inclined more towards encouraging trade rather than retarding it, much to the concern of the Reagan administration who felt that this bias in favour of trade allowed certain high technology items to be diverted to the communist bloc. Therefore in order "to improve the ability of the United States to curtail the flow of military relevant technology to the Soviet Union and her allies"[48], Reagan proposed somewhat controversial amendments to the act which was set to expire on September 30 1983.[49] Reagan's proposals for major revisions to the EAact would create far tighter restrictions on technology exports to the Soviet bloc. Among the most important changes proposed were: tougher sanctions on individuals and companies that violate export regulations; controls on foreign based U.S. subsidiary companies with strict penalties for any company suspected of violating export controls. On April 4 1983 as part of his proposed amendments to the EAact, Reagan asked Congress to allow him "to restrict imports from countries that sell to communist bloc nations in violation of an American trade sanction".[50] According to Assistant Undersecretary of State Richard Perle, Reagan's proposed legislation "would sharpen the distinction between critical and non-critical items"[51] thus making it easier to export technology with little or no military applications, while at the same time making it more difficult to sell technology that had important military uses. On September 30 1983, the Senate agreed to a 14 day extension to the EAact while the debate on proposed major revisions to the act went on. On October 14 Reagan invoked the International Emergency Economic Powers Act in order to continue the authorities of the EAact because Congress was still unable to agree on a new act. The deadlock continued and the Act was extended once again, this time to the end of February 1984. Finally on July 12, 1985 a new version of the 1979 EAact was passed into law. Some of the most important measures which this new revised version of the act provided for included: a broadening of the range of punishable offences in cases where controls were breached and the granting of power to the President to block imports from the U.S. by any party which violated American security controls. The Department of Commerce and the U.S. customs service would share the task of drafting and enforcing guidelines on the export of sensitive technology. This new version of the EAact represented a victory for Reagan in the sense that most, if not all of Reagan's major proposals, first announced in 1983, were accepted as part of the new act.

As it stands today the EAact gives the American President the power to control exports for two main purposes: (i) to protect national security[52] - commonly known as national security controls - under this the President can curtail the export of any goods and technology which would contribute to the military potential of any country; and (ii) to further significantly the foreign policy of the United States[53] - commonly known as foreign policy controls - under which the President can restrict virtually any exports whether strategic or non-strategic. It was the foreign policy controls which often led to disagreements between America and its allies when the former attempted to apply the act in unison with its allies on a multilateral basis. The allies shared concern over technology transfer and were as a result more co-operative over national security controls.

The Reagan administration even illustrated a willingness to take unilateral measures to prevent non-COCOM, non-communist industrialised countries from diverting U.S. technology they had acquired to the Soviet Union. The U.S. applied increasing pressure on these countries after 1982 over the issue of technology exports. In March 1984, Reagan gave the Department of Defense advisory authority it had been seeking to stop "diversion to the Soviet Union of US high technology products exported to non-communist industrialised countries".[54] In one serious case in 1982, the United States government threatened to impose trade sanctions against Austria if it did not stop the transfer of military sensitive technology to the Soviet bloc.[55] Pentagon officials claimed that Austria was providing the base from which many Western companies were shipping sensitive high technology to Eastern Europe.

Overall, the United States concern centred on the use of non-COCOM, non communist countries by business and smugglers to transport embargoed Western technology to the Soviet Union and its allies. This led, in early 1985, to the compilation by the United States of a list of fifteen countries which were to be affected by the new procedures announced by Reagan in 1984 giving the American Defense Department full advisory authority to review all licences for exports of high technology to these countries because of fears that they might be re-exported to the Soviet bloc. Singapore, one of the nations on the list, held talks with the United States in August 1985 on ways to prevent the use of that country as a transit point for diverting high technology to the Eastern bloc.[56] Sweden, another country on the list, took measures of its own which led to a ban on the re-export of sensitive technology.

The Americans had always expressed some reservations about the commitment of some of its allies in COCOM in applying technology controls against the Warsaw Pact countries. Throughout the 1980s the Reagan administration constantly asked its West European allies to take more steps to curb technology exports to the USSR. Indeed this led in early 1984 to controversial proposals by the United States to limit certain technological sales to other Western countries including fellow COCOM members, which were not well received. The question of sovereignty often arose, leading to a rift between America and its allies. But Reagan never appeared to refrain from taking controversial steps. In the case of the pipeline crisis of 1982 America applied sanctions against Western European companies in their home country for attempting to adhere to the terms of supply contracts in respect of the construction of the pipeline. This angered West European governments, who saw it as an attempt to enforce US law in foreign countries. Provisions in the US EAact requiring that foreign companies should seek permission from the American government before re-exporting U.S. high technology was another unilateral American measure which provoked much criticism in Western Europe. Such U.S. efforts to apply its own export controls extraterritorially were seen as unwarranted interference in the sovereignty of other nations, and thus a violation of international law.

Both Presidents Reagan and Carter, as William Root, director of the office of East-West trade (1976-83) revealed, were interested not only in controlling the transfer of strategic goods to the Soviet bloc but also "restricting the flow of knowledge" and information as well.[57] The problem was that America being a free and open society allowed information about the development and manufacture of new technologies to be readily available. This plethora of information forms the basis from which new discoveries and inventions are made. Easy accessibility to it meant that the Soviet Union exploited it to learn Western developments in science and technology. This situation threatened to erode America's technological superiority. Thus the Reagan administration throughout the 1980s took measures to control the dissemination of vital information and technical know-how. These included amendments to the EAact, to the Atomic Energy Act, and to the Invention Secrecy Act plus various national security directives (see Table 4.1).

President Reagan in particular was concerned about the transfer of scientific, technical and engineering information. In this connection the Reagan administration adopted the National Security Decision Directive 189 which was announced at the White House on September 21, 1985.[58] The directive established American policy "for controlling the flow of science, technology, and engineering information in federally funded fundamental research at colleges, universities, and laboratories".[59] The directive went on to emphasise the importance of maintaining what it said was America's leadership position in science and technology. According to many, this directive was long overdue. Leading political figures such as Senator William Cohen (Maine) had during the 1982 hearings on transfer of technology to the Soviet bloc highlighted the problem of academic exchanges which although they could be mutually beneficial often contributed to possible damage to American national security.[60] This was because the Soviets sent students on educational exchanges to study research in areas involving technologies in those fields "that have direct military applications and in which the Soviets are technologically deficient".[61] In September 17, 1984 the White House had issued another directive No. 145 - the aim of which was to protect unclassified information seen as particularly sensitive, and to protect information retrievable through databases.[62] In a bid to control the dissemination of technical data, 1984 saw the passing of the Defense Authorisation Act which had the "authority to withhold from public disclosure certain technical data" which has military or space application and was under the possession of the Defense Department "if such data may not be exported lawfully outside the United States without an approval, authorisation, or licence under the Export Administration Act of 1979 or the Arms Export Control Act".[63] In 1982 Executive Order 12356 was adopted prescribing "a uniform system for classifying, declassifying, and safeguarding national security information".[64] While acknowledging the necessity of the public to be informed of what the government was doing, the Order stressed that "certain information concerning national defense and foreign relations be protected against unauthorised disclosure".[65] In 1988 Congress amended the Invention Secrecy Act of 1951.[66] Under this act the Patent and Trademark Office may take steps to prevent the spread of technical information by exercising its authority to place patent applications under secrecy orders.

Any move to control the conduct and results of scholarly research always raises new controversies about academic freedom, and the freedom of the academic community to conduct research without excessive government interference. It also attracted criticism from a wide section of society who saw the measures intended to control information as inhibiting future research in science and other fields by withholding data and information required for continuing and advancing technical and scientific research. Thus the very base from which American advances in research are derived - the academic community and academic institutions - would be retarded by the denial of information of certain types of disclosure and dissemination. As the International Institute for Strategic Studies put it ".... restricting the academic and scientific communities' access to general information .... is as likely to hinder Western scientific breakthroughs as it is to deny those breakthroughs to potential adversaries of the West".[67]

2b. Multilateral Measures to Control the Transfer of Technology to the Soviet Bloc

U.S. sponsored efforts to control the transfer of Western technology to the Soviet bloc centred around the activities of COCOM, membership of which comprised all the NATO countries (except Iceland), Japan and more recently Australia, which joined in 1989. Created in 1949, COCOM's primary activity was to have its national delegations agree on a list of technologies and products they as individual nations would control in their trade with certain countries for reasons of national security. Proscribed destinations included the Warsaw Pact, and other communist countries such as China, North Korea and Albania. COCOM members drew up three lists:[68] the first list covered munitions and included all military items. The second list was composed of atomic energy items, while the third list covered industrial or dual use items. Items on the third list were civilian items with potential military applications. These lists were not made public in the same way as the deliberations of COCOM meetings and decisions reached were kept confidential. Initially COCOM members reviewed the three control lists every three to four years. However, in 1985 they agreed to undertake a rolling review i.e. each year some parts of the list would be reviewed in order to keep the control lists up to date in view of rapid advances in technology. During the review of lists member states put forward proposals for additions or deletions to the various lists. These proposals were then sent to the national delegations in Paris (where

COCOM was based) where negotiations were conducted on each item. Any changes to the items on a list required the unanimous consent of member states.

Only through adopting a much wider forum than COCOM provided could the United States realistically expect to exercise effective control over certain technologies. As director of office of East-West trade William Root (until his resignation in 1983) stressed "multilateral co-operation has become essential to effective security controls. The United States is no longer a unique supplier of most high technology".[69]

There were also summit meetings of the Western alliance NATO, which addressed the problems posed by the transfer of technology, and decided on steps that the allies would take in their attempts to counteract the problem through the COCOM mechanism or in conjunction with COCOM.

The 1980s was to prove a period of hectic and intense activity for COCOM, with the Americans not surprisingly taking on the leading role always encouraging and urging its allies in COCOM to do more. The United States took it upon itself to provide the lead for a hardening of strategic exports policies towards the USSR.

As early as 1980 following the Soviet invasion of Afghanistan, COCOM adopted a 'no exceptions' policy on trade with the USSR, which meant in practice that the Soviets would be denied exports of highly advanced Western technology even for civilian applications. Under the agreement between COCOM members, a country or countries could seek exemptions from particular items on the COCOM embargoed list thus allowing them to export these items to the Soviet bloc as exceptions.[70] In the late 1970s COCOM became rather lax in enforcing strategic controls and many Western countries including the United States itself began to conduct deals with the Soviet Union on the basis of exemptions.[71]

However, the events in Afghanistan and the renewed concern over technology transfer prompted the United States to revitalise COCOM, and tighten export controls.[72] On March 19, 1980 a commerce department official said that "the administration would seek few if any exemptions from COCOM controls in the future".[73] Similarly, earlier in January 1980, Deputy Secretary of State Warren Christopher, speaking in Brussels where he was attending a NATO meeting to discuss a unified response to the Soviet intervention of Afghanistan, reported that agreement had been reached that the COCOM list "should be made tighter and be more stringently applied with far fewer exceptions than in the recent period of indulgence".[74]

When Reagan assumed the Presidency in 1981 he was determined to make COCOM the centre of his efforts to enforce his policy on technology transfer to the Soviet bloc, realising the importance of allied co-operation on the matter. At the Ottawa Summit in July 1981 Reagan appealed to the allies to do more to curb transfers of Western technology to the Soviet Union. The result of this was the first top level meeting of COCOM in twenty five years.[75] It took place on January 19-20, 1982 in Paris. The central aim of the meeting was to improve export controls on high technology. The Americans put forward a number of proposals such as strict enforcement of the embargo on the sale of critical technologies embodying advanced computers, fibre optics, and some other items, and abolishing the 'exceptions' system which allowed member countries to export embargoed goods to the Soviet Union. In the end the COCOM members agreed on the need to update the list of prohibited items to include new technologies.[76] On October 4-5, 1982 another COCOM meeting was held at which the body agreed to review the existing embargo list (a study which was completed by mid-1984), as it was required to do every three to four years. The meeting saw the United States call, yet again, for tougher restrictions on technology exports to the Soviet bloc. This was expected because earlier before the meeting the United States was reported to have proposed more than one hundred changes including many additions to the COCOM control list.[77] America also pressed for a strengthening of COCOM through an increase in its budget, and an expansion of its enforcement capabilities. However, American attempts to establish a permanent subcommittee to assist the working of COCOM was rejected by leading allies such as France and West Germany. On December 9-10, 1982 a meeting of NATO foreign ministers discussed East-West trade.[78] A communique issued after the meeting stated that trade with the East would contribute to "constructive East-West relations" as long as technology exports did not endanger Western security.[79]

The third COCOM meeting in less than sixteen months took place on April 28-29, 1983. At this meeting the member states agreed to about only half of the proposals put forward by America in February, calling for tight restrictions on the transfer of oil and gas equipment to the Soviet bloc. A statement issued at the end of the meeting revealed that it had not achieved much by way of new initiatives except agreement that the joint system of checking sensitive technology exports should be effective as possible and continually adapted to developments in technology and equipment.

On December 30 1983 COCOM members agreed to embargo silicon and silicon making equipment to the Soviet bloc[80] in what was seen as a major boost to the co-ordinated allied effort since Moscow was said to be dependent on imports of silicon, and the decision was set to hamper the USSR's plan for military modernisation. This agreement was in addition to an announcement that more funding and new equipment would be available for COCOM.

At the COCOM meeting on July 12 1984 changes were revealed to the organisation's list of restricted items following the review of the list which the committee had undertaken at its October 1982 meeting.[81] The agreement reached provided for, amongst other things, sweeping changes to controls on the export of computers including an embargo on the sale of portable microcomputers; and the first ever controls on software.

Reagan's second term of office saw a continuation of COCOM's now familiar and regular meetings. The organisation met again on February 6-7 1985 and "expressed general satisfaction with the way controls on exports of sensitive technology to Soviet bloc countries have been co-ordinated" and on the "updating of the lists of controlled products and technology".[82] The meeting also decided that one third of the embargo list would be updated each year instead of a full review of the list every three to four years. Later on February 26, COCOM issued guidelines which appeared to be more liberal than previous arrangements.[83] In June 1985 COCOM drew up new rules which represented "a mixture of tightening and relaxation" of controls.[84] The new guidelines allowed computers with slow processing speeds to be exported while more advanced computers which could be used for the manufacture of microchips would be subject to continued restrictions. But America and its allies stressed that the overall controls of the committee were still heavily tilted towards restricting the export of equipment to the Soviet bloc which had military uses.

The next major COCOM meeting took place in Versailles on 27-28 January 1988 at which the member states agreed to tighten controls on the export of sensitive technology.[85] This was much to the relief of the United States which had expressed its anxiety that "its allies were becoming lax in monitoring exports" of high technology to Soviet bloc nations. The meeting actually reduced the number of high technology items banned for sale to communist countries on the basis that they were widely available (the concept of foreign availability), but tightened controls on products remaining on the list, and agreed to strengthen enforcement procedures.

Quite often COCOM sessions revealed disagreements between the United States - the most hard-line member of the organisation - and its major West European allies, particularly France, West Germany and Britain. The fundamental problem was that America was keen to tighten controls on the transfer of sensitive goods whereas many West European nations were concerned about the possible damage to their economic relations with Eastern Europe, which in some cases were very substantial. They believed that at times the U.S. went too far by wanting to ban technology items which often had very limited or no military significance. What they wanted was a fair balance between strategic and commercial interests. Furthermore the Europeans were more willing to propose a relaxation of export controls[86] as a reward for good Soviet behaviour and internal reforms in the Soviet bloc. The United States continued to resist this 'carrot' approach. In February 1988 U.S. Defense Secretary Frank Carlucci rejected West European appeals that controls on the export of high technology to the Soviet Union be loosened in response to Soviet progress on reforms and in the field of disarmament.

Towards the end of February 1988 COCOM issued tough new controls on the export of advanced technology to the Soviet Union.[87] Heading the list of embargoed products was equipment for building nuclear submarines followed by a wide range of advanced electronic equipment with possible military applications. A further meeting of COCOM on 25-27 October 1988 recommended the speeding up of the streamlining of high technology especially machine tool exports to the Soviet bloc.[88]

Despite the fact that COCOM was a multilateral body with all countries in theory having an equal say the general view throughout the 1980s was that the United States virtually ran the show, using COCOM to impose stringent controls on technology trade to the Soviet bloc. Most of the initiatives and proposals put forward at meetings came from Washington, the leading player, and only really enthusiastic member of COCOM.

In addition to working in conjunction with its NATO allies, the United States even devised a system by which it prevented neutral countries from re-exporting Western as well as their own technology to Eastern Europe. This saw the United States working together with various groups in the countries concerned. An article in the Times[89] reported the existence of a number of diverse organisations such as the Irish Government's export control delegation, the Swedish industrialists' group, the Swiss ministry of defence, and South Korean business groups who attended meetings with American defence officials. Officials in the United States claimed that the American government placed no pressure on these countries but simply reminded them that if they transferred high technology to the USSR, which was on the U.S. and COCOM list of banned technologies, they would not receive any more American technology in future. In November 1983 it was revealed that America in conjunction with the authorities of Sweden, West Germany and South Africa had foiled a well organised illegal operation by Soviet agents to "acquire key components of a U.S. produced VAX computer system used in missile guidance".[90]

3. American Unilateral and Multilateral Efforts to Control the Transfer of Technology to the Soviet Bloc - Success or Failure?

If one considers the success of U.S. efforts to stem Western technology flows to the Soviet bloc, it would be fair to say that the results were for the most part unsatisfactory (from a U.S. perspective) or even dismal. A number of factors provide proof that U.S. and Western efforts to thwart the diversion of technology to the Soviet bloc had been for the most part a failure. On the whole the United States and its allies had been unable to prevent the Soviet bloc from acquiring a significant amount of technology which had been subject to controls, and from effectively enforcing the strategic controls that were already in place.

To begin with, the United States was unable to forge an effective partnership with its allies. COCOM, which had been established for the purpose of overseeing the multilateral control of strategic exports to communist countries, turned out in many ways to be an ineffective regime. Probably the most basic problem with COCOM was that the organisation had no treaty status, no formal enforcement mechanism, and no system of imposing sanctions against violators of its controls. Instead member governments had the task of administering and enforcing agreed upon restrictions through their own laws and procedures. This made COCOM's task very difficult and the system of control weak because some member states interpreted the control list more liberally while others (particularly the United States) took a more restrictive approach, enforcing controls more actively. This "inconsistent application of COCOM controls by various member nations" coupled with the suspicion "that COCOM controls are applied unfairly because the process is surrounded by excessive secrecy"[91] was at the heart of the organisation's problems in the 1980s.

COCOM was further beset by disagreements and differences between primarily the United States and its Western European allies. Arguments centred around exactly just what to include on the embargo lists. This situation arose when COCOM decided to review the existing embargo list in October 1982. In many ways American-European differences within COCOM stemmed from their differing attitude towards the issue of trade with the Soviet bloc. The United States was keen to extend the control lists to include items whose military relevance could not be precisely verified, and thus wanted to include even civilian technologies whose military use had not been demonstrated. The European allies opposed this expansion of COCOM criteria beyond the currently accepted standard of military relevance because of the adverse effect on East-West trade. Many West European countries had (and still have) strong trade links with Eastern

Europe, and while they were appreciative and aware of Western security interests they also believed that there was something to be gained from a policy of economic detente towards the Soviet bloc.

It has to be remembered that COCOM was revived largely at the initiative of the United States, which often put stringent and at times unacceptable proposals on the table. Some Western countries such as Holland and Belgium were reported not even to be very enthusiastic about COCOM.[92] These countries were happy to go along as members on an informal basis and rejected calls from Washington to create a formal international organisation, possibly under the NATO umbrella. To add to the problems facing the American effort to curb the transfer of critical technology to the communist countries, COCOM was in need of modernisation. The organisation, as Richard Perle pointed out, had an operating budget of less than $500,000, lacked modern offices, adequate staff and "more significantly COCOM has no systematic way of evaluating proposed transfers of technology in the light of the strategic criteria it is supposed to apply ...".[93] These problems meant that the organisation was unable to carry out its task effectively and many items on the banned list found their way to the Soviet Union and other communist countries.

Evidence that technology on the COCOM control lists had indeed reached the Soviet bloc were confirmed by various reports during the 1980s. On September 18, 1985, the U.S. Defense Department released a report accusing Moscow of a "massive well organised campaign" to acquire Western technology.[94] It went on to say that about 70 per cent of military hardware obtained by Moscow was export controlled, embargoed, classified or under some control by Western governments.

American efforts to control technology transfer to the Soviet Union were also hampered by the fact some of the strategic items were widely available in neutral and non-COCOM nations which were less affected by security concerns and thus more likely to take a lax approach to any diversion of sensitive technology to the Soviet Union. Indeed there were reports of countries such as Austria and Sweden providing an outlet for the illegal or legal diversion of strategic goods to the Soviet bloc. In fact there were even rumours, which appeared to be substantiated by much evidence, of violations of COCOM rules by companies based in COCOM member states like France, West Germany and Italy. The U.S. State Department often accused Western corporations of involvement in Soviet attempts to acquire high technology. A report published in the Times said that banned exports had made their way into East European countries like Poland via the Far East.[95] At a fair in Warsaw many Polish firms displayed sophisticated hardware which it "would not have had access under COCOM's rigid export control system".[96] This highlighted the growing problems the Americans found in their attempts to prevent non-COCOM countries from re-exporting Western technology and some of their own to the Soviet bloc.

Deficiencies in the USA's own unilateral control system and enforcement mechanism allowed banned items to find their way into Soviet bloc countries. The U.S. commerce department came under increasing criticism throughout the 1980s for making "an inadequate commitment of resources and moral support to the task of controlling U.S. technology" because it was said to be more interested in promoting trade.[97] In a report based on investigations by the Senate subcommittee, and hearings into the effectiveness of the executive branch in enforcing export controls, it was noted with much concern that "advanced American microelectronics, laser, radar and precision manufacturing technologies" have been obtained by the Soviets "enabling them to make great strides in military strength ....".[98] In 1987 in a report which provoked much controversy in America, the U.S. National Academy of Sciences vehemently criticised the Reagan administration's attempts to curtail high technology exports to the Soviet Union. The findings which were compiled by former defence and intelligence officials deduced that "the administration's much publicised efforts to crack down on the diversion of technology has largely failed at a cost of more than $9billion a year to the U.S. economy".[99] The same panel of former defence and intelligence personnel had claimed in a report in 1982 that there had been "a substantial and serious" transfer of advanced technology from the USA and other non-communist countries to the Soviet bloc. Many articles claimed that the United States had indeed been "... the source of many of the most damaging technological leakages".[100]

Probably the single apparent violation of America's policy of restricting technology to the Soviet bloc nations came from the numerous reported cases of illegal shipments of banned technologies by companies, individuals and the Soviet KGB, which only served to highlight the flaws and loopholes present in the American unilateral and multilateral system for controlling and co-ordinating technology exports.

In 1988 the government of Japan and Norway admitted that companies in their countries - Toshiba and Kongsberg - had exported hi-tech computer and manufacturing equipment which had ended up in the Soviet Union.[101] More specifically these companies had provided the equipment to manufacture submarine propellers so that Russian submarines would run more quietly and be harder to detect. This would mean that NATO listening devices on patrol which could previously hear Russian submarines at a range of 200 miles would now only be able to hear them within a range of about 10 miles.[102]

In December 1988 a Dutch national was arrested and charged with the illegal export of high powered computers to East European countries.[103] He was said to be part of a operation involving some 12 U.S. and West European companies and a number of other individuals.

Articles in the American newspaper, the New York Times in July 1983 traced an upsurge in KGB espionage activities in Western Europe. One article claimed that the KGB had entered a "phase of aggressiveness in its activities...".[104] A second article published on July 25 said that "every year Western technology with military applications worth millions of dollars" disappeared beyond the borders of the Soviet Union and its allies.[105] It went on and stressed that the KGB had intensified its programme for acquiring technology with a massive input of manpower since the 1970s. The Russians were said to have scored a number of notable success by acquiring items such as advanced computers, lasers and missile guidance subsystems. In 1985 West Germany announced that it had acquired a Soviet directory ordering secret agents to obtain Western technology and information, with top priority on radar and rocket technology, anti-submarine systems, and missile guidance systems.[106] A U.S. official claimed that Soviet agents working outside the USSR had acquired Western technology for the Soviet military which had enabled Moscow to improve the accuracy of its ICBM's (intercontinental ballistic missiles).

Although the results were largely negative, the American drive to stop the flow of military technology to Eastern Europe also scored some notable successes. According to a U.S. Defense Department report released on September 18 1985 Western efforts to stem the flow of military technology had made Soviet acquisitions "more difficult and costly than at any time in the past".[107] Not surprisingly it was costing Moscow much more to acquire Western technology through illegal means. In 1988, the U.S. customs service broke up one of the largest international high technology smuggling operations involving the illegal export of high powered computers to the Soviet bloc countries.

Overall, from the evidence before us it would be fair to say that the failures outweighed the successes by a considerable margin.

Conclusions

The deterioration in the superpower relationship at the start of 1980 led to a rethinking in America on many aspects of the Soviet-American relationship. One of these was the question of technology transfer to the USSR and its allies. Throughout the 1970s and particularly during the heyday of detente liberal American policies on both strategic and non-strategic trade to the Soviet Union had allowed a substantial export of military sensitive technology to the East. Over enthusiasm to maintain peaceful and friendly nations with Moscow meant that the West underestimated the later repercussions of this rather lax approach to trade with the Soviet Union. COCOM - the multilateral body established for controlling technology exports-had virtually become obsolete (indeed it was formally disbanded on March 31, 1994), and the trend within the organisation was one tilted more towards trade promotion rather than the curtailment of strategic trade with military applications. This was witnessed by the fact that in 1979 alone it was reported that around 1500 Western deals with the USSR were exempted from COCOM controls with the United States topping the list of COCOM countries that used the exceptions procedure.[108]

As detente collapsed and the Soviets revealed their true colours at the start of the 1980s, American policy drastically hardened on the issue of technology trade with the Soviet bloc. Carter first set the tone in 1980, in what became a concerted U.S. effort to deprive Moscow and its satellite states, American and Western technology. The new administration which took office under Reagan in 1981 inherited Carter's stringent policy on technology transfer, and soon adopted it believing it to be a vital element if the United States was to challenge the Soviet threat with any real purpose.

Many unilateral steps were taken by Reagan but the President, acknowledging that the United States no longer enjoyed monopoly status on sophisticated technology with military relevance, enlisted the help of major allies in Western Europe by reviving the now defunct co-ordinating committee on strategic export controls (COCOM). Under American hegemony and pressure COCOM met frequently and adopted a restrictive role towards the export of strategic items to communist nations during the 1980s, reflecting the central premises of American policy on the issue.

However, a combination of factors rendered U.S. multilateral and unilateral measures virtually useless. On the unilateral front departments such as the Commerce Department failed to comply with policy regulations which had given them responsibility for implementing measures to control the transfer of technology because of pro-trade tendencies prevalent in the department. Indeed many political figures were unhappy at the direction of administration policy on the issue and in 1983 William Root President of the Office of East-West Trade resigned criticising American policy on trade with the Soviet bloc countries.

On the multilateral front COCOM proved to be an ineffective regulatory regime for the management of strategic export policy towards the Soviet bloc nations. There proved to be a lack of whole hearted commitment on the part of many COCOM countries which were unimpressed by American hard-line tactics to include almost all types of technologies including those with little military relevance on the embargo list, and were more concerned about the potential damage to their trade with Eastern Europe.

To add to the problems facing America in its quest to prevent Moscow and its allies from obtaining Western technology, the Soviets had devised a highly intricate and complex web of clandestine activities through its KGB agents operating in Western Europe, many under the sanctuary of embassies and protected by diplomatic immunity. What didn't help was the activities of individuals and businesses in the West and other countries which allowed a considerable consignment of illegal technology to be shipped East. As Dr. Bryen, director of the US defense technology security administration during the 1980s, put it quite simply "technology is a saleable commodity".[109]

Although there were many reported instances of the seizure of technology destined for the Soviet bloc, and the break up of major international smuggling networks this was usually after the damage had already been inflicted, and technologies had already reached their destination on the other side of the 'Iron curtain'. The success stories were far and few and virtually irrelevant in the context of the harm already done. The analysis in this chapter has shown that the school of thought illustrated by Bruce Parrott was correct. Parrott concluded that trade pressure in the form of technology denial is not usually successful, as in the case of American strategic trade pressure on the Soviet Union. We have seen that this indeed was largely the case during the years 1980 to 1988.

Notes

1. The following are on the question of technology transfer to the Soviet Union: Bruce Parrott (ed.), *Trade, Technology and Soviet - American relations* (Bloomington: Indiana University Press 1985); Gary Bertsch, *East-West Strategic Trade, Cocom, and the Atlantic Alliance* (Paris, April 1983); Philip Hanson, *Western Economic Statecraft in East-West Relations* (London: Routledge and Kegan Paul for the Royal Institute of International Affairs, Chatham House Papers No. 40, 1988).
2. Hanson, *Western Economic Statecraft in East-West Relations.*
3. Parrott, *Trade, Technology and Soviet-American Relations.*
4. *Ibid*, p.356.
5. *Ibid.*
6. See the following: *Economic Relations with the Soviet Union*, Angela E. Stent (ed.), (Westview Press 1985) Chapter 6; *Western Economic Statecraft in East West relations* by Hanson, Chapter 4 - for development of Western strategic

export controls since 1945. See also article by William Root: 'Trade Controls that work' in Foreign Policy number 56 (Fall 1984) which traces the history of US trade controls and their effectiveness since the Cold War; see also for a clear and concise look at Western efforts to coordinate controls on exports of technology to the Soviet bloc from 1945 to 1990, and the political debate this generated, Michael Mastanduno, Economic Containment (Cornell University Press 1992).

7. See Economic Warfare or Detente edited by Reinhard Rode and Hanns D. Jacobsen (Westview Press 1985), Chapter 16 for a short history of the development of US unilateral export controls. See also Office of Technology Assessment (report) of the US Congress, Technology and East-West trade (Washington D.C. 1979), Chapter 8 for analysis and history of US export control legislation.
8. *Public Law 81-11* Export Control Act 1949.
9. *Public Law 91-184* Export Administration Act 1969.
10. See *Chapter 2*.
11. In fact moves to reform existing export controls for advanced technology were already on the agenda by the late 1970s, see US Senate. 96th Congress 1st session, *Proposals for Reform of Export Controls for Advanced Technology*, American Enterprise Institute Legislative Analyses, No.5, August 1979 (Washington D.C.).
12. *NATO Review*, No. 6, December 1981, p.19.
13. *Public Law 96-72* Export Administration Act 1979.
14. Zbigniew Brzezinski, *Power and Principle: the Memoirs of the National Security Adviser 1977-81*, (New York 1983), p.323.
15. *New York Times*, March 19 1980, p.D1.
16. See Parrott (ed.), Trade, *Technology and Soviet-American relations*, pp257-259 for Reagan policy on East-West trade in the years 1981-84.
17. *Congressional Quarterly Almanac* 1982, p.21-E.
18. *New York Times*, February 8, 1982, pp.11-12.
19. *Ibid*, October 2, 1982, p.3.
20. The conduct of East-West relations in the 1980s part 11 - Adelphi Papers, No. 190 (International Institute for Strategic Studies, 1984), p.23.
21. US Senate. 97th Congress 2nd Session Transfer of United States high technology to the Soviet Union and Soviet bloc nations. *Hearings before the permanent subcommittee on Investigations of the Committee on Governmental Affairs*, (Washington D.C. 1982), p.156.
22. *Ibid.*
23. *Ibid.* p.194.
24. See for example: *New York Times* January 14 1982 p.1, and October 2 1982, p.3.
25. *New York Times*, October 1, 1982, p.1.
26. See Parrott (ed.), *Trade, Technology and Soviet-American relations*, p.270-74 on the debate and controversy over the renewal of the Export Administration Act of 1979; for the Soviet viewpoint on the revisions to the act and their belief that these would have a detrimental effect on the future prospects for East-West trade see: *SSh.A*, March 1988, No.3, pp.70-77.
27. See on this question of different groups holding diverging views on trade with the USSR, Gary Bertsch, 'US-Soviet trade: the question of leverage', *Survey* Vol. 25, No. 2 (Spring 1980) pp.66-81.

28. *Foreign Policy* No.56 (Fall of 1984), particularly pp. 62-63.
29. *New York Times*, June 26, 1982, p.6.
30. *Ibid,* January 5, 1980, p.1.
31. See Office of Technology Assessment (report) of the US Congress, Technology and East-West Trade (Washington DC 1979) pp.127-129 for information on the commodity control list, how it works and an illustrated example of it.
32. *Ibid* p.127.
33. *New York Times*, January 5, 1980, p.1.
34. *Ibid*, March 19, 1980, p.D1 and p.6.
35. *Ibid*, December 30, 1981, p.1 and p.6.
36. *Ibid.*
37. US Senate, 97th Congress, 2nd Session *Transfer of US high technology to the Soviet Union and Soviet bloc nations,* p.194.
38. *Ibid.*
39. *Ibid.*
40. *Ibid.*
41. *Ibid.*
42. See Stephen Woolcock, 'East-West trade: US policy and European interests', *World Today*, No. 38 (February 1982), pp. 51-59. This article looks at the reasons for the different approaches to East-West trade between the US and its European allies, including a background to the differences which have existed ever since the 1960s.
43. See US Senate, 97th Congress, 2nd session, *Economic Relations with the Soviet Union: The Implications of US Export Controls Related to the Soviet Gas Pipeline*, International Economic Policy, Committee on Foreign Relations, July 30 and August 12 and 13 1982 (Washington D.C. 1982).
44. *Congressional Quarterly Almanac* 1982, p.130.
45. *New York Times*, January 14, 1982, p.1.
46. US Senate. 97th Congress 2nd session, *Transfer of US high technology to the Soviet Union and Soviet bloc nations,* p.319.
47. Export Administration Act of 1979 *Public Law 96-72.*
48. *Adelphi Papers,* No.190, p.27.
49. *Ibid.*
50. *New York Times*, April 5, 1983, p.1.
51. *Adelphi Papers*, No. 190, p.27.
52. See Section 2404 of *Public Law 96-72* Export Administration Act 1979.
53. *Ibid*, Section 2405.
54. *New York Times*, March 21, 1984, p.1.
55. *Ibid,* December 14, 1982, p.12.
56. *The Financial Times*, August 16 1985, p.4.
57. *Foreign Policy*, No.56 (Fall 1984), p.70.
58. *National Security Decision Directive 189.*
59. *Ibid.*
60. US Senate, 97th Congress, 2nd Session, *Transfer of US high technology to the Soviet Union and Soviet bloc nations,* p.313.
61. *Ibid.* p.49.
62. *National Security Decision Directive 145.*
63. *Public Law 98* - 525 Defense Authorization Act 1984.

64. Executive Order 12356 of April 2, 1982 in *Federal Register*, Volume 47, No.66, Tuesday, April 6, 1982.
65. *Ibid.*
66. Authority of the Patent and Trademark office to impose secrecy orders on Patent Applications, Title 35 US code annotated.
67. *Strategic Survey* 1983-84, (International Institute for Strategic Studies, London), p.21.
68. See *Technology and East-West trade*, p.155, for more detailed information about the lists.
69. *Foreign Policy* No. 56 (Fall of 1984), p.74.
70. See *Technology and East-West Trade*, p.157 on how exceptions procedure operates.
71. *New York Times*, March 19, 1980, p.D13.
72. The United States policy of strengthening the COCOM regime and tightening controls since the beginning of the 1980s was noted in *SSh.A*, August 1984, No. 8, pp.80-85.
73. *New York Times,* March 19, 1980, p.D13.
74. *Ibid*, January 16, 1980, p.10.
75. *Ibid,* January 20, 1982, p.8.
76. *Ibid.*
77 *Ibid*, October 2, 1982, p.3.
78. *NATO Review.*
79. *Ibid.*
80. *Financial Times*, December 30, 1983, p.3.
81. *Ibid*, July 16, 1984, p.30.
82. *The Times* February 9, 1985, p.5.
83. *Ibid,* February 26, 1985, p.20.
84. Ibid, June 14, 1985, p.2.
85. *The Times*, January 29, 1988, p.9.
86. Vlad Sobell, 'Perestroika and Western Security', *Radio Free Europe / Radio Liberty background report* No. 222, 11 November 1988.
87. *Ibid,* February 29, 1988, p.8.
88. *Financial Times,* October 28, 1988, p.5.
89. *The Times,* October 15, 1988, p.9.
90. *Strategic Survey* 1983-84, p.20.
91. *NATO Review,* No. 5 October 1987, p.11.
92. See for example *The Times*, October 8, 1988, p.8.
93. *Adelphi Papers*, No. 190, p.24.
94. *The Times*, September 19, 1985, p.9.
95. *Ibid*, March 22, 1988 p.36.
96. *Ibid.*
97. US Senate, 97th Congress, 2nd session, *Report submitted by the Committee on Governmental Affairs titled Transfer of US high technology to the Soviet Union and Soviet bloc nations*, 15 November 1982.
98. *Ibid,* p.59.
99. *The Times*, January 20, 1987, p.25.
100. *The Economist*, November 20-26, 1982, pp. 21-22.
101. *The Times*, January 26, 1988, p.36.

102. *The Economist*, June 27, 1987, volume 303, p.66.
103. *Financial Times*, December 29, 1988, p.1.
104. *New York Times*, July 24, 1983, p.1.
105. *Ibid,* July 25, 1983, p.1.
106. *The Times*, January 24, 1985, p.6.
107. *Ibid*, September 19, 1985, p.9.
108. *New York Times*, March 19, 1980, p.D13.
109. *The Times*, October 8, 1988, p.8.

5 Assessing the Political Success of American Trade Pressure: 1- Soviet Policy on Human Rights

Introduction

We now come to the wider question of whether United States trade pressure on the Soviet Union actually achieved its declared political purpose.[1] The prime objective of American trade pressure was to impose economic costs on Moscow by denying the Soviets the benefits of trade, to such an extent that it would over a period of time influence the Soviet Union to change its behaviour in areas identified by the United States government, namely Soviet policy on human rights, and Moscow's direct and indirect involvement in the Third World (which will be the subject of the next chapter).

Trade pressure employed by Carter in his final year, and then by the Reagan administration, was at its most stringent during the years 1980-84 (see chapters 3 and 4). There were already other US measures such as the Jackson-Vanik Amendment[2] which had been in place since the 1970s.

It has to be remembered there is a time lag between when a policy is implemented or takes shape, and its results or effectiveness, which can only by judged over a period of years. In this case one can realistically assess the results of US trade pressure at its peak during the years 1980-84, in the period 1985-88 by which time the policy had been firmly established and had been in operation for a number of years to see if it had indeed had any impact on the relevant areas of Soviet behaviour which were the target of American trade pressure. Therefore, using the period 1985-88 as a benchmark for judging Soviet compliance with U.S. objectives is an ideal base as it allows as assessment of Soviet behaviour over a number of years rather than just one or two.

In view of all this, the chapter again will be divided into two sections. Section one will restate the political objectives of American trade pressure. In other words what the Americans specified during the period 1980-84 as what they were looking for in terms of changes in Soviet behaviour, and in what areas. In order to know whether US trade pressure achieved its political purpose it is necessary to define precisely what the objectives were as publicly stated. Section two will concentrate on the question of Soviet performance on human rights. *Part a* of this section will concentrate on the issue of dissent. *Part b* will continue on the theme of human rights but with the focus of attention shifting to the issue of emigration, in particular Jewish emigration.

1. US Trade Pressure: Restating the Political Objectives

The use of trade pressure for political aims was not a new phenomenon in American - Soviet relations during the 1980s. Indeed as was seen in the previous chapter, COCOM was set up in 1949 to regulate Western exports to the communist countries. Then in 1975 there was the passing of the Jackson-Vanik Amendment which made the granting of most favoured nation status conditional on the liberalisation of emigration policies in the Soviet Union. Throughout the early 1980s the United States government made clear the areas in which it was looking for changes with regard to Soviet domestic and international behaviour. These were the very issue areas which had been contributing to a souring of Soviet-American relations since the turn of 1980.

The first of these issues was the Soviet record on human rights (the second being Soviet involvement in the third world, which will be the subject of the next chapter). On numerous occasions and at various international forums the United States expressed its dismay at what it saw as the abysmal Soviet record on the issue. Human rights were and has always been an issue close to America[3] since the principles of freedom and democracy form the basis of US society, and on which US society was founded. It is hardly surprising that given the contrasting ideologies of communism and capitalism, which entailed differing conceptions of human rights, the issue was always one of the most contentious in the superpower relationship. For the United States the more traditional concept of human rights covering what are known as political rights have generally had precedence over the more modern concept which includes economic and social rights. On the other hand the USSR in line with Marxist conceptions of democracy placed more emphasis on social and economic rights believing them to be more important than political rights, which were severely restricted.[4] A common argument employed by Moscow to counteract Western criticism of its human rights policy was to in turn censure the West for failing to provide adequate economic and social rights for its own citizens.

However, on the basis of the adoption of international standards on human rights, and through various international forums involving the participation of European states including the USSR, the United States found a pretext to question Soviet policy on human rights in terms of Moscow not living up to its commitments. Indeed the central American concern was that the USSR had not complied with the terms of international agreements to which it was a signatory. The Conference on Security and Cooperation in Europe (CSCE) and the Helsinki Final Act[5] were a product of the period of detente in the 1970s during when the developing dialogue between East and West allowed the latter, and particularly America, to air its concern over issues such as human rights and gave them an ideal opportunity to bring such issues to the forefront. In effect by participating in the Helsinki process and in the CSCE the Soviets had acknowledged the force of Western definitions of human rights, and had assumed responsibility for establishing such rights in the Soviet Union. The West saw CSCE as a broad multilateral negotiating process aimed at not only lessening East-West tension but gradually encouraging the possibility for development of freedom and democracy (as they defined them) in Eastern Europe. The United States was keen to emphasize to Moscow the importance of the Helsinki process and the CSCE, in particular basket 111 dealing with "cooperation in humanitarian and other fields".[6] Washington stressed to Moscow the latter's obligation to meet its requirements.

As Under Secretary of state for Security Assistance Science and Technology, US Department of State, Matthew Nimetz pointed out, the Helsinki Final Act of 1975 drew

> a number of Western principles concerning human rights .... into the fabric of the East-West dialogue, establishing the performance of signatories on human rights issues as a legitimate topic for international discussion.[7]

He went on to stress that the human rights situation in the Soviet Union was giving considerable cause for concern with little movement "to resolve long standing cases involving human rights spokesmen and prisoners of conscience".[8]

In a statement before the Senate Foreign Relations Committee in 1983, on 'US-Soviet relations in the context of US foreign policy', Secretary of state George Shultz stated that amongst other things the United States would be seeking an "improvement in Soviet performance on human rights".[9]

In an address on East-West relations delivered at Eureka college (Illinois) on May 9 1982, Reagan criticised the Soviet Union for not relaxing "its hold on its own people ..." despite being a signatory to the

Helsinki agreements on human rights.[10] He went on to say that America would be willing to respond with an expansion of trade with Moscow but this would depend on Soviet actions.

Further evidence that the United States under the Reagan administration envisaged a connection between the trade and political aspects of US-Soviet relations could be seen in former president Richard Nixon's statement that trade and political issues were inexorably linked. "For the United States to increase trade ... at a time when they (the Soviets) are engaging in political activities that are opposed to our interests would be stupid and dangerous".[11]

The questions of dissent and freedom of emigration were top of the American agenda of human rights concerns.

Dissent or the expression of one's disagreement with the state, openly or publicly for political, religious, economic, cultural, national, ideological, or any other reason was sharply curtailed in a one party state like the USSR.[12] Dissidents expressing their views openly found themselves in conflict with the state, with the authorities taking measures to punish and bring into line human rights activists, and dissidents.[13]

The treatment of dissidents came under severe American criticism before and during the Reagan administration's terms of office. In its annual report to Congress on human rights practices in 1979 the American State Department noted a continuing mistreatment of prisoners, harsh conditions in prison, and the subjection of political prisoners to interrogation and psychological pressure, including threats against their families.[14] In its report for 1980, the State Department illustrated what it saw as increased repression at home, with a crack-down on human rights activities seen as more severe than ever before.[15] No improvement was seen in the following year or in 1982.[16] Instead the use of powerful drugs against political dissidents who had been admitted to Soviet psychiatric hospitals was noted. The State Department's survey for 1983 concluded that Moscow's performance in the field of human rights had fallen far short of acceptable international standards.[17] Throughout the 1970s and 1980s many prominent dissidents were sent into internal exile and labour camps. The plight of well known activists such as Yuri Orlov, Anatoly Scharansky, and Andrei Sakharov was highlighted by the West. Many Jews who formed a considerable proportion of the most outspoken activists suffered severe repression on top of the fact that many were denied the right to emigrate. Unofficial groups such as the Helsinki Group attempting to monitor Soviet compliance with the human rights provisions of the Final Act were also hit hard by Soviet repression. Many members of such groups were arrested and then imprisoned. Some were sent into exile and many were even reported missing.

The other area of human rights of most concern to the United States was the question of Jewish emigration. The treatment of Jews in the Soviet Union, in particular the Soviet authorities denying them the right to emigrate, was a major topic of concern.[18] Although there were other ethnic groups such as Germans and Armenians who also wished to emigrate, it was the plight of Soviet Jews which attracted most concern because of the United States' historic friendship with Israel and the pressure of a large Jewish community in America with significant financial and political clout. Therefore American concern on emigration was concentrated largely on the state of Jews, and such concern was often relayed to Soviet leaders.

As in the case of political dissent the Soviet authorities had once again failed to live up to their international commitments. By refusing emigration to hundreds of thousands of Jews, Moscow had shown an unwillingness to implement Basket 111 of the Helsinki process which included provisions calling for the free mobility of the populations of Europe and other civil liberties. The denial of emigration also entailed failure to comply with the concluding document of the Madrid meeting (the Madrid Conference which ran from September 1980 to July 1983) which called for the participating states to deal favourably with applications "relating to contacts and regular meetings on the basis of family ties, reunification of families...".[19]

For their part the Soviet authorities always denied that there existed any mass desire for emigration. Instead they claimed that Jews remained an integral part of Soviet society.[20] The reality however was very different. Not only was there a mass desire to leave, the Soviet authorities used various tactics such as: harassment of those applying to leave by KGB agents; a cumbersome and time consuming application procedure with applications being ".... snagged by bureaucratic technicalities".[21] Confiscation of invitations to leave through the process of interfering with private mail was also used to block potential émigrés from acquiring exit visas.[22] In addition refuseniks - those refused visas - were subjected to various forms of harassment and ill treatment.[23] The policy of intimidation against Jews wanting to emigrate was linked to the general upward trend in anti-semitism in the USSR in the early 1980s. Andropov's policy in this respect was seen as particularly hostile towards Jews, evoking memories of "the Nazi era and of Stalin's last days".[24] This culminated in 1983 in the formation of the anti-Zionist Committee of the Soviet Public which denied that there had been any curb on Jewish emigration, and linked Zionism to Nazism.[25]

While Jewish emigration had peaked in 1979 there was a steady decline thereafter with the lowest figure since 1971 attained in 1984.[26] The continued denial of exit visas for thousands of Jews wanting to emigrate led to the presence of many refuseniks in the USSR. As Senator D'Amato of New York put it during the hearing and markup before the subcommittee on human rights in 1983 ".... getting out remains one of the most difficult tasks for Jews in the Soviet Union".[27] In a statement by the Assistant Secretary of State, Elliot Abrams, it was noted that "the US Government is deeply concerned about the severe downturn in emigration, and the issue is being raised with the Soviets at every appropriate opportunity, both in public forums such as the Commission on Security and Cooperation in Europe (CSCE) and in bilateral talks".[28] He went on and stated that the US would in the short run try to help "as many individuals" as possible, "limit discriminatory practices, and obtain freer emigration".[29]

During the period 1980-84 the human rights organisation Amnesty International in its annual reports noted continued repression of those attempting to leave the USSR. In 1982 Amnesty International noted the imprisonment of eight Jews who had been campaigning for the right to leave.[30] The same organisation noted that in 1983 the authorities had continued their prosecution and imprisonment of citizens "who sought to exercise their right to leave the country".[31]

This section has pin-pointed the areas in which the United States was seeking what it regarded as improvements from the Soviet Union. The section also gives a brief account of actual Soviet practices in the issues concerned in order to illustrate that there was indeed shortcomings or problems with Moscow's behaviour in these areas which needed to be rectified and the aim of US trade pressure was to do just that. In the case of Soviet human rights practices, Washington was looking for a substantial improvement so that Soviet practices would fall in line with internationally accepted standards. In addition Washington was seeking greater tolerance of dissent by the Soviet authorities, and an end to the repression of dissidents, who were engaged in the type of activities that would pose no problem in the Western world. On top of all this America wanted Moscow to grant Soviet Jews the right to emigrate by greatly liberalizing its policy of restricting the freedom of movement.

2. The Effect of United States Trade Pressure on Soviet Human Rights Practices

This section will now analyze whether the application of trade pressure achieved the first of its political objectives of inducing a modification for the better in Soviet behaviour in the area of human rights as defined by Washington. Reports from various international organisations and bodies monitoring the progress of human rights worldwide,[32] plus the work of the U.S. government itself, as well as official pronouncements emanating from Washington, provide a useful yardstick for assessing any changes in Moscow's human rights performance over the period 1985-88. Part one of this section will concentrate on dissent, the other on the question of Jewish emigration. An important question which one must bear in mind is whether any changes were real and fundamental or just cosmetic.

Dissent in the Soviet Union 1985-1988

Open criticism of the political, economic, ideological or moral foundations on which Soviet society rested had always been severely repressed. The 1970s in particular saw a rise in dissident activity largely in response to the increased violation of human rights by the Soviet authorities. The emergence of dissident movements[33] invited a severe crack-down by the authorities characterised by full scale repression of human rights activists which continued throughout the early 1980s. The limits of permissible dissent were narrow in the Soviet Union at this time.

What we are interested in now is to see whether in the period 1985-1988 there was any improvement in the conduct of Soviet policy on dissent, and whether the Soviets were willing to expand the limits of permissible dissent by easing restrictions on dissident activities, and allowing more freedom of expression and criticism of the Soviet system. Also to what extent did Moscow take measures to free political prisoners and improve the treatment of such prisoners being held? Was the scope of political rights and civil liberties available to Soviet citizens expanded in response to Western pressure or other factors?

If we begin with the question of the imprisonment of individuals on political grounds we will find that during the years 1985-88 the situation remained the same as that which prevailed prior to 1985, with many reported cases of imprisonment on political charges. While it is true that the actual number of political prisoners held in the Soviet Union decreased considerably during 1985 to 1988, in comparison with 1980-84, this can hardly be regarded as a significant change in Soviet policy since the imprisonment of any number of such individuals is unacceptable on the basis of the generally accepted standards laid down by international law. After all such prisoners have not committed a criminal offence (in the usual sense of the term such as murder, burglary, assault etc.) but have simply exercised in a non-violent manner their civil and political rights, including their freedom of conscience, expression, and speech.

Under various articles of Soviet law individuals were arrested for political reasons. Article 70 of the criminal code dealing with "anti-Soviet agitation and propaganda" was the article under which dissidents were most frequently arrested. It carried a maximum penalty of seven years imprisonment and up to an additional five years in internal exile. There were other articles such as article 190-1: "the dissemination of deliberately hostile fabrications defaming the Soviet and social system", and article 190-3: "the organisation of, or active participation in a group actively violating public order", which all carried prison sentences, and which together were responsible for denying various internationally recognised human rights such as freedom of speech, freedom of expression, freedom of association, and freedom of conscience.

Table 5.1 Number of Political Prisoners Held in the Soviet Union, 1982-88*

Year	No. of Prisoners
1982	848
1983	903
1984	887
1985	837
1986	530
1987	300
1988	140

*The exact number of political prisoners in the USSR was not determinable. The figures are therefore estimates from the work done by organisations such as Amnesty International and the International Helsinki Federation for Human Rights. Also the figures are likely to be much lower than the real ones because of official censorship, restrictions on freedom of movement, and limitations on the flow of information which mask the real figures (political prisoners as defined by the International Helsinki Federation were those who were incarcerated in prison, labour camps, psychiatric hospitals, sent into internal exile as punishment for the non violent exercise of their civil and political rights).
Source: Figures for 1982-84 from *Violations of the Helsinki Accords: USSR* - a report prepared for the International Helsinki Federation, p176. Figures for 1985-88 from those reported in *Amnesty International Reports* for the years 1986, 1987, 1988 and 1989.

In 1985 there was a heavy crackdown on religious dissenters.[34] Amnesty International reported that at least 132 Soviet citizens were jailed under laws curtailing freedom of religion and expression. Furthermore, another 65 people were imprisoned for producing uncensored literature, thus violating the state's monopoly of publishing and censoring all printed material.[35] Many of those jailed had allegedly criticised the Soviet government's treatment of non-Russians in the USSR. Thus the continuing poor performance of the Soviet authorities in the realm of human rights saw them fail to meet "even the most elementary of accepted international standards".[36]

There appeared to be no significant improvement in the treatment of dissidents or any relaxation of Soviet policy towards dissent in 1986. As before "Soviet citizens were still at risk if they exercised their freedom of conscience in ways that did not conform to official policy",[37] and 150 individuals were prosecuted on such grounds.[38]

Amnesty confirmed that a total of about 259 political prisoners were released in 1987, the largest number to be set free in any one year since the 1950s.[39] Despite this, at least 300 (probably more; see Table 5.1) prisoners of conscience were still being held in the Soviet Union at the end of 1987. Indeed, in 1988 there were reports of new arrests on political charges.

On top of the imprisonment of prisoners on political grounds, another important issue was the treatment of 'political prisoners'. The period 1985-88 was to witness the continued mistreatment of these prisoners of conscience. Such repressive treatment was characterised by cases of torture, and the continued use of "psychiatric confinement for political purposes".[40] This saw individuals confined indefinitely in mental hospitals, and some were even beaten up and given powerful drugs "after they had refused to repudiate their views".[41] Prisoners at corrective labour camps were forced to do taxing compulsory labour, with many suffering from extreme hunger, which was prescribed in Soviet law as a means of punishment. Indeed the US Department of State reported that in 1985 political prisoners held in psychiatric hospitals against their will were subjected to "cruel and degrading treatment".[42] In addition, the Soviet authorities continued their practice of exiling political dissenters. The prominent dissident Andrei Sakharov remained in exile in the city of Gorky despite repeated calls from the West for him to be released and given adequate medical attention. In 1985 a total of 46 death sentences were passed and 16 executions took place (see Table 5.2). It appears as though the Soviet authorities were still resisting calls from international organisations like Amnesty International to work towards the eventual abolition of the death penalty.[43] The U.S State Department's report on human rights practices for 1985 reported the death of a number of individuals in Soviet custody, who were engaged in religious or political dissent. They included well-known activists from Estonia, Armenia and the Ukraine.[44]

In 1986, Dr. Andrei Sakharov and his wife, who had been in internal exile since 1980, were released, along with the early release of some 12 prisoners of conscience from labour camps. These were, however, only minor developments in a positive direction. Conditions for remaining political prisoners continued to be harsh on the colonies of the corrective labour system where most were held.[45] Poor medical care, limited rations, and high work targets which often involved heavy physical labour were the order of the day. The case of one activist, Anatoly Marchenko, who died in December 1986 following a hunger strike, highlighted the situation which dissidents in prison had to endure.[46] Marchenko had constantly complained about ill treatment at the hands of colony officials but his complaints were ignored and instead he was further punished. The abuse of psychiatry continued as well.[47] Amnesty International reported that 44 prisoners of conscience were still being held in psychiatric institutions and many had been given powerful drugs.[48]

Table 5.2 Number of Death Sentences Passed and Number of Executions in the Soviet Union, 1983-88

Year	No. of Death Sentences	No. of Executions
1983	24	8
1984	53	16
1985	46*	27*
1986	17	8
1987	25	8
1988	15	7

*Amnesty International believed that the figures for 1985 were probably much higher.
Source: *Amnesty International Reports* 1984 through to 1989.

The U.S. State Department noted with much concern that the KGB appeared to have been largely exempted from the new 'glasnost' (openness) being promoted by the Soviet leadership, a disappointing development especially since the KGB was heavily involved in the execution of the Soviet government's hardline policy on dissent, and the organisation was well known for engaging in systematic beatings of human rights activists, for spying on dissidents, setting up dissidents, and bringing false charges against critics of the government.

Further evidence that the Soviet government's performance on the question of dissent had not improved by much during the period 1985-88 in comparison with the early 1980s was provided by the *Comparative Survey of Freedom* (see Table 5.3 for explanation of the survey) published annually, and which provided a rating for political rights, civil liberties and the status of freedom in the Soviet Union. According to this survey the USSR was ranked amongst the least free nations in the world. The USSR was designated as 'not free' in each year from 1985 to 1988, representing no change from the previous 5 years (see Table 5.3). A ranking of 7 for political rights in the period 1985-88 meant that the USSR was rated as offering the lowest level of political rights. This rating of 7 in fact represented a further deterioration in the level of such rights prevalent in the Soviet Union from some of the earlier years, such as 1980 to 1983, when Moscow had been ranked 6. A rating of 7 for civil liberties was also in accordance with the low level of such rights prevalent in the USSR.

Table 5.3 Rating of Political Rights, Civil Liberties and the Status of Freedom in the Soviet Union, 1980-88

Year	Political Rights[a]	Civil Liberties[b]	Status of Freedom
1980	6	7	NF
1981	6	7	NF
1982	6	7	NF
1983	6	7	NF
1984	7	7	NF
1985	7	7	NF
1986	7	7	NF
1987	7	7	NF
1988	-	-	-

[a] & [b] In the case of political rights and civil liberties countries are ranked on a scale of 1 to 7, where a rating of 1 means the country is ranked freest in terms of political rights and civil liberties, and the lowest rating 7 means the country is least free i.e. it offers the lowest level of political or civil rights. NF designates the status of freedom as 'not free'.
Source: *Comparative Survey of Freedom* which is published annually in *Freedom in the World*.

So far the analysis has revealed much evidence that the same old policies and practices were still in operation during the period 1985-88, as they were prior to that period.

However, in all fairness there were some positive changes that did occur in the area of dissent particularly in 1987 and 1988, which are worth looking at especially since the prospect for change had been bleak for so long.

To start with the limits of permissible dissent were expanded. The Soviet authorities allowed debates on human rights issues that were previously taboo.[49] There was the broadening of the discussion of historical, social, economic, and to a lesser extent political issues in the official media, brought about by the authorities' decision to end the requirement that all publications, film and television scripts be submitted for censorship to the "main administration for safeguarding state secrets in the media".[50] Also in 1987 the Soviet government granted freedom for Soviet citizens "to demonstrate against government policies and to form independent discussion clubs ....".[51] The abuse of psychiatry was brought to public attention, raising hopes that this truly repressive practice would be brought to an end very soon. Indeed, later in March 1988, a new decree went into effect which pointed towards an end to the practice of committing healthy persons (most notably dissidents) to psychiatric institutions.[52] Abuse of psychiatry was actually made a punishable offence. On top of this a number of prominent political and religious prisoners were released from psychiatric hospitals.

The USSR was also involved in a major review of its existing criminal law in order that it meet international standards. The review included issues such as restricting the death penalty; giving defendants earlier access to a lawyer; and repealing the law which in effect restricted freedom of expression. This led to the publication in 1988 of new draft principles of criminal law "which would restrict the scope of the death penalty and give precedence to international standards over domestic law".[53]

During the course of 1987, Gorbachev made a number of pronouncements which pointed towards a change for the better in future Soviet human rights practices. In an article in *Pravda* in September, Gobachev suggested that the United Nations play a leading role in the promotion and protection of human rights.[54] He also stressed that governments had a duty to make their laws conform with international standards. 1987 also saw the Soviet Union ratify the UN convention against torture.[55]

1988 was a year which saw changes take place in the Soviet Union which would have been unthinkable at one time, as Soviet leader Gorbachev's policies of glasnost (openness) and perestroika (restructuring) began to take shape. This culminated in an expansion of the limits of permissible dissent witnessed in many ways.

On July 28 the USSR Supreme Soviet Presidium issued a decree on "procedures for the organisation and conduct of meetings, rallies .... demonstrations ....."[56] This provided a legal basis for demonstrations. Indeed in the Baltic Republics and Armenia massive demonstrations took place during the year.[57] Positive developments in the area of freedom of association saw the formation of large organisations for political action.[58]

At a major speech delivered at the United Nations on December 7 1988,[59] Gorbachev outlined his proposals and plans in a number of areas. In the area of human rights the Soviet leader pledged that "no persons would be confined or persecuted in the Soviet Union because of their political or religious beliefs".[60] He also argued that "World Court decisions regarding international agreements on human rights should be binding".[61] Earlier at the Moscow Summit in May/June even Reagan before leaving cited what he described as a "sizeable improvement" in human rights observance in the Soviet Union.[62]

Nevertheless, despite some significant changes for the better in Soviet performance on human rights particularly in the latter part of the period 1985-88, the U.S. Department of State reported that "the changes were more than cosmetic and less than fundamental".[63] And as Amnesty International noted "there was a yet no changes in law that would protect Soviet citizens from being imprisoned for peacefully exercising their rights, preventing ill treatment in places of imprisonment ....".[64] The key thing to remember as the US State Department stated was that the improvements which took place in 1987 in particular had still to be reinforced by reform laws.[65] Without changes in the law itself the reforms taking place would lack substance, and would not provide satisfactory evidence that change would not only develop further but would be irreversible. 1988 itself did not see many changes in Soviet law in areas of relevance to dissent but instead saw mainly hints of change, and more draft proposals.

On this basis the U.S. State Department in its annual report to Congress on Human Rights Practices (for 1988) around the world urged caution and stressed that it was still not possible to say "that there has been a fundamental shift in the Soviet Union's approach to human rights".[66] It is clear that the Americans were impressed with the changes that were indeed taking place, and particularly the profound implications they would have. But as before the United States was keen to see changes in Soviet law in a wide range of issues covering human rights, which would make the changes real and irreversible.

Therefore, judging the period 1985-88 as a whole it is reasonable to say that trade pressure appears not to have had the far reaching and desired effect that was intended. Soviet policy on dissent continued to give cause for concern, even under the new leadership of Mikhail Gorbachev. While Gorbachev expressed his willingness to open up the Soviet system under his programme of 'glasnost' and 'perestroika' the changes did not go far enough from the American point of view. The same old policy characterised by the repression of dissent was still largely in force. More significantly, the apparent movement towards change was not accompanied by the far reaching changes in Soviet law, which would have ultimately made Gorbachev's new initiatives more convincing. Certainly Gorbachev appeared to be moving in the right direction by the end of 1988, and if one were to compare the Soviet performance in the period 1985-88 with the years of the early 1980s there is no doubt that Moscow had made great strides forward. However, Gorbachev had gone far but not far enough.

Certainly if we were judging Soviet performance on a year by year basis it would be true to say that major strides were made by the Soviet government in the realm of human rights during 1988 which can be seen in many ways as a kind of turning point. Unfortunately it is improvements in the period as a whole that are more important rather than one single year, since it is the period as a whole which is the yardstick for measurement here.

Of course no one can or could have realistically expected all political prisoners to be released within a couple of years, and although the changes may have disappointed the U.S. officially they could in themselves be seen as significant, especially 1988 which laid the groundwork or foundation from which real and irreversible changes would later emanate.

Emigration: The Case of the Soviet Jews

The situation for Soviet Jews wishing to emigrate had been steadily deteriorating since the record number of departures occurred in 1979. In the period 1980-84 Jewish emigration from the USSR declined at an increasingly rapid rate reaching its lowest figure for 18 years in 1984 - with only 896 departing (see Table 5.4). There was nevertheless renewed optimism that the application of American trade pressure beginning in 1980 would have its effect after a number of years, even though similar pressure applied previously in the form of the Jackson-Vanik Amendment did not appear to have yielded the desired outcome.

Table 5.4 Jewish Emigration from the Soviet Union in the Period, 1979-88

Year	Emigration
1979	51,320
1980	21,471
1981	9,447
1982	2,688
1983	1,315
1984	896
1985	1,140
1986	914
1987	8,155
1988	19,292

Source: Figures for years 1979-85 from *Human Contacts, Reunion of Families and Soviet Jewry* - Report prepared by the Institute of Jewish Affairs in London. Figures for 1986-88 taken from the annual report submitted to Congress by the U.S. Department of State titled *Country Reports on Human Rights Practices* for the years 1986, 1987 and 1988.

We now come to the question of Soviet policy on emigration in the period 1985-88 in order to assess the performance of Moscow during these years. What will matter in this analysis is not so much the Soviet performance on emigration year by year but the overall Soviet performance in the period 1985-88 in relation to this annual analysis.

The year 1985 saw the first increase in the level of Jewish emigration for 5 years (see Table 5.4). It saw 244 more Jews being allowed to leave than was the case in 1984, representing an increase of 27%. In terms of numbers this represented a very small increase if one considered that according to the U.S. State Department there remained more than 200,000 Jews who possessed the letters of invitation (known as Vyzovs) from Israel required for all applications for emigration but who were still being denied their right to leave.[67] The State Department concluded that Jewish, as well as emigration of other major ethnic groups wishing to emigrate "remained at severely restricted levels..."[68]

The human rights organisation Amnesty International in its annual report covering the year 1985 also noted the difficulties which Soviet citizens continued to endure in their quest to emigrate, with those attempting to leave illegally risking the possibility of up to 3 years in jail.[69] Amnesty cited the case of eleven Jews who were imprisoned for appealing abroad asking for help in emigrating. According to the Helsinki Federation[70] "even those allowed to leave the USSR in 1985 did not for the most part include veteran refuseniks who had been waiting for more than ten years".[71] Robert Bernstein, chairman of Helsinki Watch human rights organisation, said that the old type of repression was continuing under Gorbachev's regime.[72]

At the Geneva summit in November 1985 there was a unscheduled session between Gorbachev and American Senator Jesse Jackson.[73] At this session Jackson raised the plight of Soviet Jews complaining about the treatment of Jews, especially with regard to the question of freedom to travel. Gorbachev rejected Jackson's accusations, instead arguing that there existed no Jewish problem. Clearly Gorbachev did not share or recognise international, particularly American concern over the question of Jewish emigration.

If 1985 saw only a insignificant increase in the level of Soviet-Jewish emigration, 1986 proved to be a disaster for Soviet Jewry. The downward trend in Jewish emigration evident since 1979, and only momentarily disrupted in 1985, reappeared in 1986 with a further fall of 19.8%. Not a significant fall but a drop nevertheless, taking the number of departures below the one thousand mark for the second time in 3 years (see Table 5.4). According to Jewish sources there were about 383,000 Jews in the Soviet

Union in possession of a vyzov by 1986 (the first step in the emigration process) whose application had been rejected over the years, making the figure of 914 departures for the year seem even more miniscule by comparison.[74] This point was also noted by Dr. William Korey, public member of the American delegation to the Berne experts' meeting on human contacts in 1986.[75] Later at the Helsinki Commission hearing on June 18, 1986, Dr. Korey expressed shock and dismay at what he called "... the almost total non-compliance of Basket 111 provisions on reunion of families by the Kremlin with respect to Soviet Jews seeking emigration to Israel...".[76]

President Reagan raised the issue of Jewish emigration with Soviet leader Gorbachev at the Reykjavik summit meeting in October 1986. The President presented a list of 1200 Jews who he said wanted to leave the Soviet Union, repeating that "Soviet human rights policies were impeding the improvement of our relationship".[77] Earlier before the summit, the *New York Times* reported that the status of Soviet Jews had emerged as the central topic of the summit meeting in advance of proceedings, saying that the U.S. was set to give a high priority to the issue.[78]

1987 saw somewhat of a turn-round. More than eight thousand Jews were allowed to emigrate (see Table 5.4), the largest figure since 1982. However, as before this increase masked the considerable number (possibly up to 50,000) who were denied exit visas.[79] Nevertheless the 1987 figures did represent movement in a positive direction of a more substantial nature than before with many well-known refuseniks being allowed to leave as well. Throughout 1987 Reagan had "publicly excoriated the Soviets for refusing to allow Jews and dissidents to emigrate"..[80] and the upcoming summit in Washington later in the year may have contributed to the softening of Soviet emigration policy in 1987.

In February 1987 a number of prominent Jewish activists held an illegal press conference in Moscow calling for increased pressure to be applied on the Soviet authorities "to adopt a more sympathetic approach to their problem".[81]

They expressed concern about new Soviet laws which were likely to make the process of emigration more difficult. The activists were referring to new Soviet regulations which came into force in January 1987, which according to the U.S. State Department made "...family reunification the only legal basis for emigration". These new regulations as a result "... codified Moscow's long-standing refusal to recognise the right to leave..".[82]

1988 provided the first signs of real evidence that the Soviet authorities were opening their doors to allow a more sustained exodus of Jews from the Soviet Union.[83] 19,292 Jews were allowed to emigrate in

1988, the largest number since 1980 (see Table 5.4), representing an increase of 136% from the previous year. 1988 was to begin an irreversible process which was to see emigration for Jews increase to unprecedented levels. Many political observers saw the liberalisation of Soviet policy on emigration as not entirely unexpected in view of the changing political climate in the USSR which had been gathering pace ever since Gorbachev launched his reform programme.

Throughout 1988 there was much attention focussed on the question of human rights including the treatment of Soviet Jews. At the Moscow summit - the fourth Reagan and Gorbachev summit - held between May 29 - June 2, Reagan criticised the Soviet record on human rights as abysmal, accusing Moscow of violating its commitments under the Helsinki Accords, with most criticism centred on "the government's refusal to allow Jews ... other minorities and dissident to emigrate...".[84] In a move which irritated the Soviet authorities and was accordingly denounced by the Soviet press,[85] Reagan met 98 Soviet citizens including some well known refuseniks who had been denied permission to leave.

However, Reagan acknowledged that Gorbachev had made great strides in the area of improving human rights, and blamed the bureaucracy rather than the Soviet leadership for restrictions on emigration.[86] At the summit, Reagan had once again highlighted America's deep concern on the issue of Jewish emigration, and had shown that American support for Soviet Jewry was stronger than ever, and that Washington always regarded the Jewish question as one of the top issues in any superpower negotiations. Reagan's confidence in Gorbachev regarding the latter's commitment to improving Soviet human rights performance was to be further boosted later in the year.

On December 7, at the United Nations, Gorbachev delivered a speech, where along with an announcement of major troop cuts the Soviet leader outlined his proposals in a number of other issues including human rights.[87] In the field of human rights, Gorbachev announced that "the ban on emigration by persons possessing secret information would expire after a specified time limit".[88] This represented a significant development since one of the reasons often cited by the Soviet authorities for denying exit visas to some individuals was that they had had access to classified military information.

Total Jewish emigration for the period 1985-88 as a whole amounted to 29501. This represented a fall of 18% from the previous period 1980-84 during which 35817 Jews had been allowed to leave. Furthermore, the fall from 1980-84 to 1985-88 would have been even greater if there had not been such a sizeable increase in emigration in 1988.

The evidence before US has shown that American attempts to improve Soviet policy on Jewish emigration by the application of trade pressure had limited success. The period 1985-88 actually witnessed a fall in the level of emigration from the previous period 1980-84. This is hardly surprising given that there was no indication of any progress in the years 1985 and 1986, with only a slight increase in 1985 and a decline in 1986. The first real sign of substantial progress was seen in 1987 with a large increase in the number of exist visas granted. This progress was further enhanced in 1988 with an even larger increase.

However, as the Institute of Jewish Affairs pointed out in a 1986 report "even during the years of rising emigration the number of refuseniks was growing", reflecting the fact "..... that the number of applications constantly exceeds the number of exit visas granted ...".[89] In other words one has to be careful to concentrate not only on the number allowed to emigrate but also on the number of rejected visas in order to get a more accurate picture of the real changes in Soviet policy. Also, despite the increases in Jewish emigration in 1987 and 1988 it has to be remembered that there were no actual changes in Soviet law in the direction of easing restrictions on emigration. If anything the new Soviet laws which came into effect on January 1987 regarding emigration were seen as placing further obstacles to the freedom of emigration, to add to the continuing discrimination faced by Soviet Jews in society.

Therefore, an overall view of Soviet emigration policy towards the Jews in the period 1985-88 has to be that there was still some way to go before Soviet progress on the issue could be deemed satisfactory. This was illustrated by the continuing concern conveyed by the Americans to Moscow even by 1988, as at the Moscow summit. So if trade pressure was indeed a determinant of Soviet policy on emigration it is fair to say that it had achieved very limited results in the years 1985 to 1988.

Conclusions

In conclusion it can be said that the use of United States trade pressure to secure political objectives - namely improvements in Soviet policy on human rights, in the areas of dissent and Jewish emigration had if any very limited success.

Beginning with the question of dissent, the Soviet authorities throughout 1985 to 1988 displayed their customary harshness towards dissidents through the continued use of imprisonment, internal exile and incarceration in psychiatric hospitals, on top of the general mistreatment of political prisoners involving harsh conditions at labour camps, forced starvation, torture and the use of powerful drugs. Soviet citizens continued to be denied basic freedoms enjoyed in the West, and the country was ranked among the least free nations in the world with its citizens having to endure the lowest level of political rights and civil liberties as measured by Freedom House in New York in its annual publication the *Comparative Survey of Freedom* (see Table 5.3).

The launch of Gorbachev's programme of perestroika and glasnost provided some optimism that lasting change could be on the way in 1987 but this never really materialised, largely because Soviet laws remained basically unaltered, thus there still were no legal or constitutional guarantees protecting individuals from political arrests and safeguarding fundamental freedoms.

Moving on to the issue of Jewish emigration, improvements in the rates of Jewish emigration, in terms of the number of Jews wanting to emigrate, were largely not forthcoming with the exception of 1987 and 1988, two years which saw large increases in Jewish emigration. But even these increases failed to satisfy the Americans who cited the growing number of refuseniks in proportion to those granted exit visas. To add to this, the number of Jews who emigrated in the years 1985-88 fell by 6,316 from the period 1980-84 (see Table 5.4).

All in all, United States trade pressure had not achieved its political goals in the area of human rights, something acknowledged even by the Americans themselves. In March 1988, Deputy Secretary of State John Whitehead indicated that Soviet actions on human rights, while promising, had not gone far enough to justify an easing of U.S. restrictions on trade.[90] Similarly in April 1988 the U.S. Commerce Secretary Verity pointed out that the United States was unlikely to grant most-favoured nation status to Moscow until it had made more progress in human rights such as Jewish emigration.[91] President Reagan at his summit meetings with Gorbachev was quick to denounce Soviet human rights practices, seen quite vividly during the Moscow summit when both leaders were engaged in a heated discussion on the issue, providing further evidence that the Americans were far from satisfied with the changes that had taken place in Soviet human rights behaviour. Any improvements in Soviet domestic behaviour had been more cosmetic than real. The use of trade pressure throughout the 1980s had not succeeded in altering Soviet policies to the desired extent as witnessed by the analysis earlier in the chapter. By the end of 1988 the Soviet Union under Gorbachev was still some way behind in meeting its international obligations on human rights, such as satisfying the criteria set out in the Helsinki Final Act, something which the United States had stressed all along Moscow had to achieve.

Notes

1. On this question, and on the general concept of trade pressure applied for political purposes see the following: David W. Hunter, *Western Trade Pressure on the Soviet Union* (Macmillan 1991); Gary Hufbauer, and Jeffrey J. Schott, *Economic sanctions in Support of Foreign Policy Goals* (Washington 1983); Philip Hanson, *Western Economic Statecraft in East-West Relations* (London: Routledge and Kegan Paul for the Royal Institute of International Affairs, Chatham House Papers no. 40, 1988); David Baldwin, *Economic Statecraft* (Princeton University Press 1985).
2. Public Law 93-618, *The Jackson - Vanik Amendment* 1975.
3. This was illustrated by Ambassador Walter Stoessal Jr., Under Secretary for Political Affairs, in a statement before the subcommittee on human rights and international organisations of the House Foreign Affairs Committee on July 14 1981 (see *Department of State Bulletin* Vol. 81, September 1981, pp.42-43) when he said that "this commitment to human rights ... is an expression of values deeply held by the American people themselves". He went on "our commitment to human rights is fundamental". During this statement he also emphasised that "the protection and enhancement of human rights" was "a principal goal of the Reagan administration" and an integral element of its foreign policy.
4. On Human Rights in the Soviet Union and Eastern Europe see: David Lane, 'Human Rights Under State Socialism', *Political Studies*, Volume 32, No. 3, September 1984 pp.349-368; Jane L. Curry, *Dissent in Eastern Europe* (New York: Praeger, 1983); Albert Szymanski, *Human Rights in the Soviet Union* (London, Zed press, 1984).
5. For excerpts of the Final Act see: *International Human Rights - Documents and Introductory Notes* (Vienna 1993), pp.103-118; See also T. Buergenthal (ed) *Human Rights, International Law and the Helsinki Accord* (1977).
6. See p.106 of *International Human Rights - Documents and Introductory Notes*, which deals with basket 111.
7. *NATO Review*, No. 2 April 1980, p.6.
8. *Ibid*, p.7.
9. *Department of State Bulletin*, Vol. 81 (July 1983), pp.65-72.
10. *Congressional Quarterly Almanac 1982*, pp.22-E.
11. *Foreign Affairs*, Volume 64 (1985-86) Fall 1985, pp.1-12.
12. On dissent in the Soviet Union and Eastern Europe see: Rudolf L. Tokes (ed), *Dissent in the USSR* (Baltimore, Maryland: John Hopkins University Press, 1975); Curry, *Dissent in Eastern Europe*; F.J.M. Feldbrugge, *Samizdat and Political Dissent in the Soviet Union* (Leyden: Sijthoff, 1975); Peter Reddaway, 'Dissent in the USSR', *Problems of Communism*, Volume 32, No.6 (November-December 1983), pp.1-15.
13. Amnesty International released a report detailing the conditions and treatment endured by political prisoners in the USSR in 1979 - an updated version of a 1975 report. The report is titled *Prisoners of conscience in the USSR*, 2nd edition, (London: Quatermaine House, 1980).
14. U.S. Department of State, *Country Reports on Human Rights Practices 1979*

(Washington, D.C., U.S. Government Printing Office, 1980).

15. *Ibid*, 1980.
16. *Ibid*, 1981 and 1982.
17. *Ibid*, 1983.
18. See Nora Levin, *The Jews in the Soviet Union since 1917*, Volume 2 (New York University Press, 1988). This book provides a fairly comprehensive treatment of the condition and position of Jews in the Soviet Union since 1971, with Chapters 31 and 32 dealing specifically with Jewish emigration; see also US Senate 98th Congress, 1st session '*Soviet Jewry - Hearing and Markup*' before the Subcommittee on Human Rights and International Organisations of the Committee on Foreign Affairs and the Commission on Security, and Cooperation in Europe House of Representatives', June 23 and 28, 1983 (Washington D.C. U.S. Government Printing Office, 1984). These hearings were held to review the plight of Jews in the Soviet Union; Victor Zaslavky and Robert J. Brym, *Soviet-Jewish Emigration and Soviet Nationality Policy* (Macmillan 1983).
19. See p.118 of *International Human Rights: Documents and Introductory Notes* for excerpts of the Concluding document of the Madrid meeting of September 6, 1983.
20. On a representative statement of the Soviet position see A. Rukhadze, *Jews in the USSR* (Moscow: Novosti 1982). In theory there was no discrimination according to the Soviet authorities' since it was outlawed in the constitution. Furthermore the Soviets claimed that there were no unreasonable obstacles set in the way of individuals wanting to emigrate.
21. *Violation of the Helsinki Accords: USSR* (International Helsinki Federation for Human Rights, November 1986, Vienna) p.88.
22. *Human Contacts, Reunion of Families and Soviet Jewry* (report prepared by the Institute of Jewish Affairs in London, 1986) - see pp.29-31 for some of the official reasons given by Soviet authorities for denying exist visas.
23. *Ibid*. pp.31-39. See also pp.103-119 of *Violations of the Helsinki Accords: USSR* which cites evidence of actual cases involving harassment and mistreatment of refuseniks and Jews who have applied to emigrate.
24. p.40, *Soviet Jewry - Hearing and Markup*... see also: Theodore H. Friedgut, 'Soviet Anti-zionism and Anti-semitism - Another cycle', *Soviet-Jewish Affairs*, Vol.14, No.1, 1984. This article looks at what it calls the background to the current campaign against Jews initiated under Andropov.
25. See *Pravda*, April 22, 1983, p.4; see also pp.41-47 of *Soviet Jewry - Hearing and Markup* ..... which analyses and comments upon the purpose and creation of the anti-zionist committee.
26. *Human Contacts, Reunion of Families and Soviet Jewry*, p.25.
27. *Soviet Jewry hearing and markup* ....., p.2; see also *The Economist*, April 16-22 1983, p.64.
28. *Soviet Jewry hearing and markup*...., p.10.
29. *Ibid.*
30. *Amnesty International Report 1983*, p.284.
31. *Ibid*, 1984, p.314.
32. For a list of some of the International organisations and bodies working for the protection of human rights in the Soviet Union see *Human Rights Internet Directory: Eastern Europe and the USSR* (Harvard Law School, 1987).

33. See *Ibid*, for a list of some of the human rights movements in the Soviet Union and Eastern Europe.
34. On religion and politics in the USSR since the 1917 revolution see: R.F. Millar and T.H. Rigby (ed), *Religion and Politics in Communist States* (Canberra, 1986), Chapters 2, 3, and 9; Sabrina P. Ramet, *The Politics of Religion in Eastern Europe and the USSR* (Indiana University Press, 1987), Chapter 1.
35. *Amnesty International Report 1986,* p.312.
36. *Country Reports on Human Rights Practices 1985*, p.1122.
37. *Amnesty International Report 1987*, p.323.
38. *Department of State Bulletin,* Vol. 81 (July 1983), pp.65-72.
39. *Amnesty International Report 1987*, p.219.
40. *Ibid,* 1986, p.312.
41. *Ibid,* p.310.
42. *Country Reports on Human Rights Practices 1985*, p.1122.
43. *Amnesty International Report 1986,* p.309.
44. *Country Reports on Human Rights Practices 1985,* p.1123.
45. *Amnesty International Report 1987*, p.322.
46. *Ibid.*
47. On the abuse of psychiatry in the Soviet Union see Robert Von Voren (ed), *Soviet Psychiatric Abuse in the Gorbachev Era* (Amsterdam, 1989); Sidney Bloch, *Soviet Psychiatric Abuse: The Shadow Over World Psychiatry* (London Gollancz, 1984).
48. *Amnesty International Report 1987*, p.324.
49. *Ibid.*
50. *Country Reports on Human Rights Practices 1987*, p.1054.
51. *Amnesty International Report 1988*, p.220.
52. *Country Reports on Human Rights Practices 1988,* p.1215.
53. *Amnesty International Report 1989*, p.237.
54. *Pravda*, September 17, 1987, pp.1-2.
55. *Amnesty International Report 1988*, p.218.
56. See *Country Reports on Human Rights Practices 1988,* p.1221; see also for text of the decree in *Izvestia* July 29 1988, p.2.
57. *Country Reports on Human Rights Practices 1988*, p.1221.
58. *Ibid,* p.1222.
59. This speech is in *Pravda*, December 8, 1988, pp.1-2; it is also analysed in the *New York Times* December 9 1988, p.17.
60. *Congressional Quarterly Almanac 1988*, p.463.
61. *Ibid.*
62. *Ibid*, p.462.
63. *Country Reports on Human Rights Practices 1987*, p.2.
64. *Amnesty International Report 1988,* p.218.
65. *Ibid.*
66. *Country Reports on Human Rights Practices 1988*, p.2.
67. *Ibid,* 1985, p.1133.
68. *Ibid,* p.1123.
69. *Amnesty International Report 1986*, p.313.
70. The International Helsinki Federation is a non - governmental organisation that seeks to promote compliance of the signatory states with the human rights

provisions of the Helsinki Final Act.

71. *Violation of the Helsinki Accords: USSR*, p.99.
72. *New York Times* July, 8, 1985, p.17.
73. *Soviet Diplomacy and Negotiating Behaviour - 1979-88: New Tests for U.S. Diplomacy,* Committee on Foreign Affairs Volume 11, p.284, (Washington D.C. Government Printing Office, 1988).
74. *Human Contacts, Reunion of Families and Soviet Jewry*, p.27.
75. U.S. Government, *Implementation of the Helsinki Accords. Hearings before the Commission on Security and Cooperation in Europe*. 99th Congress, Bern Human contacts experts' meeting, March 18 and June 18 1986, (Washington, D.C. U.S. Government printing office, 1986), p.53.
76. *Ibid,* p.55.
77. Ronald Reagan, *An American life* (New York, Simon and Schuster, 1990), p.705.
78. *New York Times,* October 11, 1986, p.1.
79. According to Jewish activists - reported in *New York Times* February 20, 1987, p.8.
80. *Congressional Quarterly Almanac 1988*, p.462.
81. *New York Times*, February 20, 1987, p.8.
82. *Country Reports on Human Rights Practices 1987*; see also *New York Times* November 8, 1987, p.1.
83. See Sidney Heitman 'The Third Soviet Emigration', *Soviet Jewish Affairs*, Vol. 18, No.2, 1988 in which Heitman foresees the possibility of a significant increase in Jewish emigration in the years ahead if 1988 levels continue.
84. *Congressional Quarterly Almanac 1988*, p.462.
85. *Izvestia* June 1, 1988, p.5.
86. *Congressional Quarterly Almanac 1988*, p.462.
87. *Pravda,* December 8, 1988, pp.1-2.
88. *Congressional Quarterly Almanac 1988* p.463.
89. *Human Contacts, Reunion of families and Soviet Jewry*, p.27.
90. *New York Times,* March 6, 1988, p.10.
91. *Ibid*, April 15, 1988, p.17.

6 Assessing the Political Success of American Trade Pressure: 2 - Soviet Involvement in the Third World and Regional Conflicts

Introduction

This second chapter assessing the political success of American trade pressure will look at what was the second issue of concern to the United States - the level of Soviet involvement in the third world and regional flashpoints.[1] The format used in the previous chapter will be applied again.

Section one will restate American concern about the scale of Soviet intervention in the third world by giving a brief account of the high level of Soviet involvement in the third world in the 1970s which continued into the 1980s[2] and which attracted retaliatory American measures such as trade pressure. Section two, the main section, will judge whether U.S. trade pressure had the desired effect of inducing a change for the better as the U.S. saw it in the period 1985-88, by making the USSR limit or substantially decrease its military involvement in the third world.

To do this will require a fairly comprehensive statistical analysis in order to determine the level of Soviet involvement in the third world, and to assess whether Moscow had increased or decreased its commitments in the region. Constant comparison of the years 1985-88 with the period 1979-84 when the Soviets were particularly active in the third world will be necessary. Such indicators as: the value of arms sales; the share of Soviet arms exports to the regions of the third world; and the presence of Soviet military personnel in various developing countries will help to aid the analysis. The main aim of this chapter is not to look at Soviet involvement in the global community but instead to focus attention on the key client states of Moscow in each part of the third world, especially those countries whose close military association with Moscow was of particular concern to Washington. In view of this the analysis will be confined largely to: Cuba and Nicaragua in Central America; Angola, Mozambique, and Ethiopia in Africa; and Afghanistan in Asia. In addition there will be some analysis of Soviet military assistance to the third world countries as a whole, which will be referred to in this context as developing countries, as well as Soviet arms transfers, and deliveries by regional breakdown.

1. Restating American Political Objectives and Concerns over Soviet Third World Behaviour

Like human rights, Soviet involvement in the third world had attracted considerable American criticism and was a major bone of contention in Soviet-American relations.[3] Indeed it was the direct Soviet involvement in Afghanistan which had triggered the rapid deterioration in Soviet-American relations, and which had invited a harsh American response under Carter and then Reagan.[4] This tough American response involved the use of trade pressure in order to induce more acceptable Soviet behaviour in the international arena (as well as in domestic policy e.g. the issue of human rights - see chapter 5). The United States' more short term and immediate response to Soviet involvement in the third world saw President Reagan initiate a more offensive policy which came to be termed the 'Reagan doctrine',[5] and which involved American support for guerilla forces who were struggling to overthrow communist regimes.

U.S. concern in the 1980s over Soviet activities in the third world stemmed from the growing, direct and indirect Soviet involvement in the countries of the third world, which was posing an ideological, political, economic and military challenge to American interests, as well as to America's own third world allies. Over a period of six years between 1974-80, Ethiopia (1974), South Vietnam (1975), Angola and Mozambique (1975), Afghanistan (1979) and Nicaragua (1980) fell successively into the hands of ruling groups closely aligned with the USSR. Moscow continued to provide military assistance and support to these countries well into the 1980s as shown in Table 6.1. Table 6.1 shows that the USSR's arms transfers to major allies in Africa and Latin America increased considerably in value from the period 1974-78 to the period 1979-83. In the case of the major African allies of Moscow - Angola, Mozambique, and Ethiopia - the Soviets consolidated their active involvement in Sub-Saharan Africa which had occurred during the 1970s by increasing their arms transfers to these countries by large amounts. Also, in Latin America after 1979 and up to 1983 Nicaragua had become the joint second major recipient of Soviet military support along with Peru in terms of its overall share of arms transfers (after Cuba) in that region.[6] The Soviets supplied Managua with 36% of all arms transfers to that country in the period 1979-83.[7] This was in notable comparison to the pre-1979 period during which Moscow supplied no arms to Nicaragua, which was ruled by a right wing government at that time.[8] In the case of Cuba, Moscow accounted for 98% of the value of arms transfers to that country during 1979-83[9] which was about the same as for the previous period 1974-78.[10]

Table 6.1 Value of Arms Transfers by the Soviet Union to Key Soviet Clients, 1974-78 and 1979-83 (in millions of current dollars)

Recipient Country	Supplier: Soviet Union	
	1974-78[a]	1979-83[b]
Nicaragua	-	100
Angola	410	1500
Mozambique	130	525
Ethiopia	1300	1800
Cuba	675	3100

[a] *Source*: United States Arms Control and Disarmament Agency (ACDA), *World Military Expenditures and Arms Transfers, 1969-1978* (Washington D.C., U.S. Government Printing Office, 1980).
[b] United States ACDA, *World Military Expenditures and Arms Transfers 1985* (Washington D.C., U.S. Government Printing Office, 1985).

Not only did the Soviet Union continue to provide substantial military assistance to individual key allies in the third world, its overall value of arms transfers to the developing world as a whole remained very high. This can be revealed by the fact that in the period 1974-78, the USSR's value of arms transfers to the developing countries amounted to 20800 million current dollars, and it was the second largest supplier (after the United States) of arms to the third world during that period.[11]

However, by 1979 through to 1983 Moscow had not only increased its value of arms transfers to the developing world by a staggering 147% to 51280 million current dollars,[12] it had also taken over as the leading supplier to that part of the world, with a clear lead over the United States. If we look at the picture in terms of deliveries of arms by the Soviet Union to the developing countries, the story is much the same. While between and prior to the period 1973-76 the United States was the leading arms deliverer to the third world,[13] the USSR overtook America for the period 1977-80,[14] a trend which continued into the next period - 1981-84 - by which time the Soviets had delivered a further 38 billion current dollars worth of arms to the third world.[15]

The American Department of Defense estimated that by 1984 the Soviet Union had around 139000 military personnel in various third world regions.[16] These Soviet personnel comprised of troops engaged in direct combat as in Afghanistan, and military and technical advisers who were present in many third world countries. In addition there were proxy allies of the Soviet Union, chiefly the Cubans fighting on behalf of Moscow. It was estimated that by 1984 there were around 40,000 Cubans, mainly troops present in the client states of the Soviet Union such as Angola, Ethiopia, and Nicaragua.[17]

The Soviet-Cuban axis dominated by massive Soviet military and economic support for Cuba was a major irritant in American - Soviet relations ever since Castro's regime came to power on the island. This was especially because of Cuba's close proximity to the United States, and Washington's suspicions that increased Soviet military aid to Cuba and then Nicaragua after 1979 stemmed from the fact that "Moscow recognises that political instability in America's backyard furthers Soviet interests".[18]

Since 1960 to 1985 the Soviet Union supplied almost $6 billion worth of military aid to Cuba.[19] This military support comprised of significant weapons systems with Moscow undertaking to upgrade Cuban forces.

In addition the value of arms transfers from the Soviet Union to Cuba in the period 1974-78 amounted to 675 million dollars.[20] Since the overall value of arms transfers to Cuba was also 675 million dollars for that period, Moscow had accounted for 100% of all arms transferred to Cuba.[21] In the period 1979-83 the total value of arms transfers to Cuba was 3140 million dollars of which 3100 million dollars worth came from the USSR, a share of 99% for Moscow.[22]

Cuba's importance to the Soviet Union as an vital strategic ally in the third world was further highlighted by the presence of a Soviet combat brigade in Cuba, and the presence of Soviet military advisers. In return for Soviet military and economic aid, Havana sent its troops to fight in order to promote and protect Soviet interests in regional conflicts, particularly in Africa. As the US Defense Department noted "Soviet proxies are particularly active in Sub-Saharan Africa", the most important of these being Cuba and East Germany.[23]

Soviet involvement in the third world was part of the superpower rivalry which was a characteristic of the Cold War. The increased Soviet activity in the third world in the 1970s saw Moscow take advantage of the weakness of the United States in the international arena at the time. For the Soviet Union the third world offered ".... ripe opportunities for expansion and lower risks of superpower confrontation".[24] According to the United

States the USSR took advantage of the period of detente between the two countries to expand its power and influence in the third world, and at the same time establish a political, military and economic foothold in the region.

Furthermore, Washington believed that Moscow exploited third world nations, and in its bid to expand its influence the USSR vigorously promoted the anti-colonial cause. All this was done at the expense of Western interests. The transfer of substantial arms to third world countries, many of whom were engaged in civil wars, saw Washington accuse Moscow of precipitating regional instability and helping to destroy the chance of any peaceful resolution of third world disputes. Moscow was also seen as forcibly imposing Marxist regimes on third world countries through the direct and indirect use of force.

When taking office, Reagan was quick to express strong objections, and denounce the Soviet Union's direct and indirect use of force in the third world. The Reagan administration characterised the USSR as the "key instigator and exploiter of conflict throughout the third world"[25] and the root cause of the instability affecting many parts of Latin America and Southern Africa. Reagan argued that detente had not served the purpose of moderating Soviet behaviour. Instead, he noted that the Soviets had taken advantage of the increase in trade which had occurred during the detente years without moderating their behaviour. Rather "the USSR had continued to pursue a foreign policy that includes an aggressive expansion of Soviet influence abroad"[26] and "over the past decade, the USSR had become increasingly active in the third world..".[27] Reagan stressed that such aggressive Soviet policies would now meet "a firm Western response".[28]

However, he also emphasised that if the Soviet leadership was willing to improve "its people's lives rather than expanding its armed conquests" this would attract a positive Western response in the form of "expanded trade and other forms of cooperation".[29] During this address on East-West relations, Reagan also stressed that "regional stability with peaceful change" would be an essential element in establishing peace with the Soviet Union.[30]

In a statement to the Senate Foreign Relations Committee on June 15, 1983, Secretary of State George Shultz heavily criticised what he called "the unconstructive Soviet involvement, direct and indirect in unstable areas of the third world" which had blocked peaceful solutions there.[31] The fact was that the Soviet Union's extension of its influence in the third world ran counter to American and Western interests in general because it saw Moscow impose the very ideology and system based on Soviet style communism and characterised by repression of human rights and essentially totalitarian in nature, which the U.S. and its allies were working to alter in the Soviet Union itself.

Therefore on the question of Soviet involvement in the third world, the United States was seeking an end to Soviet activism in the developing world through the use of proxy allies and Soviet military advisers. In addition it wanted to see an end to the Soviet occupation of Afghanistan and a diminishing of arms transfers to third world clients.

In response to the substantial Soviet military involvement in the third world during the 1970s, the United States had largely done nothing. However the invasion of Afghanistan by Soviet troops saw Moscow extend its third world 'adventurism' to an unprecedented level, through the direct use of force. Thus, the Americans in the 1980s, first under Carter, and then most notably under Reagan, formulated a more active policy in response to "Soviet aggression" in the third world than mere verbal condemnation. Trade pressure was to be one of the instruments of this more active American approach by which Washington hoped to relay its concern to Moscow, and hope to influence future Soviet conduct. Although trade pressure did not deter the USSR from continuing its substantial involvement in the third world in the early 1980s, the question is, did trade pressure eventually show signs of success from 1985 onwards when Gorbachev came to power? This is the question which we will address in the following section.

2. The Effect of United States Trade Pressure on Soviet Involvement in the Third World and Regional Conflicts 1985-88

As mentioned before this final section will analyse whether the USSR showed any willingness to withdraw from the substantial military commitments it had undertaken in parts of the third world, especially during the 1970s, and which had continued into the 1980s.[32]

When Mikhail Gorbachev came to power in 1985 the Soviet Union was still directly and indirectly engaged in many regional conflicts throughout the world. These included the presence of Soviet troops in Afghanistan, indirect involvement in the Horn of Africa, with Moscow supplying substantial military aid to Marxist regimes which it had helped to prop up in countries like Angola, Ethiopia, and Mozambique, and where Cuban troops were involved in direct fighting to protect Soviet interests. In Central America there was Soviet military assistance to the Sandinistas in Nicaragua and support for left wing guerillas in EI Salvador.[33]

However, Gorbachev's rise to power appeared to herald an imminent change in Soviet policy towards the third world, which would involve a significant de-emphasis on the concept of military aid to Moscow's client states in the developing world.[34]

The 27th CPSU Party Congress which opened in February 1986[35] provided optimism that the Soviet Union was seeking to extricate itself from involvement in the third world, where many of the countries were characterised by instability, and the transfer of military resources to these countries had arguably damaged the chances of peaceful settlement of civil wars that were raging there. At the Party Congress Gorbachev emphasised that Moscow would be looking for ways to shift emphasis from the military to other instruments of policy such as political and economic. Soviet leaders also expressed interest in finding political solutions to third world conflicts.

At a speech on March 11 1985 to the Central Committee on his election as General Secretary, Gorbachev called for sympathy rather than aid for the third world.[36] Gorbachev's seemingly changing position regarding the third world was based on a number of factors such as a negative evaluation of the cost of Soviet involvement in the region over the years, the priority attached to internal domestic needs, and the need for far reaching domestic reforms with domestic policy being more important than foreign policy; and his interest in improving East-West relations, realising that Soviet activities in the third world had harmed relations with the United States and had attracted Western political and economic pressure.

Actions speak louder than words. Were Gorbachev's pronouncements in 1985 and 1986 signalling a reduction of military involvement by Moscow in the developing world, and a commitment to peaceful settlement of regional conflicts, backed up by Soviet behaviour in the areas?

Figure 6.1 (a)

Value of Arms Transferred by the USSR to Key Third World Client States, 1979-83

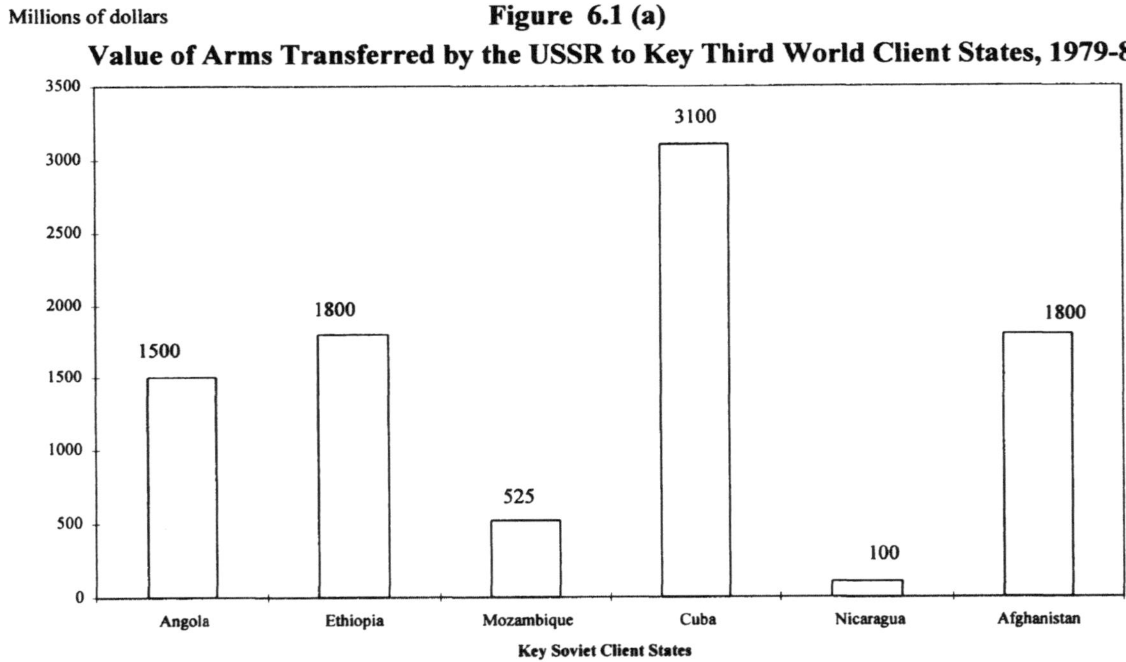

Source : United States ACDA, World Military Expenditures and arms Transfers 1985 (Washington DC US Govt. Printing office 1985)

Figure 6.1 (b)

Value of Arms Transferred by the USSR to Key Third World Client States, 1984-88

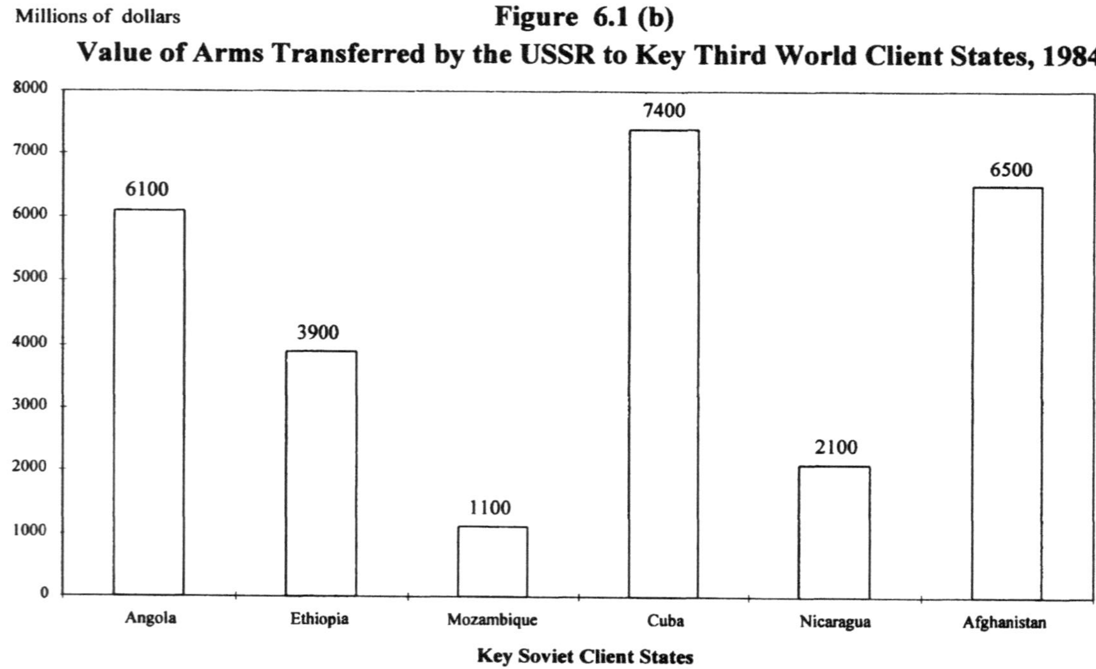

Source : United States ACDA, World Military Expenditures and arms Transfers 1989 (Washington DC US Govt. Printing office 1990)

Figures 6.1 (a) and 6.1 (b) illustrate the value of arms transferred by the USSR to key third world client states in the two periods 1979-83 and 1984-88 (in million of dollars).

Taken together, figures 6.1 (a) and 6.1 (b) reveal a continually intensified level of Soviet involvement in the countries illustrated from the period 1979-83 to 1984-88. Far from backing off, Moscow increased arms transfers to its major allies in the period 1984-88 by substantial amounts from the previous period 1979-83. In the case of all countries shown in figure 6.1 (b) Soviet arms transfers to these nations increased by more than 100% from 1979-83 to 1984-88. Nicaragua saw a staggering increase of 2000% in arms from the Soviet Union. For Angola the increase was a massive 306%, while Afghanistan saw an upward movement of 261%. The other three nations: Cuba, Ethiopia, and Mozambique all saw substantial increments of over 100%.

If we look at the picture in terms of the Soviet Union's share of arms transfers to the developing countries concerned each of the countries (except for Cuba) increased the proportion of supplies they received from Moscow.[37] The USSR accounted for 86% of all arms transfers received by Angola in 1979-83. The figure rose to 88% for the period 1984-88. Mozambique received 97% of all arms from the Soviet Union during 1984-88 up from 77% in the previous period 1979-83. While Nicaragua, which only received 35% of its arms supplies from Moscow during the period 1979-83, increased this proportion to 92% in the period 1984-88.

Table 6.2 shows the % share of arms transfers from the USSR to developing countries by regional breakdown during the periods 1979-83 and 1984-88.

An analysis of Table 6.2 reveals that all third world regions increased their share of arms imported from the Soviet Union in 1984-88 as compared with the period 1979-83. Moreover, Africa, Latin America, and South Asia all imported more than 50% of all these arms from the Soviet Union during the period 1984-88. In other words Moscow accounted for over half of all arms received by the developing regions in the period 1984-88. Even East Asia, although it received less than 50% of its arms from the Soviet Union during 1984-88, had actually increased its supplies from Moscow as compared with the period 1979-83.

So we have seen yet again the importance of Moscow as a source of arms for all parts of the developing world. This is hardly surprising considering that the Soviet Union had major client states dispersed throughout the third world. In Africa there were the traditional Marxist orientated allies in the Sub-Saharan region - Ethiopia, Mozambique, and Angola. In Latin America there was of course Cuba but also Nicaragua, which had become an even more important recipient of Soviet arms in the mid and late 1980s. As the U.S. Defense Department noted, Gorbachev's new thinking had not stopped the Soviet Union "... from increasing military aid to Nicaragua from $280 million in 1985 to well over $500 million in 1988...".[38] Furthermore "Cuba remains the Soviet Union's principal client in the Western Hemisphere and a huge recipient of Soviet military aid ....." which amounted to $1.5 billion in 1988.[39] In South Asia there was the Soviet backed regime in Afghanistan which received a constant supply of Soviet military assistance. In East Asia there was the usual military assistance to communist countries such as Vietnam, Cambodia, Laos, and North Korea. As we have seen therefore, Moscow continued under Gorbachev in the post 1985 period to be the dominant supplier of arms to the third world nations.

Table 6.2 Share of Arms Supplied by the USSR to Third World Regions, 1979-83 and 1984-88

Period	Share of Arms Supplied to Third World Regions	
1979-83[a]	Africa	49%
	Latin America	30%
	South Asia	61%
	East Asia	34%
1984-88[b]	Africa	65%
	Latin America	55%
	South Asia	73%
	East Asia	41%

[a] *Source:* U.S. ACDA, *World Military Expenditures and Arms Transfers* (Washington D.C. US Government Printing Office,1985).
[b] *Source*: U.S. ACDA, *World Military Expenditures and Arms Transfers* (Washington D.C. US Government Printing Office, 1990).

If we look at arms deliveries by the Soviet Union to the developing world in terms of regional breakdown, the story is again familiar. Africa, Latin America, South and East Asia all saw increases in arms deliveries from the Soviet Union in the period 1985-87.[40] There were falls in arms deliveries in 1988 in the case of Africa and East Asia but these were minor.[41] By 1986 the USSR was delivering well over 50% of all arms to the different regions of the third world with this situation continuing more or

Figure 6.2

Arms Transfer Deliveries by the USSR to the Third World, 1980-88

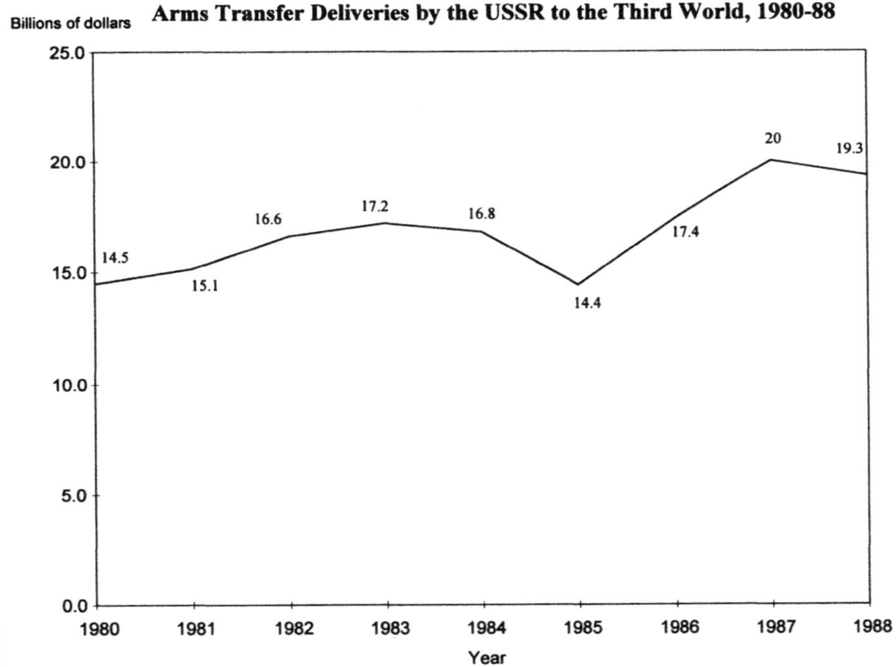

Source : *US ACDA, World Military Expenditures and Arms Transfers 1989 (Washington DC US Govt. 1990)*

less unchanged in 1987 and 1988.[42] Therefore, there is no surprise when we look at arms deliveries by the USSR to the developing world *as a whole*, that there is no evidence of a reduction in Moscow's deliveries of arms to the third world in the period 1985-88, (see Figure 6.2). Apart from a fall in 1985, arms deliveries assumed the pattern prevalent throughout the pre-1985 period with an increase of 20% in 1986 followed by another increase in 1987, this time of 15%. The fall in 1988 was a small one of only 4%. Perhaps more significantly Soviet arms deliveries were worth $20 billion in 1987, the largest figure in the whole of the period 1980-88. The figure of $19.3 billion for 1988 was the second largest in the whole of the period.

Even more significantly the Soviet Union's share of arms deliveries increased in the years 1985, 1986, 1987, and 1988.[43] In fact by 1988 the USSR was supplying over 50% of all arms deliveries received by the developing world.[44] Indeed the USSR's share of 51% for 1988 was the highest since 1980.[45] In other words not since 1980 had the USSR delivered over 50% of arms to the developing countries.

Table 6.3 (a) Number of Arms Delivered by the USSR to the Developing World by Major Weapon Type, 1979-83

Weapon Type	Number Delivered
Land Armaments	23605
Aircraft	3680
Missiles	12280
Naval Craft	214

Note: The category Land Armaments include tanks, artillery, and armoured personnel carriers while Aircraft include combat aircraft and helicopters.
Source: U.S. ACDA, *World Military Expenditures and Arms Transfers 1985* (Washington D.C. U.S. Government Printing Office, 1985).

A look at the number of arms supplied by the Soviet Union by major weapon type will give an indication of Moscow's contribution to the weapons arsenal of third world countries. The major categories of weapons delivered by the Soviet Union to third world nations is illustrated in Tables 6.3 (a) and 6.3(b). We can see from Tables 6.3 (a) and 6.3 (b) that although the actual number of different weapons supplied by the USSR to developing countries fell in quantity terms (except for missiles) in the period 1984-88 as compared with the period 1979-83, this was due largely to the fact that there was an overall decline in the import of such weapons by the developing countries in the 1984-88 period.[46] Furthermore, despite the fall in the number of such weapons supplied, the Soviets actually increased the proportion of such weapons supplied.[47] This is highlighted by the fact that Moscow increased the proportion of land armaments it was supplying from 37% to 46%. The proportion of aircraft supplied increased from 43% to 47%, while the supply of missiles increased from 57% to 58% from the period 1979-83 to 1984-88.

Table 6.3 (b) Number of Arms Delivered by the USSR to the Developing World by Major Weapon Type, 1984-88

Weapon Type	Number Delivered
Land Armaments	15940
Aircraft	2538
Missiles	16480
Naval Craft	149

Note: The category Land Armaments include tanks, artillery, and armoured personnel carriers while Aircraft include combat aircraft and helicopters.
Source: U.S. ACDA, *World Military Expenditures and Arms Transfers 1989* (Washington D.C. U.S. Government Printing Office, 1990).

The presence of military personnel, whether actual troops involved in combat or military or technical advisers involved in training the local military in maintenance and tactics, and in the construction of military facilities in a country, can help to provide a clearer picture of the human rather than material involvement by a country in a region. In the case of the Soviet Union and its proxy ally, the Cubans, the number of military personnel present in various third world regions is shown in Tables 6.4 (a) and 6.4 (b). Tables 6.4 (a) and 6.4(b) reveal that by the end of 1988 the Soviet Union had (excluding Afghanistan where Soviet troops had already begun withdrawing following the signing of a peace accord earlier in 1988) approximately the same number of military personnel in each of the regions indicated as it did at the end of 1984 (see Table 6.4 (a)) indicating a continuing Soviet military presence in its by now traditional heartland regions of Africa, Asia and Latin America. The same can be said largely for the number of Cuban military personnel in the third world. The Cubans in fact had increased their number of personnel in the third world by the end of

1988 in comparison to the pre-1985 period (see Tables 6.4 (a) and 6.4 (b), while the number of Cuban military personnel in Latin America in 1988 had fallen since 1984, Havana increased its military personnel in its traditional stronghold - Sub Saharan Africa. In early 1988, the Cubans admitted they had some 40,000 military personnel in Angola, 3000 troops and advisers in Ethiopia, and about 1500 advisers in Nicaragua (this can be seen in Table 6.4 (b).

As a result, even under Gorbachev's leadership the Soviet Union was clearly not interested in scaling down (with the exception of Afghanistan in 1988) its commitment to the third world in the form of military personnel stationed there.

Table 6.4 (a) Soviet Military Personnel in the Third World - 1984 and Cuban Military Personnel in the Third World - 1984

	Soviet Military Personnel	Cuban Military Personnel
Latin America (including Cuba)	7,900	2500 - 3500
Sub-Saharan Africa	3,600 - 4,000	35000 - 37000
Mid-East and North Africa	9,000	500
Asia (including Vietnam)	3,500	-
Afghanistan	115,000	-
Total around	139,400	41,000

Source: United States Department of Defense, *Soviet Military Power 1985* (Washington D.C. U.S. Government Printing Office, 1985).

The analysis has revealed that in terms of the projection of military power in the third world through the supply of arms, and the presence of military personnel,[48] the level of Soviet involvement in the third world remained similar to the pre-Gorbachev years, and which had attracted American trade pressure. It is obvious that even under Gorbachev, Moscow had shown little sign of lessening its military commitment to the third world despite words to the contrary from the Soviet leader in 1985. Washington's continued criticism that the Soviet Union's involvement in the third world, whether through the shipment of arms or through the use of proxies, was contributing to regional conflicts was given some credence by Moscow's continued position of dominant supplier of arms to the third world. By 1987 there was no sign of resolution of any of the major regional conflicts in which the Soviets were directly or indirectly involved. Despite discussion of regional issues by Reagan and Gorbachev at successive summit meetings there had been little movement on the matter.

Table 6.4 (b) Soviet Military Personnel in the Third World - 1988 and Cuban Military Personnel in the Third World - 1988*

	Soviet Military Personnel	Cuban Military Personnel
Latin America (including Cuba)	7,500	1000-1500
Sub-Saharan Africa	4,000	40000-45000
Mid-East and N. Africa	6,000-7000	400
Asia (including Vietnam)	4,000-4,500	-
Afghanistan	less than 200	-
Total around	23,200	47,000

* These figures are Department of Defense Estimates.
Source: United States Department of Defense, *Soviet Military Power 1989* (Washington D.C. U.S. Government Printing Office, 1989).

However, the year 1988 can be regarded as an exception to some extent. It was a year which provided some hope of progress and the possibility that U.S. pressure was beginning to work. In line with peace accords reached at Geneva, Moscow agreed to withdraw its troops from Afghanistan. Also in line with an agreement reached on November 15, 1988 between Angola, the U.S., Cuba, and South Africa, Cuban troops agreed to leave Angola over a period of 27 months. Moreover in 1988 arms transfer agreements between the Soviet Union and the developing world for the supply of Soviet arms fell for the first time since 1983 to 10.3 billion dollars down from 21 billion dollars in 1987. Central America, where a regional peace process collapsed, proved to be a difficult area for resolution of conflict, particularly Nicaragua, on which America and the USSR made no headway. At the Washington summit in 1987, Gorbachev hinted at the possibility of the USSR ceasing arms supplies to Nicaragua but later on it was revealed that such a move was conditional on the United States suspending aid to all other Central American countries, as well as stopping aid to the Contra rebels.[49]

It is clear that while Gorbachev was willing to back negotiated settlements to third world conflicts, he was not willing to curtail to any great extent the Soviet Union's involvement in the region. This is shown by the continued Soviet military aid to third world countries. Perhaps Moscow was keen to strengthen the bargaining position of its client states at any future round of peace talks. The strategy would therefore appear to have been: to continue high levels of military assistance as long as civil wars raged but at the same time back peace efforts in the cause of improving international relations, particularly relations with the United States. The United States Department of Defense noted a disparity between Gorbachev's 'new thinking' and the Soviet Union's actions in the third world.[50] In a speech marking the 70th anniversary of the Russian revolution, a statement by Gorbachev "confirmed that support for revolutionary movements and wars of 'national liberation' is consistent with both the 'new thinking' in foreign policy and with the declared Soviet goal of peaceful coexistence".[51]

As early as 1986 the US Defense Department predicted that:

> there is little chance that the General Secretary's moves to improve the Soviet economy portend a modification of Moscow's fundamental goals. The USSR still seeks to divide the West and destabilise much of the third world through its foreign policy and military actions.[52]

It seems as though this prediction came true if we judge Soviet conduct in the third world over the whole period 1985-88 rather than in any one year. On this basis it is fair to say that improvements in Soviet behaviour as stipulated by Washington did not materialise, and American trade pressure had little impact in dissuading continued Soviet involvement in the third world.

Conclusions

The analysis in this chapter has revealed that Soviet policy on regional issues remained largely unchanged if one looks at the level of military assistance given by Moscow to the various third world Marxist regimes during the period 1985-88. While Gorbachev acknowledged that the USSR's involvement in the third world had been costly, and that he was keen extricate the Soviet Union from regional conflicts in order to concentrate resources on domestic restructuring, the USSR remained the leading supplier of arms to the developing world, while publicly Gorbachev was supporting peaceful settlement of third world disputes. As the US Department of Defense noted "Gorbachev's 'new thinking' primarily reflects a change in style, while his diplomatic initiatives embody new tactics .....".[53] It went on and said that "..... by cultivating a less threatening international image Moscow aims to deflect attention away from Soviet militarism and adventurism in its foreign policy".[54]

Looking at the overall question of Soviet actions in the third world during the 1985-88 period we can see that the conditions which had existed during the years 1980 to 1984 and which had attracted United States trade pressure still existed at the end of 1988 (with the exception of Afghanistan from where the Soviets had began to withdraw). For a start Moscow was still by far the leading exporter of arms to the third world having overtaken the United States in this respect in the mid and late 1970s. This is illustrated in Table 6.5.

Table 6.5 Soviet Union's Share of Total Arms Exports to the Developing Countries, 1980-88

Year	Share of Total Arms Exports (%)
1980	51.8
1981	43.0
1982	42.0
1983	43.8
1984	39.6
1985	40.3
1986	49.2
1987	45.4
1988	51.3

Source: U.S. ACDA, *World Military Expenditures and Arms Transfers 1989* (Washington D.C. US Government Printing Office, 1990), p14.

We can see from Table 6.5 that the USSR actually enjoyed a greater share of arms exports to the developing countries in the years 1986-88 than it did during the years 1981-84. In fact the Soviet Union's share of exports in 1988 matched its share of 1980 when Moscow accounted for more than half of all arms received by the developing world.

Traditional Soviet client states, many of which Moscow had helped to bring to power in various third world regions, were far from abandoned by the USSR under Gorbachev. Instead shipments of conventional arms consisting of land armaments, aircraft, missiles and naval craft continued to pour into third world countries. Cuba as always remained the most important Soviet ally in the third world while support for Nicaragua in the form of military assistance continued to grow. In the first eight months of 1988 "the Soviets provided Nicaragua with over twice the amount of economic and military assistance provided by the United States to all of Central America".[55] Moscow persisted with deliveries of arms to third world regions despite the fact that they represented regional flashpoints in US-Soviet relations. Active Soviet involvement in the third world of a pre - 1985 scale was also portrayed by the continued presence of Soviet, as well as Cuban military personnel in key client states.

There is no doubt that if one compares Soviet activities in the third world during the years 1985-88 with the period 1980-84 there is nothing to suggest that Moscow had diminished its involvement in any way. Civil wars were still raging in countries where the Soviet Union was still heavily involved, e.g. Angola, Nicaragua, Ethiopia, Mozambique. While there was success in Afghanistan the Soviets were still believed to be supplying the Kabul regime with arms even after having agreed to withdraw its troops. Therefore it is fair to say that trade pressure failed to influence changes in Soviet behaviour in the third world as it had failed to do so in the case of Soviet policy on human rights. This view was also largely reflected by the United States government, which noted under Gorbachev only a change in style not substance in the execution of Soviet policy in the third world.

Notes

1. See the following on this: M. Katz (ed.), *The USSR and Marxist revolutions in the Third World* (Cambridge University Press 1990) particularly Chapters 1 and 2; S. Hosmer and T.Wolfe, *Soviet Policy and Practice towards Third World Conflicts* (Lexington Mass: Lexington Books, 1983); Robert Litwak and Neil Macfarlane, 'Soviet Activism in the Third World', *Survival* (International Institute for Strategic Studies (IISS), Volume 29, no. 1 (Jan-Feb 1987)), pp.21-39.
2. See *Ibid.*
3. In an address on May 24, 1981 the then Secretary of State Alexander Haig severely criticised Moscow's involvement in the third world viewing it as having a detrimental effect on the conduct of Soviet-American relations. See *Department of State Bulletin,* Volume 81 (July 1981), pp.9-11.
4. See *chapter 1.*
5. On this see Raymond L. Garthoff, *The Great Transition: American-Soviet relations and the End of the Cold War*, (Brookings institution 1994), pp.692-716.
6. U.S. Arms Control and Disarmament Agency (ACDA), *World Military Expenditures and Arms Transfers 1985* (WMEAT) (Washington D.C. US

Government Printing Office, 1985).

7. *Ibid.*
8. *Ibid. 1969-78* (Washington D.C. U.S. Government Printing Office, 1980).
9. *Ibid, 1985.*
10. *Ibid, 1969-78.*
11. *Ibid.*
12. *Ibid, 1985.*
13. *Ibid.*
14. *Ibid.*
15. *Ibid.*
16. *U.S. Department of Defense, Soviet Military Power 1985.*
17. *Ibid.*
18. *Ibid, 1988*, p.28.
19. *Ibid, 1986*, p.128.
20. U.S. ACDA, *WMEAT 1969-78.*
21. *Ibid.*
22. *Ibid, 1985.*
23. *Soviet Military Power 1983.*
24. *Ibid*, p.92.
25. *Strategic Survey 1982-83*, p.31.
26. *Soviet Military Power 1984.*
27. *Ibid*, p.113.
28. *Congressional Quarterly Almanac 1982*, p.22-D.
29. *Ibid.*
30. *Ibid.*
31. *Department of State Bulletin* Vol. 81 (July 1983), pp.65-72.
32. See *note 2.*
33. In Central America the Soviets were aided by its proxy Cuba. On this question of Soviet and Cuban military power and intervention in Central America see *The Soviet - Cuban connection in Central America and the Caribbean,* Department of State and Department of Defense, March 1985 (Washington D.C. GPO 1985); see also *Cuba's renewed support for violence in Latin America*, US Department of State, Special report, No. 90, December 14, 1981.
34. See Francis, Fukuyama, 'Gorbachev and the Third World', *Foreign Affairs* Volume 64[2], (Spring 1986), pp.715-732.
35. *Pravda*, February 26, 1986, p.1.
36. *Ibid*, March 12, 1985, p.3.
37. See U.S. ACDA, *WMEAT* editions 1985 and 1989.
38. *Soviet Military Power 1989*, p.19.
39. *Ibid*, p.24.
40. U.S. ACDA, *WMEAT 1989.*
41. *Ibid.*
42. *Ibid.*
43. *Ibid.*
44. *Ibid.*
45. *Ibid.*
46. *Ibid.*
47. See *Ibid*, Volumes for 1985 and 1989.

48. For figures on the level of Cuban involvement in the third world and the amount of Soviet military personnel in the Third World see various editions of *Soviet Military Power*.
49. *Congressional Quarterly Almanac 1988*, p.464.
50. *Soviet Military Power 1988*, p.19.
51. *Ibid*, p.19.
52. *Ibid*, 1986, p.123.
53. *Ibid*, 1988, p.31.
54. *Ibid*, 1988, p.31.
55. *Ibid*, 1989, p.126.

7 U.S. Trade Pressure on the Soviet Union: Reconsidered

Introduction

The beginning of the 1980s witnessed a new era of decline in Soviet-American economic relations, with Washington instigating trade pressure against Moscow in response to the downturn in political relations which followed Soviet intervention in Afghanistan. While the deterioration in superpower relations contributed directly to an adverse effect on trade and economic relations, the emerging rapprochement, when Gorbachev took power in the Soviet Union failed to have any real positive effect on Soviet-American trade and economic relations.

The use of trade pressure embodying the concepts of leverage and linkage was not an entirely new phenomenon in the 1980s. Trade measures against the USSR in pursuit of political goals were used in the 1970s, and in the 1950s and 1960s trade controls, in particular those designed to check the transfer of strategic goods and technology, were very much in operation.

However, the practice of 'economic statecraft',[1] to use Baldwin's term, was executed with more vigour under the Reagan administration, and in a way that led to serious tensions in U.S.-Western European relations.[2] At the heart of this conflict was the differing importance attached to economic relations with the USSR by the United States and by its European allies. The US government believed that improvements in Soviet behaviour could only be achieved through economic punishment, whereas its allies in Europe believed that behaviour could be influenced through economic incentives, i.e. economic detente.

This book has sought to demonstrate that United States inspired trade pressure on the Soviet Union during the years 1980-88 was more of a failure than a success. The measures taken by the United States failed to impose the necessary economic costs on the Soviet Union and as a result failed to alter Soviet domestic and international behaviour during the period 1985-88, with only limited progress (in the US view) made on the domestic front, and that only in 1988, a year which appeared to herald a significant movement towards a liberalisation of Soviet human rights policies.

A combination of factors contributed to the failure of United States trade pressure. Lack of cooperation of allies, stemming partly from alliance disunity, was important, with the role of politics in East-West trade being at the centre of allied friction. Lack of market power in the goods being targeted for trade pressure meant that Moscow could obtain goods from alternative supplier countries. Special features of the Soviet Union have to be remembered - vast resources and a great capacity for autarky. In reality there was a low level of Soviet dependence on Western goods and markets. The Soviet Union's superpower status could not be overlooked. A country like the USSR was unlikely to give in to what it saw as economic blackmail. Soviet leaders throughout the 1980s constantly complained about the American policy of linkage and leverage. As a result if the Soviets were indeed genuinely considering altering their behaviour then they might at the last minute refrain from doing so if they believed that such a move would be perceived as having been made in response to U.S. pressure.

American trade pressure had failed from an economic viewpoint not only in respect of non-strategic goods but also in attempts by the United States to deny strategic goods or technology to the Soviet Union. U.S. unilateral and multilateral measures to restrict technology flows were rendered ineffective by illegal shipments of banned items, limited implementation of laws and regulations by the departments of government, and the problems that beset the multilateral regulatory regime - COCOM.

1. Analysis of the Literature on the use of Economic Measures in Support of Political Goals

This section will analyse the work of various writers on the question of using economic measures to achieve political objectives. The literature on this issue is vast, and this chapter will accordingly make no attempt to refer to all the literature connected to the subject matter of this thesis. Instead it will concentrate on arguably some of the most important works like those of David Baldwin, Margaret Doxey, and more recently David Hunter's book.

If we begin firstly with those who have written in general terms on the question of the use of economic instruments for political goals we could probably divide them into two categories: the OPTIMISTS and PESSIMISTS. The Optimists led by David Baldwin, (and Philip Hanson who wrote in connection with East-West relations) who provides in his work Economic Statecraft[3] a very comprehensive survey of "economics as an instrument of politics".[4] Baldwin's line of argument represents a school of thought which believes that "the utility of economic techniques of statecraft has been ..... underestimated since 1945".[5] He argues that writings on this topic in the past 40 years or so have left the impression that economic measures such as sanctions don't work. Through his thesis Baldwin believes that he has shown the inadequacies of the conventional wisdom that measures of economic statecraft have little use.

However, Baldwin points out that he has by no means argued that the use of economic instruments for foreign policy reasons is necessarily a desirable option. Instead Baldwin's work has aimed "to provide an analytical framework within which reliable knowledge about economic statecraft can be developed to replace the conventional wisdom".[6] In view of this Baldwin sets out his own nine point set of guidelines which according to him should help in forging a more adequate evaluation of the utility of economic techniques of statecraft.[7] Baldwin draws attention to the fact that some successful cases of the use of economic statecraft have been overlooked by scholars because of a lack of understanding of the concept. Baldwin goes on to say that attempts to develop more knowledge about economic statecraft have been hindered by the fact that writers have been too quick to dismiss economic statecraft as useless. "Economic statecraft often works slowly, but this is not necessarily the inherent weakness it is often made out to be".[8]

Despite the optimism prevalent in Baldwin's work, most other writers take a much more sceptical view about the efficacy of economic measures for political purposes. In clear contradiction to Baldwin, Robert Gilpin argues that "the utility of economic sanctions tends to be greatly exaggerated" and that they are of little utility.[9] In other words Gilpin argues that the effectiveness of economic sanctions is overestimated. Similarly Margaret Doxey stated unequivocally that "in none of the cases analysed .... have economic sanctions succeeded in producing the desired political result".[10]

Furthermore, Doxey outlines a number of measures which the target country can take in order to minimise the effect of sanctions, and which can render them virtually useless.[11] These include "adaptation, reduction of external dependence, and possibly the development of new links with non-sanctioning states".[12] Therefore according to Doxey it is hardly surprising that scepticism about their efficacy and concern over their drawbacks are widespread. Doxey stresses that policymakers must consider not only that economic sanctions may fail to alter the target's behaviour "but that they could produce the opposite effects from those intended",[13] for example "the target may be driven to adopt defiant and perhaps more extreme positions as a result of sanctions".[14] Doxey notes however that despite the shortcomings of economic sanctions they continue to be used by governments possibly because they serve purposes other than simply to alter the target nations' political behaviour. They may serve a symbolic purpose in the manner depicted by Hunter,[15] by sending a signal to third states, and to the domestic audience and by demonstrating a willingness to take action, showing leadership qualities, and raising the visibility of an issue.

A very authoritative and clear analysis of the use of 'economic sanctions in support of foreign policy goals' is provided by Gary Hufbauer and Jeffrey Schott,[16] who note that success in the use of sanctions "has proven much more elusive in recent years than in earlier decades".[17] They emphasise that part of the reason for this has been the fact that the frequent use of economic measures to achieve what they call 'modest' political goals have led target nations to become "immune to their impact".[18] This development is connected with the fact that target nations are nowadays less dependent on trade with states imposing the sanctions with "ties between target and sender countries" having become weaker.[19]

Despite this Hufbauer and Schott do not suggest that sanctions should be dismissed outright as instruments of foreign policy. Instead they suggest nine conditions which they argue that policymakers should seriously consider before deploying economic sanctions.[20] Briefly these are the following:

- Don't expect sanctions to achieve too much: The sender nation must not set itself virtually unattainable goals, and should have fairly modest and not inflated expectations.
- The chances of sanctions having the desired impact are greatly enhanced if the target country is much smaller than the sender.
- The weakest and helpless target countries are more likely to yield to the policy objectives of the sender states.
- "The shorter the duration of the sanctions the greater the likelihood of success"[21] since sanctions applied over a longer time period may allow the target nation to develop a greater capacity for self sufficiency, and thus make it immune to the economic hardship implicit in sanctions.
- Comprehensive sanctions that inflict heavy cost on the target are more likely to be successful.
- A country should not use sanctions when the costs to itself are high.
- Sanctions used in conjunction with additional measures such as military will not ensure success, and the accompanying policies will probably not succeed either.
- The greater the number of nations required to implement economic sanctions the less likely that sanctions will be effective.
- Finally Hufbauer and Schott advise that "the sender

government should think through its means and objectives before taking a final decision to deploy sanctions".[22]

Much has also been written on the use of economic instruments to further political objectives in the context of East-West relations, to which we will now turn our attention.

Once again most writers express a less than positive viewpoint on the exercise of trade pressure, in this case by the United States and its European allies against principally the Soviet Union.

Gordon B. Smith offers an analysis of the role played by politics in the East-West economic relationship.[23] Smith outlines his reservations about the use of trade pressure by the Western nations against the USSR since the Second World War, arguing that evidence since 1945 suggests that Soviet international and domestic behaviour can be moderated through a policy of economic detente which offers Moscow positive inducements, making the Soviet Union more cautious about undertaking actions in the future which may threaten the material benefits it gains from cooperation with the West. Whereas a policy of sustained trade pressure against Moscow is likely to elicit more aggressive international behaviour from the Soviets, and harsher domestic policies with the Soviet leadership seeing itself in a position where it has nothing to lose from further provoking the West.[24] Smith goes on to stress that "Western nations must recognise the limits of their ability to moderate Soviet policies".[25]

Others such as Reinhard Rode, Hanns Jacobsen[26] and Peter Knirsch[27] highlight the failure of Western trade pressure against the USSR on the grounds that Western-Soviet economic relations are not suitable for use as instruments of Western policy. This is particularly because the USSR is not "a suitable target for economic pressure because of its remarkable capacity for autarky and independence".[28]

In a view similar to that adopted by Smith, Rode and Jacobsen conclude that the history of US-Soviet economic relations has shown that "economic incentives can be more effective than negative sanctions in the form of embargoes or boycotts....".[29] While Peter Knirsch states clearly that the policy of sanctions used by America against the Soviet Union did not work as it failed to alter the Soviet Union's political conduct.[30]

Despite Smith's reservations about the use of economic punishment to achieve political results, he acknowledged that because there was strategic parity between the United States and the USSR the use of military force in order to satisfy political objectives such as moderating Soviet domestic and international behaviour was no longer an option for the United States. Precisely because of this "economic policies have taken on added significance in East-West relations".[31]

Gunnar Adler-Karlsson, one of the staunchest critics of the effectiveness of Western trade pressure, and someone who has analysed Western trade policies towards Eastern Europe from the early years of the Cold War, sums up his views rather aptly in his statement that "the burden of proof is clearly on those who claim that an embargo policy is an efficient instrument of foreign policy. Experience seems to indicate the contrary".[32] In later works Karlsson extended this view further and concluded that economic sanctions as instruments of foreign policy almost never worked.[33] In the context of US-Soviet relations this view is given further credence by Bruce Parrott's summary that "the 1980s American policy of economic sanctions, or negative linkage has proved even less successful politically...".[34]

Some writers such as Stephen Woolcock expressed concern about the detrimental effect that the frequent use of economic leverage would have on the scale of East-West economic relations, which were already on a very small scale.[35] Woolcock pointed out that since leverage depended on there being East-West trade on a scale that could be exploited for political purposes, the frequent resort to economic leverage threatened to damage East-West relations to such an extent that there would be no leverage to exploit. Like Smith, Woolcock acknowledged that "trade is of limited value as a means of regulating political relations between East and West",[36] and argued that the West should give priority to the economic gains rather than the political advantages to be made from mutual trade. In other words, economic factors and not political factors should dictate trade. Woolcock also mentions that these are precisely the criteria which America's European allies apply in their trade with the Eastern bloc. They see trade as an important stabilising element in East-West relations, and doubt the effectiveness of using trade links as an instrument of East-West politics.[37]

The effectiveness of economic sanctions may also be dependent upon the type of sanctions imposed and the objective. This is the foundation of David Hunter's study: *Western trade pressure on the Soviet Union.*[38] Hunter distinguishes between symbolic and instrumental sanctions. He defines symbolic sanctions as those which are aimed at: deflecting international criticism; appearing concerned about an issue and drawing attention to it; "demonstrating the willingness to take some action"; showing leadership qualities; "and assigning moral judgement or responsibility".[39] Hunter's instrumental objectives include: "encouraging internal resistance or political reforms; deterring undesired action; punishing past errors or extracting reprisals; undermining a political regime; encouraging acceptance of international reforms; ....".[40] In the context of US-Soviet relations examples of symbolic action include Carter's boycott of the Moscow Olympics in

1980 following the Soviet invasion of Afghanistan. Examples of instrumental sanctions can be found in the passing of the Jackson-Vanik Amendment by Congress which was designed to encourage Jewish emigration reforms in the USSR.

According to Hunter, instrumental sanctions provide a "reasonable prospect of success".[41] But their overall success is conditional on factors such as: the sanctioner's power resources; the target nation's level of need for the values being controlled; and the costs of compliance to the target.[42]

Hunter appears to adopt a more neutral stance on the question of using economic means for foreign policy reasons, arguing neither that economic measures such as sanctions are never effective at all nor embracing the view that they have a high success rate. For Hunter it is really a question of satisfying the necessary conditions laid out. Even though it is difficult to establish the political consequences as against the publicly stated objectives of sanctions Hunter believes that "this should not undermine the resort to sanctions as an instrument for achieving political objectives".[43] Having said this Hunter stresses that in the case of American trade pressure on the Soviet Union "there is simply insufficient leverage in trade and economic relations between the USSR and Western nations at the present time to influence key Soviet foreign policy decisions".[44]

Writings on trade pressure in the context of East-West relations have largely revealed, so far, a great deal of scepticism about the successful application of economic pressure against the USSR by Western nations.

However, Philip Hanson is an exception.[45] He is unwilling to write off Western economic measures against Moscow as outright failures, and in this sense provides support for Baldwin's line of argument that the use of economic measures for political goals should not be underestimated. Hanson states that U.S. attempts at economic leverage against the USSR cannot be dismissed as failures. He believes that U.S. sanctions should be judged by their long - term effects on Soviet behaviour, and not just by their apparent influence on the policy which served as the original pretext for each sanction.[46] It is possible that U.S. economic measures may have been successful in inducing caution in subsequent Soviet behaviour in the long term. This is particularly true, Hanson says, in the case of Soviet involvement in the third world where the use of sanctions over the events in Afghanistan and Poland, although it failed to alter Soviet policy in these areas, may have had the long-term effect of instilling caution in future Soviet actions abroad.[47]

Apart from arguing "that U.S. sanctions against the USSR should be judged by their cumulative effect over a lengthy period",[48] Hanson also argues in similar fashion to Hunter on this point that one cannot judge sanctions solely on the basis of what economic effects are achieved since sanctions also serve the purpose of sending signals (what Hunter terms as 'symbolic sanctions') and thus "their outcomes must be interpreted with that in mind".[49]

The overwhelming conclusion that one derives from the selected literature on this topic is that the use of economic instruments to attain political goals is seen largely as an ineffective policy both in the framework of U.S.-Soviet relations, and also in the general context of its usage in international relations. Only a few writers, such as Baldwin and Hanson, have more positive than negative remarks to make about the utility of trade pressure.

2. United States Trade Pressure on the Soviet Union: Conclusions Revisited

The use of trade pressure by the United States in the judgement of this book, failed both in its objective of imposing economic penalties on Moscow for its political behaviour, and also in the overriding aim of altering Soviet political behaviour in both the international and domestic arenas.

Despite this it would be incorrect to conclude that the use of economic pressure by America had no influence whatsoever on Soviet political thinking. There is no doubt that U.S. trade pressure had some bearing on the conduct of Soviet behaviour, with Gorbachev in particular sensitive to the damage to East-West relations and to the Soviet Union's reputation done by international criticism of its actions in the domestic and international arenas.

Nevertheless, the evidence before us suggests - with the possible exception of 1988 - that during the course of 1985-88 there was little to indicate any positive changes in Soviet behaviour as desired by Washington. Even the changes in 1988 represented only the beginning of possible changes to come. Therefore if one is measuring the success of trade pressure in terms of whether it satisfied the political goals of the state deploying it then one can rightly take the line that trade pressure largely failed to produce the desired impact in the period 1985-88. The type of economic measures taken by the United States against the USSR falls more into the category of what Hunter calls 'instrumental sanctions' in the period 1980-88. In the case of human rights (dissent and emigration) the objective was to encourage political reforms and liberalisation. In the case of regional conflicts the aim was to deter undesired action, and end Soviet involvement in the areas concerned.

If we look at the failure of trade pressure to impose the necessary economic costs on Moscow by denying the Soviets access to various commodities, both strategic (technology) and non-strategic, a whole host of reasons may help to explain why this was so.

Not least, one cannot overlook the relatively low level of American-Soviet trade and the corresponding level of economic interdependence between the two countries. The basic fact is that as Peter Knirsch puts it ".... East-West economic relations are relatively insignificant in terms of trade volume, which is particularly true for the Soviet Union, and this greatly limits the effectiveness..." of measures such as sanctions.[50] Hunter makes a similar point in this statement .... that "there is simply insufficient leverage in trade and economic relations between the USSR and Western nations to influence key Soviet foreign policy decisions".[51] If we look at U.S. trade pressure on Soviet exports any success there was overshadowed by the very small level of exports by Moscow to America prior to trade pressure. As a result any effect on the Soviet Union was almost negligible. Similarly for this reason denial of most favoured nation status to the Soviet Union by the United States also had little negative impact on Moscow.

Coupled with the relative insignificance of Soviet-American trade is the fact that goods denied to the Soviet Union were obtained by Moscow through alternative sources. Since U.S. trade pressure was a unilateral policy action (multilateral only to the extent that it was supported by some key allies in Western Europe) it was unlikely to have universal support. Most countries were more than willing to fill the gap vacated by the United States as was illustrated by the U.S. grain embargo of 1980-81. As Hunter says "only if sanctions are supported on a multilateral basis will they be able to generate a substantial level of economic impact on the target country".[52] The key idea here is that it is not multilateral support from allies which was essential but more importantly the support of other countries who were also major suppliers of the goods which were at the centre of U.S. trade denial measures. The availability of substitute countries for most commodities meant that only the formation of a cartel by leading supplier countries could make commodity denial successful.[53] A related problem for the United States was the structure of the market for the various goods which were the target of trade pressure. The markets for these commodities were characterised by a perfectly competitive structure rather than a monopoly one, which greatly diminished the chances of success since no one country could on its own influence the market for these goods.

It also has to be remembered that the United States suffered economic costs itself from its use of trade pressure against Moscow, particularly in the early 1980s when its agricultural sector suffered during the embargo against the USSR, especially as agricultural products dominated its trade with the Soviet Union. In keeping with the conditions laid down by Hufbauer and Schott, one of which states "the more it costs a sender country to impose sanctions, the less likely it is that the sanctions will succeed",[54] it is hardly surprising that American attempts at trade pressure proved unsuccessful, particularly in the early 1980s.

Disagreements, and a conflict of interests to a degree between the United States and its allies in Western Europe on the conduct of trade with the East, and in particular with the Soviet Union, did not help Washington in its bid to use trade pressure against Moscow in order to extract political concessions. The West lacked a coherent policy to tackle this issue with the West Europeans more inclined to use economic incentives to promote changes in Soviet policy, while the United States rejected any use of the 'carrot' but favoured the use of policies symptomatic of economic warfare. As Angela Stent pointed out ".... European states rejected the utility of economic sanctions as an acceptable means of changing Soviet behaviour..".[55]

American unilateral and cooperative attempts with its allies to deprive the Soviet Union of Western technology also proved a failure. The multilateral enforcement mechanism - COCOM - was beset by problems, and U.S. unilateral measures were hampered by a clash of interests within the various U.S. governmental departments between those with pro-trade tendencies and that believed in a more liberal interpretation of technology controls, and those that were concerned about the advantages that were accruing to Moscow from strategic trade with the United States.

The second task of trade pressure is to determine if it was successful in achieving its political goals. The major aims of the United States in its use of trade pressure against the Soviet Union were to alter Soviet performance on human rights (with specific interest in the areas of dissent and Jewish emigration), and to moderate Moscow's involvement in regional conflicts. On this basis trade pressure failed to produce the desired political impact on the Soviet Union. Why? The inability of U.S. trade pressure to change Soviet behaviour is not altogether surprising.

In the first place the failure of U.S. trade pressure to have the desired economic impact limited any prospects of inducing the necessary political changes.

Furthermore, the Soviets had made it clear in the past that they were unlikely to give in to any form of pressure, political or economic. In the early 1980s Soviet officials made it known that any form of linkage between issues such as trade and human rights was unacceptable, and American public criticism of Soviet actions served only to make Moscow more stubborn and less susceptible to change.

Also the changes initiated by Gorbachev were more cosmetic than fundamental. The Soviet leader embarked on a process of change which was more effective in the perception of change which it put across than in the actual results it yielded. Gorbachev had to be careful not to be seen as compromising the Soviet Union's superpower status if he was to be seen as bowing to U.S. pressure. The question of pride and reputation no doubt played some part. Gorbachev's realisation of the need for change in Soviet policy on human rights and in its involvement in areas of regional instability was driven by domestic concerns, and was certainly influenced by the adverse effect of U.S. trade pressure on the USSR which was depriving Moscow of much - needed Western technology and credits. However, even then he was only ready to initiate the process of change not carry it through to the extent that would have satisfied the United States.

The failure of U.S. trade pressure to have the necessary political result could also be linked to the fact that as Hufbauer and Schott outline in their list of advice for the successful application of economic sanctions, sanctions cannot "force strong target countries into making fundamental changes".[56] Furthermore the chances of sanctions having an impact are greater if the target country is much smaller than the sender.[57] In the case of the Soviet Union and the United States it was actually the other way round. In addition it is the weakest and helpless target countries which are more likely to yield to the policy objectives of the sender countries.[58] This was certainly not true of the Soviet Union.

There is no doubt that trying to measure the political success of trade pressure is a difficult task. As Hunter correctly points out "it is not easy to identify and measure political consequences against the publicly stated sanctions goals".[59] If a trade pressure measure is applied in response to a particular action taken by the target, for example an invasion of a country, then one must establish the purpose of the measure. Is it intended simply to express displeasure and anger? In other words is it simply intended to send a 'symbolic' message? Or is its goal to force the target to reverse its action? If it is the latter then it is not difficult to measure effectiveness.

Problems still arise because of the very fact that governments do not always make public or state precisely their intended political goals which makes measuring success even more difficult.

Further problems arise because often the nation practising trade pressure has much wider goals which cannot be met in the short run. What is required then is to monitor the targets' behaviour over a long-term period. The success of trade pressure when it is applied continuously is best judged from an overall perspective and over a long run period rather than episode after episode. This is particularly relevant in the study of the use of U.S. trade pressure against the Soviet Union in the 1980s, which although was initially used in response to specific Soviet behaviour for example the Afghanistan invasion and the Polish crisis, became a systematic policy involving the constant use of trade pressure throughout the 1980s whose success could only be measured over a number of years.

However, a further question has to be addressed when attempting to measure the political success of trade pressure in the long run: where change in targets' actions and behaviour did occur, to what extent can it be attributed to trade pressure? Could it be that other factors played a more decisive role in effecting the change that occurred? This is certainly a complex question, and it is not at all easy to determine the relative influence which various factors had on the conduct of Soviet policy in certain areas. While Moscow may have publicly claimed that U.S. economic pressure was unacceptable and would have no bearing on the execution of Soviet domestic and foreign policy, in its private decision making the Soviet leadership may have had to concede that the cost of U.S. trade pressure was proving detrimental to Soviet interests, and as a result could not be dismissed lightly. At the same time Moscow could claim publicly that changes in policy had not been influenced by U.S. trade pressure but that other factors such as domestic had been responsible for initiating change.

Also, as one would expect, there were no official statements from Soviet officials indicating that U.S. economic pressure had indeed made them rethink their policies. If anything the Soviets often criticised the United States for even contemplating that trade pressure could exert leverage on them.

In the case of Soviet involvement in the third world during the 1980s such problems about the role played by various factors in changing Soviet policy do not really arise since the extent of Moscow's involvement in this area remained largely unaltered. Only in 1988 did there appear to be signs of a rethink in Soviet policy towards the third world. In the case of Soviet human rights performance, changes fairly significant in nature did occur in 1987 and 1988. It is safe to say that these changes can be attributed to a change of leadership since before Gorbachev took power there were no signs of changes to come in the years preceding 1985 or even in the early months of 1985. It appears as though the changes can be attributed to Gorbachev's own initiatives.

Equally it could be argued that since changes were more pronounced in 1987 and 1988, it could be that trade pressure did play a part since it could imply that Gorbachev who came to power in 1985 had by 1987-88 assessed the overall situation and realised that trade pressure was causing unnecessary harm to the USSR, and then undertook changes that would ease such pressure.

A study of the key literature on the use of economic measures for political goals reveals that many writers have neglected to offer an assessment of the political success of trade pressure but have instead paid too much attention to the economic impact generated by trade pressure. An example of this can be seen in Gordon Smith's study[60] in which he concentrates more on the economic impact of trade pressure on various sectors of the Soviet economy rather than on the political reasoning behind Western trade pressure and the Soviet response to it. Doxey[61] herself provides only a brief framework for analyzing the political effect of economic sanctions, and even this is confined to a couple of pages in the final chapter.

Some writers may be forgiven for the absence of a thorough analysis of the political success of trade pressure on the grounds that their study is essentially a work of economics, but even this cannot be accepted as a valid excuse if one takes into account the inseparability of politics and economics in East-West relations.

In fairness there are some such as Hunter who devotes a chapter to the political significance of economic sanctions,[62] and in particular Philip Hanson[63] who offers a concise and coherent analysis of whether different economic measures such as sanctions and embargoes have been successful in altering Soviet behaviour in various areas. Probably most importantly of all Hanson's view that "U.S. sanctions against the USSR should be judged by their cumulative effect over a lengthy period"[64] coincides very closely with the advice on assessing the political effect of trade pressure offered in this thesis, which is that the effectiveness of trade pressure applied in the early 1980s and mid 1980s can only be adequately measured in subsequent years by which time the economic measures implemented have had the chance to make an impact (however the longer the period of time we use to show whether the measures work, the greater the danger that other factors may enter the equation and modify the results, as a result of all this it can be harder to show the intended effect). Furthermore Hufbauer and Schott[65] also devote a chapter in which they concentrate solely on the political variables involved in economic sanctions, and provide a measurement of success that the pursuit of various political goals have had.

Another noticeable deficiency in the literature on trade pressure is that there has as yet been no detailed study specifically on U.S. trade pressure on the Soviet Union, although U.S. trade pressure on the Soviet Union has of course been looked at in the broader context of Western trade pressure on the USSR. However, this is not wholly adequate because of the differences between various members of the Western alliance, most notably between the United States and its European allies. The fact is that the likes of for example Germany and the United States both have differing viewpoints as to the conduct of economic policy towards Moscow.[66] Lack of a single Western policy towards the Soviet Union and differing approaches to achieve political goals means that a separate country by country study would be most appropriate.

In addition most writers tend not to employ the term 'trade pressure' or 'economic pressure' (an exception being David Hunter), which I believe are more comprehensive and accurate terms. This is because the term trade pressure encompasses everything from economic sanctions and embargoes to the denial of most favoured nation status, which is a true reflection of the various economic measures which countries like the United States had at their disposal. Instead most writers appear to have preferred to concentrate on economic sanctions, with little attention having been devoted to other instruments of trade pressure.

Shortcomings can also be detected in the writings of those who have offered something on the political success of trade pressure. The writers have largely failed to take into account the underlying cause of change in Soviet policies. In other words they have failed to establish whether changes in Soviet policy were the result of trade pressure or whether other factors may have played a more decisive role.

There have been many instances where economic pressure to satisfy political objectives has been used by countries like the United States. The application of trade pressure by Washington against the Soviet Union during the 1980s proved to be a failure as the policy objectives were not achieved. This then leads one to a perfectly fair question: does the sanctioning state - in this case the United States - really consider or give much time to the important thinking behind a strategy of trade pressure? Perhaps not. The United States ought to have examined more carefully the probable outcome of such a policy. "The sender government should think through its means and objectives before taking a final decision to deploy sanctions".[67] The failure of trade pressure in this instance does not mean that trade pressure is a redundant policy which has no role to play in international diplomacy. It simply means that caution is required before exercising it, and in some cases the target country is of such a kind that economic pressure may not be the most effective policy instrument. However, in a highly militarized world where the use of force would be highly destructive and as a result is not feasible, trade pressure may be the only suitable or alternative means of influencing another country, which is the position the United States found itself in with regard to the Soviet Union during the period considered in this book.

Notes

1. 'Economic Statecraft' is a term used by David Baldwin in his book of the same name. It means the use of economic instruments to influence or attempt to influence some dimension of the behaviour of other international actors. It is used by Baldwin in the same sense that the term trade pressure is used in this thesis. The concept of 'Economic Statecraft' is analysed in detail in chapter 3 of David A. Baldwin, *Economic Statecraft* (Princeton: Princeton University Press, 1985).
2. A particularly appropriate source on this is: Angela E. Stent (ed.), *Economic Relations with the Soviet Union* (Boulder Co: Westview Press, 1985). Also see Angela E. Stent 'Technology Transfers in East-West Trade The Western Alliance Studies', AE1- *Foreign Policy and Defense Review*, Volume 5, No. 2, 1985.
3. Baldwin, *Economic Statecraft*.
4. *Ibid*, p.3.
5. *Ibid*, p.4.
6. *Ibid*, p.371.
7. *Ibid*, These 9 points are set out by Baldwin on pp.371-374.
8. *Ibid*, p.111.
9. Robert Gilpin, *The Political Economy of International Relations* (Princeton, New Jersey: Princeton University Press, 1987), p.76.
10. Margaret Doxey, *Economic Sanctions and International Enforcement* (Oxford, England: Oxford University Press, 1971), p.139. See also Makio Miyagawa, *Do Economic Sanctions Work?* (Basingstoke Macmillan 1992) in which the author notes a very small number of cases when sanctions were effective. On the whole he sees them largely as failed instruments of policy.
11. Margaret Doxey, *International Sanctions in Contemporary Perspective* (Macmillan Press, 1987), p.111.
12. *Ibid*.
13. *Ibid*, p.146.
14. *Ibid*.
15. David W. Hunter, *Western Trade Pressure on the Soviet Union* (London: Macmillan 1991). Hunter in this book distinguishes between instrumental and symbolic sanctions and objectives.
16. Gary Clyde Hufbauer and Jeffrey Schott, *Economic Sanctions in Support of Foreign Policy Goals* (Institute for International Economics, Washington D.C., October 1983).
17. *Ibid*, p.75.
18. *Ibid*.
19. *Ibid*.
20. *Ibid*, These are described in some detail by Hufbauer and Schott on pp.76-85.
21. *Ibid*, p.80.
22. *Ibid*, p.84.
23. Gordon B. Smith (ed.), *The Politics of East-West Trade* (Westview Press, 1984).
24. *Ibid*, p.27.
25. *Ibid*.

26. See Reinhard Rode and Hanns-D. Jacobsen, (ed), *Economic Warfare or Detente* (Westview Press, 1985).
27. See Peter Knirsch's Chapter in *Ibid*, pp. 86-99.
28. Rode and Jacobsen, *Economic Warfare or Detente*, p.297.
29. *Ibid*, p.295.
30. *Ibid*, p.94.
31. Smith (ed), *The Politics of East-West Trade*, p.1.
32. Gunnar Adler-Karlsson, *Western Economic Warfare 1947-1967* (Stockholm: Almqvist and Wiksell, 1968), p.10.
33. Gunnar Adler-Karlsson, 'The US Embargo, Inefficient and Counterproductive'. *Aussenwirtschaft* (June 1980).
34. Bruce Parrott, (ed), *Trade, Technology and Soviet-American Relations* (Bloomington: Indiana University Press, 1985), p.360.
35. Stephen Woolcock, *Western Policies on East-West Trade* (London: Routledge and Kegan Paul for the Royal Institute of International Affairs, Chatham House Papers 15, 1982).
36. *Ibid*, p.81.
37. *Ibid*, p.79.
38. Hunter, *Western Trade Pressure on the Soviet Union.*
39. Symbolic sanctions are defined by Hunter on pp.44-48 of *ibid.*
40. Instrumental sanctions are defined by Hunter also on pp.44-48 of *ibid.*
41. *Ibid*, p.47.
42. *Ibid.*
43. *Ibid*, p.83.
44. *Ibid*, p.100.
45. Philip Hanson *Western Economic Statecraft in East-West Relations*, (London: Routledge and Kegan Paul for the Royal Institute of International Affairs, Chatham House Papers No. 40, 1988).
46. *Ibid*, pp.71-72.
47. *Ibid*, p.49.
48. *Ibid*, p.71.
49. *Ibid.*
50. Rode and Jacobsen, *Economic Warfare or Detente*, p.94.
51. Hunter, *Western Trade Pressure on the Soviet Union*, p.100.
52. *Ibid*, p.70.
53. See chapter by James Millar in *Trade, Technology and Soviet-American Relations*, edited by Bruce Parrott, pp.324-351; also see pp.519-529 of the following: *US Senate. 97th Congress 2nd session,* Soviet Economy in the 1980s: Problems and Prospects - Part 2, Selected papers submitted to the Joint Economic Committee, Congress of the United States, December 31, 1982 (Washington: GPO 1983).
54. Hufbauer and Schott, *Economic Sanctions in Support of Foreign Policy Goals*, p.81.
55. Stent, 'Technology Transfers in East-West Trade', *Foreign Policy and Defense Review,* Volume 5, No. 2, 1985, p.48.
56. Hufbauer and Schott, *Economic Sanctions in Support of Foreign Policy Goals,* p.76.
57. *Ibid*, p.77.

58. *Ibid,* p.78.
59. Hunter, *Western Trade Pressure on the Soviet Union*, p.83.
60. Smith (ed.), *The Politics of East-West Trade.*
61. Doxey, *International Sanctions in Contemporary Perspective.*
62. Hunter, *Western Trade Pressure on the Soviet Union*, Chapter 6 is devoted to this matter.
63. Hanson, Western *Economic Statecraft in East-West Relations.*
64. *Ibid,* p.71.
65. Hufbauer and Schott, *Economic Sanctions in Support of Foreign Policy Goals*, Chapter 3 is devoted to this.
66. See Stent (ed.*), Economic Relations with the Soviet Union,* op.cit.
67. Hufbauer and Schott, *Economic Sanctions in Support of Foreign Policy Goals.*

Bibliography

Archives

Centre for the Conservation of Contemporary Documentation, Moscow: *Transcripts of relevant material.*

Data Archives

Soviet treaties project, Department of Politics, University of Glasgow.

Official Documentary Sources

Authority of the Patent and Trademark Office to Impose Secrecy Orders on Patent Applications, 1988 (Title 35 U.S. Code Annotated).

Committee on Foreign Affairs, Soviet Diplomacy and Negotiating Behaviour 1979-88, Volume II (Washington D.C. U.S. G.P.O. 1988).

Congressional Quarterly Almanac (Washington, annual).

Congressional Research Service, *An Assessment of the Afghanistan Sanctions: Implications for Trade and Diplomacy in the 1980s. Report prepared for the Subcommittee on Europe and the Middle East of the Committee on Foreign Affairs,* US House of Representatives (Washington D.C. U.S. Government 75-985, 1981).

Congressional Research Service, Library of Congress: *Soviet Policy and the United States Response in the Third World, report prepared for the committee on Foreign Affairs* (Washington D.C. U.S. G.P.O. 1981).

Executive Order 12356 April 2 1982, In Federal Register, Volume 47, no. 66, Tuesday, April 6 1982.

International Food Policy Research Institute, *Estimates of Soviet Grain Imports in 1980-85: Alternative Approaches* - research report 22 (February 1981).

International Human Rights, Documents and Introductory Notes (Vienna 1993).

National Security Decision Directive 145 (Unclassified version, 1984).

National Security Decision Directive 189, 1985.

Public Law 81-11 - *Export Control Act 1949.*

Public Law 91-184 - *Export Administration Act 1969.*
Public Law 93-618 - *The Jackson - Vanik Amendment 1975.*
Public Law 96-72 - *Export Administration Act 1979.*
Public Law 98-525 - *Defence Authorisation Act 1984.*
U.S Congress, Office of Technology Assessment (report), *Technology and East-West Trade* (Washington D.C. 1979).
U.S Congress, Office of Technology Assessment, *Technology and East-West Trade: an Update* (Washington D.C. 1983).
U.S. Department of State Bulletin (now called U.S. Department of State Dispatch).
U.S. Department of State Country Reports on Human Rights (Washington, annual).
U.S. Department of State, *Cuba's Renewed Support for Violence in Latin America: Special report No. 90*, December 14 1981.
U.S. Department of State and Department of Defense, *The Soviet - Cuban Connection in Central America and the Caribbean* (Washington D.C. March 1985).
U.S. Government Implementation of the Helsinki Accords: *Hearings before the Commission on Security and Co-operation in Europe*, 99th Congress, Berne Human Contacts Experts' Meeting, March 18 and June 18, 1986 (Washington D.C. U.S. G.P.O., 1986).
U.S. Senate, 96th Congress. 1st session, *Proposals for Reform of Export Controls for Advanced Technology*, American Enterprise Institute Legislative Analyses no. 5. August 1979 (Washington D.C.).
U.S. Senate, 97th Congress, 1st Session, *Human Rights - Ukraine and the Soviet Union. Hearing and Markup before the Committee on Foreign Affairs and its Subcommittee on Human Rights and International Organisations*, House of Representatives July 28, 30 and September 17 1981 (Washington U.S. G.P.O. 1981).
U.S. Senate, 97th Congress, 2nd session, *Economic Relations with the Soviet Union: The Implications of U.S. Export Controls related to the Soviet Gas Pipeline*, July 30 and August 12 and 13 1982, U.S. Senate Subcommittee on Foreign Relations (Washington DC U.S. GPO. 1982).
U.S. Senate, 97th Congress 2nd Session, *Soviet Economy in the 1980's: Problems and Prospects* - part 2, selected papers submitted to the Joint Economic Committee Congress of the United States, December 31 1982 (Washington DC U.S. GPO 1983).
U.S. Senate, 97th Congress, 2nd session, *Transfer of United States High Technology to the Soviet Union and Soviet Bloc Nations. Hearings before the Permanent Subcommittee on Investigations of the Committee on Governmental Affairs,* 15 November 1982 (Washington DC: U.S.

GPO 1982).
U.S. Senate, 98th Congress, 1st session, *Soviet Jewry: Hearing and Markup before the Subcommittee on Human Rights and International Organisations of the Committee on Foreign Affairs and the Commission on Security and Co-operation in Europe,* House of Representatives, June 23 and 28 1983 (Washington DC. U.S. GPO. 1984).
U.S. Senate, 100th Congress, 2nd session, *The INF Treaty: Hearings before the Committee on Foreign Relations* (Washington D.C. U.S. GPO. 1988).
Weekly Compilation of Presidential Documents (Washington).

Russian Language Documentary Sources

Andropov, Yu.V., *Izbrannye rechi i Stat'i* (Moscow: Politizdat 1983).
Brezhnev, L. I., *Leninskim Kursom* (9 Vols.) (Moscow: Politizdat, 1970-83).
Gorbachev, M. S., *Izbrannye rechi i Stat'i* (7 Vols.) (Moscow: Politizdat, 1987-90).
Gorbachev, M. S., *Perestroika i Novoye Myshlenie Dlya Nashei Strany i Dlya Vsego Mira* (Moscow: Politizdat 1987).
Istoriya Mezhdunarodnykh Otnoshenii i Vneshnei Politiki SSSR (3 Vols.) (Moscow: Mezhdunarodnye Otnosheniya 1986-87).
KPSS O Perestroike, Sbornik Dokumentov (Moscow: Politizdat 1988).
Sobranie Postanovlenii Pravitel'stva SSSR (Moscow, annual).
Sovestsko - Amerikanskaya Vstrecha na Vysshem Urovne, Zheneva *19-21 noyabrya 1985* goda, Dokumenty i Materialy (Moscow 1985).
Sovetsko - Amerikanskaya Vstrecha na Vysshem Urovne Reik'- yavik 11-12 Oktyabrya 1986 goda, Dokumenty i Materialy (Moscow 1986).
Sovetsko - Amerikanskaya Vstrecha na Vysshem Urovne, Moskva 29 Maya - 2 iyuni 1988 goda, Dokumenty i Materialy (Moscow 1988).
SSSR i Mezhdunarodnye Ekonomicheskie Otnosheniya, Sbornik Dokumentov i Materialov (Moscow: Mezhdunarodnye Otnosheniya 1985).
SSSR V borb'e Za bezopasnost' i Sotrudnichestvo V Evrope 1964-87, Sbornik Dokumentov (Moscow: Mezhdunarodnye Otnosheniya 1988).
Vizit general'nogo Sekretarya Tsk KPSS M. S. Gorbachova SSh.A, 7-10 dekabrya 1987 goda, Dokumenty i Materialy (Moscow 1987).
Vneshnyaya Politika Sovetskogo Soyuza, Sbornik Dokumentov (Moscow, annual).
Za Mir i bezopasnost' narodov Dokumenty Vneshnei Politiki SSSR: 1985 and 1986 {each in 2 parts) (Moscow: Politizdat, 1988 and 1989).

Zasedaniya Verkhovnogo Soveta SSSR (Moscow, various years).

Official Statistics

Economist Intelligence Unit, 1987-88 (London Economist Intelligence Unit 1987), *Country Profile: USSR no. 48.*
International Wheat Council (London, monthly), *International Wheat Council Grain Market Report.*
Ministry of Foreign Trade, Moscow annual, *Vneshnyaya Torgovlya.*
Pockney, B. P. (New York: St. Martins 1991), *Soviet Statistics since 1950.* United Nations (New York), *Economic Survey of Europe.*
United Nations (New York, annual), *Statistical Yearbook of the United Nations.*
U.S. Arms Control and Disarmament Agency (Washington), *World Military Expenditures and Arms Transfers.*
U.S. Department of Commerce, Bureau of Census (Washington, annual) *Statistical Abstract of the United States.*
U.S. Department of Defense (Washington), *Soviet Military Power.*
Vienna Institute for Comparative Economic Studies (London: Macmillan), *Comecon Data.*

Organisational Publications

Amnesty International, *Amnesty International Report* (London, annual).
Amnesty International (Sunbury - on - Thames Quatermaine House Ltd. 1980), *Prisoners of Conscience in the USSR (2nd edition).*
Freedom House (New York), *Freedom in the World.*
Harvard Law School (Cambridge: Mass U.S.A., 1987), *Human Rights Internet Directory: Eastern Europe and the USSR.*
Institute of Jewish Affairs (London 1986), *Human Contacts Reunion of Families and Soviet Jewry.*
International Helsinki Federation for Human Rights (Vienna 1986), *Violations of the Helsinki Accords: USSR.*
International Institute for Strategic Studies, annual Conference papers, Adelphi papers no. 190, *The Conduct of East-West relations in the 1980s, part 11.*
International Institute for Strategic Studies (London, annual), *Strategic Survey.*

Newspapers and Journals

English Language

Atlantic Community Quarterly.
Current Digest of the Soviet Press.
Economist.
Financial Times.
Foreign Affairs.
Foreign Broadcast and Information Service (FBIS).
Foreign Policy.
International Herald Tribune.
Military Balance.
Nato Review.
New York Times.
The Times.
Wall Street Journal.
Washington Post.
World Affairs.

Russian Language

Ekonomicheskaya Gazeta.
Izvestia.
Kommunist.
Krasnaya Zvezda.
Literaturnaya Gazeta.
Mirovaya Ekonomika i Mezhunarodnye Otnosheniya.
Pravda.
Sotsialisticheskaya Industria.
Sovetskaya Torgovlya.
SSh.A.
SSSR i Zarubezhnye Strany.
Trud.
Vneshnyaya Torgovlya.
Voprosy Ekonomiki.
Voprosy Istorii.

Memoirs

English Language

Brzezinski, Zbigniew, *Power and Principle: Memoirs of the National Security Adviser, 1977-81* (New York, Farrar, Strauss and Giroux 1983).
Carter, Jimmy, *Keeping Faith* (New York, Bantam, 1982).
Haig, Alexander M., *Caveat: Realism, Reagan and Foreign Policy* (New York, Macmillan, 1984).
Kissinger, Henry, *Years of Upheaval* (London Weidenfeld and Nicolson 1982).
Nitze, Paul H., *From Hiroshima to Glasnost* (New York, Grove, Weidenfeld, 1989).
Reagan, Ronald, An American Life (New York, Simon and Schuster, 1990).
Shultz, George P., *Turmoil and Triumph: My years as Secretary of State* (Charles Scribner's Sons, 1993).
Vance, Cyrus, *Hard Choices: Critical Years in American Foreign Policy* (New York, Simon and Schuster, 1983).
Weinberger, Caspar, *Fighting for Peace: Seven Critical Years in the Pentagon* (New York, Warner Bros, 1990).

Russian Language

Gromyko, A.A., Pamyatnoye (book one), (Moscow: Politizdat 1988).
Gromyko, A.A., Pamyatnoye (book two), (Moscow: Politizdat 1988).
Shevardnadze, Eduard, Moi Vybor V Zashchitu Demokratii i Svobody (Moscow: Novosti 1991).

Books

Adler - Karlsson, Gunnar, (1968), *Western Economic Warfare 1947-1967*, Stockholm: Almqvist and Wiksell.
Baldwin, David A.(1985), *Economic Statecraft,* Princeton: Princeton University Press.
Baldwin, D.A., (1993), *Key Concepts in International Political Economy*, Volumes 1 and 11 Aldershot, England, Brookfield, USA: Elgar.
Bertsch, Gary K. (1983), *East-West Strategic Trade, COCOM, and the Atlantic Alliance,* The Atlantic Papers no. 49, Paris, April.

Bialer, S and Mandelbaum, M. (1988), *The Global Rivals,* New York Knopf.
Bloch, Sidney, (1984), *Soviet Psychiatric Abuse: the Shadow over World Psychiatry,*London: Gollancz.
Boyle, Peter E. (1993), *American - Soviet Relations from the Russian Revolution to the Fall of Communism*, London, New York.
Buergenthal, T. (ed.), (1977), *Human Rights, International Law and the Helsinki Accord*, Montclair, N. J. Allanheld, Osmun, New York distribution, Universe books.
Crockatt, Richard, (1994), *The Fifty Years War, The United States and the Soviet Union in World Politics 1941-1991*, Routledge.
Cullen, Robert (ed.), (1990), *The Post Containment Handbook:Key Issues in U.S.-Soviet Economic Relations*, Westview Press.
Curry, Jane L. (1983), *Dissent in Eastern Europe*, New York Praeger.
Dallin, Alexander, (1985), *Black Box KAL 007 and the Superpowers*, University of California Press.
Doxey, Margaret, (1971), *Economic Sanctions and International Enforcement*, Oxford: Oxford University Press.
Doxey, Margaret, (1987), *International Sanctions in Contemporary Perspective*, Macmillan Press.
Feldbrugge, F.J.M. (1975), *Samizdat and Political Dissent*, Leyden: Sijthoff.
Frei, Daniel and Ruloff, Dieter, (1983), *East-West Relations: Volume 1 - a Systematic Survey,* Oelgeschlager, Gunn and Hain.
Frei, Daniel and Ruloff, Dieter, (1983), *East-West Relations: Volume 2 – Methodology*, Oelgeschlager, Gunn and Hain.
Garthoff, Raymond L. (1985*), Detente and Confrontation: American - Soviet Relations from Nixon to Reagan,* Brookings Institution.
Garthoff, Raymond L. (1994), *The Great Transition: American - Soviet Relations and the End of the Cold War*, Brookings Institution.
Gilpin, Robert, (1987), *The Political Economy of International Relations*, Princeton, New Jersey: Princeton University Press.
Grigoriev, E.E. and Kolesnichenko, T. A., Vashington, Moskva, (1988), *CHTO DAL'SHE?,* Moscow: Mezhdunarodnye Otnosheniya.
Hanson, Philip, (1981), *Trade and Technology in Soviet - Western Relations*, London: Macmillan.
Hanson, Philip, (1998), *Western Economic Statecraft in East-West Relations*, London: Routledge and Kegan Paul for the Royal Institute of International Affairs, Chatham House Papers no. 40.
Horelick, A. (ed.), (1986), *US - Soviet Relations: the Next Phase,* Cornell UP.

Hufbauer, Gary Clyde and Jeffrey Schott, (1983), *Economic Sanctions in Support of Foreign Policy Goals*, Institute for International Economics, Washington D.C.

Hufbauer, Gary C. and Schott, J.F. and Elliott, K.A. (1990), *Economic Sanctions Reconsidered*, Washington D.C. Institute for International Economics.

Hulett, Louisa S. (1988), *From Cold Wars to Star Wars: Debates Over Defense and Détente*, University Press of America.

Hunter, David W. (1991), *Western Trade Pressure on the Soviet Union*, London: Macmillan.

Jones, Chris, (1988), *Superpowers: Relations Between the Soviet Union and the USA Since 1945*, Melbourne: Longmans.

Jones, James R. (ed.), (1986), *East-West Agricultural Trade*, Westview Press: Boulder and London.

Katz, Mark (ed.), (1990), *The USSR and Marxist Revolutions in the Third World*, Cambridge University Press.

Knorr, Klaus, (1973), *Power and Wealth: The Political Economy of International Power*, London: Macmillan.

Levin, Nora, (1988), *The Jews in the Soviet Union Since 1917, Volume 2*, New York University Press.

Light, Margot, (1998), *The Soviet theory of International Relations*, Wheatsheaf Books, Brighton.

Mandelbaum, M and Bialer, S (eds.), (1998), *Gorbachev's Russia and American Foreign Policy,* Boulder: Westview.

Mandelbaum, M and Talbott, S. (1987), *Reagan and Gorbachev*, New York, Vintage Books.

Mastanduno, Michael, (1992), *Economic Containment,* Cornell University Press.

McDougall, D. (1990), *Soviet-American Relations since the 1940s, 2nd edition*, Melbourne: Arnold.

Medvedev, Zhores, (1988), *Gorbachev,* Oxford and New York.

Miller, R. F. and Rigby T. H. (ed.), (1986), *Religion and Politics in Communist States,* Canberra.

Miyagawa, Makio, (1992), *Do Economic Sanctions Work?,* Basingstoke, Macmillan.

Ovinnikov, R. S. (1986), *Zigzagi Vneshnei Politiki SShA*, Moscow IPL.

Parrott, Bruce (ed.), (1985), *Trade Technology and Soviet - American Relations*, Bloomington: Indiana University Press.

Podlesnyi, P. T. (1983), *SSSR i SShA: 50 let diplomaticheskikh otnoshenii*, Moscow: Mezhdunarodnye Otnosheniya.

Ramet, Sabrina Petra, (1987), *The Politics of Religion in Eastern Europe*

and the USSR, Indiana University Press.
Rigby T. H., Brown Archie, and Reddaway, Peter (ed.), (1980), *Authority, Power, and Policy in the USSR, essays dedicated to Leonard Schapiro*, Macmillan.
Rode, Reinhard and Jacobsen, Hanns - D. (ed.), (1985), *Economic Warfare or Detente: An Assessment of East-West Economic Relations in the 1980s*, Westview Press.
Rogov, S. M. (1989), *Sovetskii Soyuz i SSh.A: Poiski balansa interesov*, Moscow Mezhdunarodnye Otnosheniya.
Rukhadze, A. (1982), *Jews in the USSR*, Moscow: Novosti.
Smith, Gordon B. (ed.), (1984), *The Politics of East-West Trade*, Westview Press.
Stent, Angela E. (1985), *Economic Relations with the Soviet Union*, Westview Press.
Szymanski, Albert, (1984), *Human Rights in the Soviet Union*, London: Zed Press.
Talbott, Strobe, (1984), *The Russians and Reagan*, New York, Vintage Books.
Tokes, Rudolf L. (ed.), (1975), *Dissent in the USSR*, Baltimore, Maryland: John Hopkins University Press.
Trofimenko, G. A. (ed.), (1987), *Sovetsko-Amerikanskie Otnosheniya V Sovremennom Mire*, Moscow Nauka.
Voren, Robert Von (ed.), (1989), *Soviet Psychiatric Abuse in the Gorbachev Era*, Amsterdam.
White, Stephen, (1991), *Gorbachev and After*, Cambridge University Press.
Wilczinski, Jan, (1969), *The Economics and Politics of East-West Trade*, London: Macmillan.
Wolfe, T and Hosmer, S. (1983), *Soviet Policy and Practice Towards Third World Conflicts*, Lexington Mass: Lexington Books.
Woolcock, Stephen, (1982), *Western Policies on East-West Trade*, London: Routledge and Kegan Paul for the Royal Institute of International Affairs, Chatham House Papers 15.
Woolf, Thomas, (1973), *US-East-West Trade Policy: Economic Warfare Versus Economic Welfare*, London: Lexington books.
Zaslavsky, Victor and Brym, Robert, (1983), *Soviet-Jewish Emigration and Soviet Nationality Policy*, Macmillan.

Articles

Adler - Karlsson, Gunnar, (1980), 'The US Embargo Inefficient and

Conterproductive', *Aussenwirtschaft,* June.
Barber, James, (1979), 'Economic Sanctions as a Policy Instrument', *International Affairs*, vol. 55, no. 3, July, pp. 367-385.
Bialer, S and Afferica, J. (1982/83), 'Reagan and Russia', *Foreign Affairs*, vol. 61, Winter, pp. 249-271.
Bialer, Seweryn, (1988), 'New Thinking and Soviet Foreign Policy', *Survival*, vol.30, no.4, July/August, pp.291-310.
Bertsch, Gary, (1980), 'US-Soviet Trade: The Question of Leverage': *Survey,* vol. 25, no.2 Spring, pp.66-81.
Brym, Robert. J. (1985), 'Soviet Emigration Policy: the Changing Rate of Jewish Emigration From the USSR: some lessons from the 1970s', *Soviet - Jewish Affairs*, vol. 15, no. 2, pp.22-44.
Cullen, Robert B. (1986-87), 'Soviet Jewry', *Foreign Affairs*, vol. 65, Winter, pp.252-266.
Doxey, Margaret, (1980), 'Economic Sanctions: Benefits and Costs', *World Today*, vol. 36 no.12, December, pp. 484-489.
Friedgut, Theodore H. (1984), 'Soviet anti - Zionism and anti - Semitism - another cycle', *Soviet - Jewish affairs*, vol. 4, no. 1, pp. 3-23.
Friedgut, Theodore H. (1991), 'Soviet Emigration Policies', *Coexistence*, June, pp.319-335.
Fukuyama, Francis, (1986), 'Gorbachev and the Third World', *Foreign Affairs*, vol. 64[2], Spring, pp.715-732.
Gubin, Sandra, (1993), 'The Evolution of Soviet Emigration Policies and Law: Toward a Law Governed or Rule of Law State?', Unpublished manuscript.
Hanson, Paul, (1985), 'Economic Aspects of Helsinki', *International Affairs*, vol. 61, Autumn, pp. 619-629.
Heitman, Sidney, (1988) 'The Third Soviet Emigration', *Soviet - Jewish Affairs,* vol. 18, no. 2, pp. 17-43.
Holloway, David, (1989), 'Gorbachev's New Thinking', *Foreign Affairs*, vol. 68, no. 1, pp.66-81.
Kaiser, R. G. (1981), 'U.S. - Soviet Relations: Goodbye to Détente', *Foreign Affairs*, vol. 59, no. 3, pp.500-521.
Lane, David, (1984), 'Human Rights Under State Socialism', *Political Studies*, vol. 32, no. 3, September, pp.349-368.
Macfarlane, Neil and Litwak, Robert, (1987), 'Soviet Activism in the Third World, *Survival*, vol. 29 no. 1, Jan/Feb, pp.21-39.
Millar, James, (1985), 'The Impact of Trade and Trade Denial on the U.S. Economy', In Bruce Parrott (ed), *Trade Technology and Soviet - American Relations*, Bloomington: Indiana University Press, pp.324-351.

Reddaway, Peter, (1983), 'Dissent in the USSR', *Problems of Communism*, vol. 32, no. 6, November-December, pp.1-15.

Schelling, T. C. (1985/86), 'What Went Wrong With Arms Control?', *Foreign Affairs*, vol. 64, Winter, pp.219-233.

Shearman, Peter, (1993), 'The New Political Thinking Reassessed', *Review of International Studies*, vol. 19, no. 2, April, pp.139-158.

Sobell, Vlad, (1988), 'Perestroika and Western Security, *Radio Free Europe / Radio Liberty background report/222*, 11 November.

Stent, Angela E. (1985), 'Technology Transfers in East-West Trade: The Western Alliance Studies', *AEI - Foreign Policy and Defence Review*, vol. 5, no. 2, pp.44-52.

Talbott, S (1980), 'U.S. - Soviet Relations: From Bad to Worse', *Foreign Affairs*, vol. 58, no. 3, pp.515-539.

Tismaneanu, V. (1987), 'Dissent in the Gorbachev Era', *Orbis*, no. 31, Summer, pp.234-243.

Woolcock, Stephen, (1982), 'East-West Trade: US Policy and European Interests, *World Today*, vol. 38, February, pp.51-59.

For Product Safety Concerns and Information please contact our EU representative GPSR@taylorandfrancis.com
Taylor & Francis Verlag GmbH, Kaufingerstraße 24, 80331 München, Germany

www.ingramcontent.com/pod-product-compliance
Ingram Content Group UK Ltd.
Pitfield, Milton Keynes, MK11 3LW, UK
UKHW022202190926
475702UK00003B/165
* 9 7 8 1 1 3 8 3 3 7 7 9 4 *